A Poetics of Trauma

HBI Series on Jewish Women

Shulamit Reinharz, General Editor
Sylvia Barack Fishman, Associate Editor

The HBI Series on Jewish Women, created by the Hadassah-Brandeis Institute, publishes a wide range of books by and about Jewish women in diverse contexts and time periods. Of interest to scholars and the educated public, the HBI Series on Jewish Women fills major gaps in Jewish Studies and in Women and Gender Studies as well as their intersection.

For the complete list of books that are available in this series, please see www.upne.com

Susan M. Weiss and Netty C. Gross-Horowitz
Marriage and Divorce in the Jewish State: Israel's Civil War
Ilana Szobel
A Poetics of Trauma: The Work of Dahlia Ravikovitch
Ronit Irshai
Fertility and Jewish Law: Feminist Perspectives on Orthodox Responsa Literature
Elana Maryles Sztokman
The Men's Section: Orthodox Jewish Men in an Egalitarian World
Sharon Faye Koren
Forsaken: The Menstruant in Medieval Jewish Mysticism
Sonja M. Hedgepeth and Rochelle G. Saidel, editors
Sexual Violence against Jewish Women during the Holocaust
Julia R. Lieberman, editor
Sephardi Family Life in the Early Modern Diaspora
Derek Rubin, editor
Promised Lands: New Jewish American Fiction on Longing and Belonging
Carol K. Ingall, editor
The Women Who Reconstructed American Jewish Education: 1910–1965
Gaby Brimmer and Elena Poniatowska
Gaby Brimmer: An Autobiography in Three Voices
Harriet Hartman and Moshe Hartman
Gender and American Jews: Patterns in Work, Education, and Family in Contemporary Life
Dvora E. Weisberg
Levirate Marriage and the Family in Ancient Judaism
Ellen M. Umansky and Dianne Ashton, editors
Four Centuries of Jewish Women's Spirituality: A Sourcebook

The Schusterman Series in Israel Studies

Editors: S. Ilan Troen, Jehuda Reinharz, Sylvia Fuks Fried

The Schusterman Series in Israel Studies publishes original scholarship of exceptional significance on the history of Zionism and the State of Israel. It draws on disciplines across the academy, from anthropology, sociology, political science and international relations to the arts, history and literature. It seeks to further an understanding of Israel within the context of the modern Middle East and the modern Jewish experience. There is special interest in developing publications that enrich the university curriculum and enlighten the public at large. The series is published under the auspices of the Schusterman Center for Israel Studies at Brandeis University.

For a complete list of books in this series, please see www.upne.com

Ilana Szobel
A Poetics of Trauma: The Work of Dahlia Ravikovitch
Anita Shapira
Israel: A History
Orit Rozin
The Rise of the Individual in 1950s Israel: A Challenge to Collectivism
Boaz Neumann
Land and Desire in Early Zionism
Anat Helman
Young Tel Aviv: A Tale of Two Cities
Nili Scharf Gold
Yehuda Amichai: The Making of Israel's National Poet
Itamar Rabinovich and Jehuda Reinharz, editors
Israel in the Middle East: Documents and Readings on Society, Politics, and Foreign Relations, Pre-1948 to the Present

A Poetics of Trauma

The Work of Dahlia Ravikovitch

Ilana Szobel

BRANDEIS UNIVERSITY PRESS

Waltham, Massachusetts

Brandeis University Press

An imprint of University Press of New England

www.upne.com

© 2013 Brandeis University

Manufactured in the United States of America

Designed by Eric M. Brooks

Typeset in Calluna by Integrated Publishing Solutions

Frontispiece photo by Dina Guna

University Press of New England is a member of the
Green Press Initiative. The paper used in this book meets
their minimum requirement for recycled paper.

For permission to reproduce any of the material in this book,
contact Permissions, University Press of New England, One Court
Street, Suite 250, Lebanon NH 03766; or visit www.upne.com

*The publication of this book was generously supported by the
Lucius N. Littauer Foundation.*

Excerpts from *Hovering at a Low Altitude: The Collected Poetry of
Dahlia Ravikovitch*, by Dahlia Ravikovitch, copyright © 2009 by
Chana Bloch, Chana Kronfeld, and Ido Kalir, English translation
copyright © 2009 by Chana Bloch and Chana Kronfeld, are used
by permission of W. W. Norton & Company, Inc.

Chapter 1 was originally published as "Forever Beholden: Orphanhood in the Work of Dalia Ravikovitch," in *Nashim: A Journal of
Jewish Women's Studies & Gender* 19 (2010): 228–47 and is reprinted
here by permission of Indiana University Press.

Library of Congress Cataloging-in-Publication Data
appear on the last printed page of this book.

Contents

Acknowledgments

Writing a book is a personal process, which could not be possible without the support and the advice of so many dear people: family, friends, teachers, colleagues, and students. I would like to express my gratitude to the many people whom I had the good fortune of encountering throughout the years, and who helped me shape and reshape this book.

I am so grateful to Yael Feldman for her guidance, wisdom, and support. I cannot say enough about her willingness to listen and to give insightful and useful advice. I am deeply grateful to Hannah Naveh, who always lent a sympathetic ear when my thoughts became tangled. Our long-term dialogue has been and is a constant source of inspiration and stimulation.

It is my pleasure to express gratitude to my friend Taly Ravid, for carefully reading and commenting on countless revisions of this book. I thank Daniel Banai for his help with the translations. I greatly cherish the friendship of both, and I deeply value their constant support.

I am also indebted to Dan Miron, Marianne Hirsch, Mary Louise Pratt, David Engel, and Nili Scharf Gold, who read earlier drafts of this book, for their shrewd suggestions. I owe a debt of gratitude to Sylvia Fuks Fried, executive director of the Tauber Institute and director of publications at the Schusterman Center for Israel Studies at Brandeis University, for her enthusiastic support, to Giles Harvey for his profound editing, to Phyllis Deutsch, editor-in-chief of the University Press of New England for her insights, and to the Skirball Department of Hebrew and Judaic Studies at New York University.

Brandeis University has become my academic home over the last few years. I am fortunate to enjoy the encouraging support of my colleagues in the Department of Near Eastern and Judaic Studies. In particular I wish to thank those who have shown a special interest in the development of this book: Sylvia Barack Fishman, Ilan Troen, Jonathan Sarna, Marc Brettler, David Wright, Tzvi Abusch, Bernadette J. Brooten, ChaeRan Freeze, Eugene R. Sheppard, Jonathan Decter, Sharon Feiman-Nemser, and Vardit Ringvald.

Excerpts of some chapters have been previously published elsewhere. An earlier version of chapter 1 was originally published in *Nashim: A Journal of Jewish Women's Studies & Gender* 19 (2010): 228–47 as "Forever Beholden: The

State of Orphanhood in the Work of Dahlia Ravikovitch." Earlier versions of chapters 4 and 7 were originally published in *Teoryah uvikoret* 28 (2006): 127–55 as "'She Tried to Escape and Lost Her Senses': Alienation and Madness in the Stories of Dahlia Ravikovitch." An earlier version of part 4 was originally published in *Khitmei or* [Sparks of light: Essays about Dahlia Ravikovitch's oeuvre], eds. Hamutal Tsamir and Tamar S. Hess, 444–69, Tel Aviv: Hakibbutz Hameuchad, 2010, as "'Hovering at a Low Altitude: Testimony and Complicity in the Political Writing of Dahlia Ravikovitch." I thank each of these publishers for their generous permission to include the pieces in this book.

I am thankful to Ido Kalir for his kind permission to use unpublished drafts of the poems "The Love of an Orange" (Ahavat tapuach hazahav), "On the road at night" (Omed al hakhevish), and "Clockwork Doll" (Bubah memukenet). I was deeply touched by his kindness in allowing me an unforgettable glance into Ravikovitch's literary bequest.

Finally, I greatly appreciate the financial support of the Near Eastern and Judaic Studies Department at Brandeis University, the Henry M. MacCracken Fund, and the Memorial Foundation for Jewish Culture.

What Must Be Forgotten

Photo: Dina Guna

Dahlia Ravikovitch (1936–2005) is one of the most widely admired and beloved writers among both readers and scholars of modern Hebrew literature, and one of the most influential figures in the Israeli canon. Between 1959 and 2005 she published eight books of poetry (which have been translated into twenty-three languages), three collections of short stories, eight children's books, and various translations of children's classics and English poetry. Her rich literary corpus has won her a coveted place in the "Generation of the State," the group of writers who came of age in the years following the establishment of the State of Israel in 1948.

This group, which includes Yehuda Amichai, Nathan Zach, David Avidan, Yona Wallach, and Dahlia Hertz, transformed Hebrew poetry in the 1950s and 1960s. The Generation of the State, also known as the post-1948 Statehood Generation (*Dor hamedinah*), revolted against the modernism of Avraham Shlonsky, Nathan Alterman, and Leah Goldberg, questioning their ideology, structure, rhythm, and language. The works of Amichai, Zach, Avidan, Wallach, Ravikovitch and other poets of the *Likrat* literary group emerged as a new form of poetry that challenged the previous generation's tendency toward a collective voice and a national heroic ethos. Instead, it embraced the personal and endowed it with universal valence. Although Ravikovitch was one of the leading poetic voices of this literary generation, she did not fully identify with the rebellion against her predecessors, but rather felt a tender affinity with the poetics and aesthetics of poets such as Alterman, Goldberg, and Yonatan Ratosh. Accordingly, her mode of poetry deviated in various ways from the stylistic norms of her generation,[1] consequently leading to her establishment as a unique and inimitable voice in Hebrew literature.

Like many of her contemporaries, Ravikovitch achieved canonical status in her own lifetime. She was awarded the Bialik Prize in 1987, the Israel Prize in 1998, and the Prime Minister's Prize in 2005, the year of her death. This canonization has consolidated certain narrow assumptions about the direct connection between her personal history and her poetic persona. As is often the case with women writers, her work was read as representing her private, feminine—and hence limited—experience. Like Rachel Bluwstein Sela (1890–1931) and Yona Wallach (1944–1985), Ravikovitch had to endure a good deal of public scrutiny. Her biography became entwined not just with her writing but with her public persona. Even in the absence of a scholarly biography, Israeli readers are familiar with the main events of her life. She was born in Ramat Gan on November 27, 1936. Her mother, Michal Hominer (who would later adopt her second husband's surname, Ben-Arie), was a much-loved teacher and the great-granddaughter of Rabbi Samuel Hominer (1845–1907), who was among the founders of the ultraorthodox *Mea shearim*, the fifth Jewish neighborhood to be built in Jerusalem outside the wall of the Old City in 1874. Her father, Levi Ravikovitch, was a Russian-born Jewish engineer and an amateur poet who immigrated to Palestine from China in the early 1930s. When Dahlia Ravikovitch was six years old, her father was killed in a car accident. She moved with her mother and twin brothers to Kibbutz Geva and, after years of misery, moved at age thirteen to different foster homes in Haifa. She studied linguistics and both Hebrew and English literature at the Hebrew University of Jerusalem and English literature at Oxford University. She married twice (in 1957 and 1961) and in 1978 had a son, Ido Kalir, who from the age of eleven remained under the custody of his father Haim Kalir. Even though she suffered from clinical depression throughout her life, with the outbreak of the First Lebanon War in 1982 and the First Intifada in 1987, Ravikovitch became active in different Israeli peace movements, collaborating with Israeli and Palestinian artists and politicians, exposing injustice, and struggling for peace and human rights.

Her much-gossiped-about private life did not detract from the widespread appreciation her work received from readers and fellow writers alike. Nevertheless, given her centrality to Israeli culture, there is an incongruously small amount of research on her work (only two books in Hebrew that are dedicated to the poetry,[2] and no book at all in English). This book attempts to fill a critical gap by thoroughly examining the Ravikovitch oeuvre—both prose and poetry—as a whole. Although Ravikovitch discussed some of her life experiences in interviews, this volume focuses solely on her literary work, as Ravikovitch herself would probably have wanted. In one of her most provocative and controversial interviews, Ravikovitch was asked by Ayelet Negev: "If you were to write an autobiography, how would you title it? How would you summarize your life in one single line?" Ravikovitch answered: *What Must Be Forgotten.* Whatever happened to me, aside from the poems, must be forgotten."[3]

In December 2005, a few months after Ravikovitch's death, Tel Aviv University held an academic conference on her work. Titled "'True Love': An Academic Conference on the Literary Work of Dahlia Ravikovitch," the conference revealed the growing academic interest in Ravikovitch. It presented discussions about her poetics in relation to other major Hebrew writers, illuminated moral and political aspects of her writing, and raised important questions about the dominance of trauma and disaster in her poetry. Some of these presentations have been published in the recent anthology *Khitmei or* [Sparks of light: Essays about Dahlia Ravikovitch's oeuvre], edited by Hamutal Tsamir and Tamar Hess. The variety of issues, themes, and interpretations discussed in this collection, as well as the diversity of academic backgrounds represented by the writers, testify both to significant progress in the scholarly work on Ravikovitch and to the enormous amount of research that remains if we are to arrive at a full understanding of her work.

The publication of Chana Bloch and Chana Kronfeld's profound new translation of Ravikovitch's poems into English indicates that the increasing interest in her work is not limited to Hebrew speakers. My aim is to offer both Hebrew and non-Hebrew speakers a deeper look into Ravikovitch's poetic world, a look that is explicitly concerned with the very act of translation, with the innovative potential embodied in a foreign language, with the exciting, sometimes frustrating, challenge of understanding and exploring the Hebrew world of Ravikovitch in English, a language she herself read and translated into Hebrew.

A Traumatic Deviant Subjectivity

Ravikovitch's opulent literary corpus of poems and short stories raises questions about trauma, gender, subjectivity, and nationalism. From a holistic perspective, her writing portrays the emotional structure of traumatized and victimized individuals. Ravikovitch's entire oeuvre (both the lyrical and the political works) gives expression to her characters' inner psychic mechanism, and presents a process that moves back and forth between personal and national trauma. The theoretical, ideological, and emotional challenge of this book is to analyze the deep structure embodied in Ravikovitch's work—a vortex of estrangement, madness, and politics—and to unearth the interconnectedness of her private-poetic subjectivity and Israeli national identity. Furthermore, focusing on the symptoms of a traumatized psyche enables a deeper understanding of the various ways in which the subjectivity of a deviant might undermine the foundations of hegemony—that is, of the symbolic order. This book thus attempts a theoretical discussion of both the poetics of trauma and the politics of victimhood.

The infrastructure of the typical Ravikovitch character's imaginary biography is presented through a juxtaposition of the symbolic order (namely, the Law of the Father) and the deviant subjectivity. Read critically, the option of emotional, cultural, and ideological deviations enable an exploration of questions of identity and visibility within modern Hebrew literature. Furthermore, a conceptualization of the traumatized personality in terms that create a unique (almost idiosyncratic) space within the symbolic order enables an examination of various presentations of otherness and marginality that have been overshadowed by aspects of the hegemony in the Israeli context. Through its unique poetics, Ravikovitch's work thus reveals uncommon ways of understanding victimhood and can help readers overcome cultural biases and engage with otherness.

The political nature of a deviant and traumatized personality and the attempt "to examine how trauma unsettles and forces us to rethink our notions of experience and communication" are central to this book.[4] Nevertheless, since such an aim tends to generalize the notion of victimhood, and to include various types under the umbrella of "trauma," let me identify the boundaries of my discussion: it is concerned specifically with the victimhood of a Jewish Israeli orphan woman, written in Hebrew, by Dahlia Ravikovitch, in the years 1959–2005.

In the Israeli context, which addresses victimhood mainly with reference to the Holocaust and Zionist nationalism, Ravikovitch's oeuvre enables the reader to think about victimhood from a different perspective, by giving her insight into the world of those for whom estrangement is a way of living, an involuntary existential condition. From its inception, the nationalist-Zionist movement and early Israeli society allowed only a finite period of time for victims to experience the weakness and helplessness inherent to victimhood—even or especially victimhood of the Holocaust—after which it was expected that a *tkuma*, a recovery and revival, would follow. The victimhood of the Ravikovitch character, however, is permanent; lack of control is her existential position. In the reality of many of Ravikovitch's poems and short stories—and certainly in Western thought and in the Zionist movement—victimhood is considered a powerless position, a state of weakness. Nonetheless, an in-depth reading of Ravikovitch's literary corpus exposes her multifaceted approach to this subject, an approach that challenges the very notion of victimhood's inherent weakness. It is not that Ravikovitch's characters speak and act from a position of power (not just because such an option would maintain the same understanding of weakness, but mainly because it is not what occurs in the texts), but rather that they assert an immovability, a weight, a presence in the world, a kind of struggle. It is a struggle between pushing away and internalizing, of repeating and progressing; it is the existential project of a traumatized personality.

Generally speaking, Israeli society integrates a "trauma and recovery" approach, which posits the possibility of healing from a traumatic event, into an "ongoing trauma" approach, namely one that denies any real option of escaping the traumatic state. Zionist ideology conceives of trauma in terms of weakness and imagines itself as a movement toward rehabilitation, a process of recovering from the Diaspora and from the Holocaust. At the same time, the Israeli national project preserves and maintains the discourse of victimhood (characterized by tropes such as Jews as victims, the few against the many, etc.) as a fundamental legitimatization of its existence. Although this double disposition seems paradoxical, the two actually share a common premise regarding victimhood: that the one who possesses the power uses it against the one who lacks it (and it does not matter if the dynamic works according to a simple Hegelian or a sophisticated Foucauldian mechanism). A significant effect of this concept of power is that it leads to a whole set of binary valuations, such as passive vs. active, master vs. slave, or object vs. subject.

Within this cultural context, Ravikovitch conceives of a form of victimhood that does not adopt this basic assumption, or at least not entirely. It is impossible to read Ravikovitch's victimhood in terms of powerful/weak, active/passive. Even though her characters are largely passive, waiting for a change achievable only in their fantasized world, to settle for a claim about the passive feminine would be to ignore other layers in her writing. Her work contains mental and poetic strategies that subvert the passive image, albeit without renouncing it. The insistence on a subversive voice and on the right to self-identification (the project of establishing subjectivity) is an active move, even if not always conscious.

Ravikovitch thus creates activity that does not erase passivity—what might be called "active passivity." Her work does not necessarily ascribe power to activity and weakness to passivity. Hence, spurts of activity or moves toward establishing independence do not change anything in the concrete world of her characters, nor do they endow her characters with power in their life or environment; moreover, what might seem like passive and mute reactions sometimes indicate a vigorous breakthrough for a character. The complexity and multiplicity of layers that one can find in Ravikovitch's poetic decisions do not betray any preference for one or another of the categories, activity or passivity. Rather, the movement between the two categories is itself a central aspect of the subjectivity of her characters. Thus Ravikovitch's work undermines not just binary opposition in the process of self-construction but also the valued and ideological dimension ascribed to each of the categories in a hierarchy of the symbolic order.[5]

Echoing Jacques Derrida's *Différance*,[6] Ravikovitch's meaning of trauma and victimhood is forever "deferred" through an endless chain of poetic signifiers, and the "differed" binary oppositions and hierarchies, which underpin the very meaning of trauma and victimhood, are challenged. The conventional terms usually ascribed to trauma—victimhood and estrangement—are therefore not always adequate for describing the experience in Ravikovitch's work, which both adopts and challenges, maintains and disrupts, dichotomies. Ravikovitch opens wide interspaces between them that enable her (and subsequently us) to examine those dichotomies over and over again, from inside, outside, and in between. In this way she constructs dichotomies and most of our familiar concepts as sites of performances, sometimes ossified and other times unstable, occasionally repressing, at times releasing.

Stressing this point enables me to raise the question that stands at the center of my project: how can a situation without choice be part of a process of self-construction? How can a state of emotional imprisonment function not as a limitation that covers up a repressed subjectivity, but rather as the subjectivity itself? Instead of referring to this possibility as paradoxical, this book offers a rethinking of the notions of choice, activity/passivity, and strength/weakness. In other words, it is a study of a personality for whom the term "choice" is not relevant, but who nonetheless struggles for her own subjectivity and for an individual existence. It is about a woman whose actions cannot be anything but what they are, who can only be what she is, and who understands the world and interacts with her surroundings through her own perceptions, however idiosyncratic they may be.

Poetics and Identity

This volume raises questions about a coherent self's relation to deviant subjectivity: What are the relationships between a firm self and trauma, involuntary eruption, mad speech, and madness? Ravikovitch reveals a complex mental structure of estrangement and presents a subjectivity founded on the struggle between the symbolic order and a dissident, deviant existence. This book delineates the female character's deviances, as they emerge in four major axes of her identity formation: orphanhood, estrangement, madness, and national identity. By focusing on the features, effects, and, in particular, on the poetic construction of a traumatic personality, I illustrate Ravikovitch's unique mental-poetic literary subjectivity, and the ways in which her work offers a distinctive way of thinking about trauma, selfhood, and nationalism.

With the intention of providing an intellectual and emotional analysis of Ravikovitch's oeuvre, I read her work closely, paying attention to her literary expression and its link to Israeli society. At the same time, I explore her work using gender, psychoanalysis, and trauma theories as prisms through which to view the larger shape of her writing. This multi-layered structure enables me to examine the juxtaposition of poetics and identity, and to look into the linguistic and poetic presentations of identity construction (the identity of a woman, a poet, a nation etc.).

Hence, I look at the central female figure developed throughout Ravikovitch's poems and short stories. I conceptualize this imaginary character and present a psychological picture of her by gathering, examining, and integrating her main representations and behavioral patterns. The methodology of my project is thus a synthesis of the character's various representations in Ravikovitch's work. In other words, although each of Ravikovitch's poems and stories is open to independent reading, my interpretation focuses on the connections among the texts. Such a reading integrates Ravikovitch's writing into a fragmented "novel" of sorts, at the center of which is a female protagonist who is portrayed at diverse phases in her life. The construction of this character lies in certain similarities and parallels between the diverse texts (emotional mechanisms, types of recurring events and behavior, repeated ethical and political approaches taken by the character, etc.). Throughout the book I will use the terms "Ravikovitch's character," "Ravikovitch's speaker," or "Ravikovitch's poetic persona," as a reference to this central female figure who is developed throughout Ravikovitch's oeuvre.

Since different texts emphasize different elements of the character's self-construction, the book is organized around four major cores of identity—orphanhood, estrangement and alienation, madness, and national identity—and not according to the chronological development either of the Ravikovitch character (from childhood to maturity) or of Ravikovitch's books (from her first book, *The Love of an Orange*, published in 1959, to her last, *Come and Gone*, published in 2005).

Part 1 of this volume examines the character's father's death, a traumatic event to which Ravikovitch often returns. The state of orphanhood destines the speaker to feelings of discrimination, yearning, and vulnerability. I explore the continued retelling of the wound of orphanhood and try to understand the way in which it works with the illusion of reformation as the underlying basis for the relationship between the symbolic order and traumatic repetition in Ravikovitch's poetics.

It often seems as though Ravikovitch's work, as it were, chooses the state of orphanhood as a founding experience, as the primal cause, as the core of being. From the point of view of the role that orphanhood serves in Ravikovitch's work, there is almost a desire for it. Orphanhood becomes a major part of the fantasy that establishes the character's subjectivity, and thus is transformed from a real state into an imaginary one. As part of her autosuggestion, the character converts orphanhood from a sign of social deviation to one of excellence and superiority.

The mechanism of this alteration, as well as the character's estrangement that functions both as a marker of social inferiority and as a feature of identity, is the main issue developed in part 2. This part focuses on the permanent feeling of estrangement, which permeates the character's identity and which also manifests in her ongoing struggle between the desire to integrate and the need to be distinct.

The gap between society and the character grows steadily wider, causing a web of external definition and signification to tighten around her until she can no longer escape the signification of madness. This movement from estrangement to insanity stands at the center of part 3. Here I look at the ways in which Ravikovitch's oeuvre presents a unique perspective on madness, and explore the way Ravikovitch's so-called madness subverts the hegemonic system. In order to constitute the mad Other as a subject within the very system that otherwise objectifies madness, Ravikovitch portrays the dominant system in its attempts to separate speech *about* madness from *mad speech,* to use Shoshanna Felman's terms.[7] While seeming to operate within the boundaries of this distinction, Ravikovitch's work ultimately reveals a blurring of the demarcation, which undermines the stability of the dominant system.

Part 4 of this book is dedicated to the deconstruction of national identity in Ravikovitch's work. Ravikovitch's poetic reactions to the First Lebanon War (1982) and to the First Intifada (1987) focus on the suffering of Palestinian Arabs and present intellectual criticism of Israeli behavior and politics. Furthermore, while referring to the political aspects of the war and to the suffering she witnesses, Ravikovitch also defines her way of seeing and raises questions about the actual position of witnessing and testimony. This part focuses on Ravikovitch's poetic and moral position of witnessing and depicts the connections between responsibility, guilt, complicity, immorality, and national identity.

The complex and layered emotional structure of Ravikovitch's character, as explored in parts 1–3, forms the basis of my understanding of Ravikovitch's political writing. I refer to her protest poetry and stories not as an isolated subgenre within her body of work but rather as poetry that is derived from the same emotional structure as the rest of her writing. Since the character's identity is constituted as a maladjustment, her existence creates a subject with acute and paralyzing sensitivity, which functions as a victim and, as such, exposes the suffering and the victimization of the other. In that way, Ravikovitch's protest poetry can be seen as a manifestation, an acting-out, of this emotional mechanism. As a poetic and metaphoric acting-out, it may be seen to challenge the dominant discourse in terms of such fundamental themes as the Israeli sense of self and its boundaries, national ethics and conscience, Jewish identity and responsibility, and the relationship between Palestinian identity and the definition of contemporary Zionism.

Part One

Forever Beholden

The State of Orphanhood

I am her father—though she is an orphan

Joseph Ibn Hasday, "Shirah Yetoma"

[A female orphan poem][1]

Poetics of Orphanhood

When Dahlia Ravikovitch was six years old, her father was killed in a car accident—a traumatic event that would fundamentally orient her writing and play a central role in the way she established her poetic self. This incident and its repercussions, which scholars have described as "a fatal forcibleness"—a force that ties the speaker to her orphanhood[1]—appear in various guises throughout Ravikovitch's work. Indeed, as Hannah Naveh suggests, for the speaker in Ravikovitch's writings the work of mourning is an endless quest.[2]

In her first book of poetry, *The Love of an Orange* (1959), in an untitled poem beginning with the words "On the road at night" (Omed al hakhevish), Ravikovitch articulates this experience: *veratziti lishol et haish ad matai chayevet ani/veyadaati zot merosh shetamid chayevet ani.* In Chana and Ariel Bloch's translation, these lines read: "And I want to ask the man how long will I have to./And I know, even as I ask, I will always have to."[3] The translation of the second line, however, does not capture its full meaning. I prefer to render it: "I always knew, I was forever beholden"—a statement that embodies Ravikovitch's personal experiences and poetic commitments, as well as providing a prophetic definition of her writing as a whole. Although the line can be read in multiple contexts—ars poetica, femininity, nationality—one cannot ignore its original appearance in a section of the book primarily concerned with her father's death. In this context, "I was forever beholden" becomes a poetic articulation of the nature of her trauma.

This early declaration reemerges almost four decades later, in the poem "There Is No Fear of God in This Place" (Ein yirat elohim bamakom hazeh). The father speaks to his daughter:

When I was run over and killed on that black road,
in an eyeblink, alone,

struck to the ground, startled and shamed,
in that eyeblink I knew:
In all the years to come
like me you'd remain startled,

(CP, 255; BK, 231)

First published in Nathan Zach's periodical *Hinneh* in January 1995, this poem was republished a few months later in *The Complete Poems So Far.* There is, however, a significant difference between the two versions. Where the earlier reads, "instantaneously, I knew that *until the end of your days*/like me, you would be petrified," the later poem has, "in that eyeblink I knew:/*In all the years to come*/like me you'd remain startled" (emphasis added). In her reassessment of the speaker's orphanhood, the author ultimately decides on a period that goes beyond the speaker's human limits; the second version resounds like an ancient curse, as though orphanhood is a state that will transcend the orphan's own life time.

This chapter examines the psychological and poetic "curse" at the heart of Ravikovitch's writings, in which traumatic loss creates an emotional mechanism of psychological imprisonment whereby the Ravikovitch speaker is condemned to an existence inescapably defined by orphanhood. Trauma, as Cathy Caruth explains, "is not experienced as a mere repression or defense, but as a temporal delay that carries the individual beyond the shock of the first moment. The trauma is a repeated suffering of the event, but it is also a continual leaving of its site."[4] By investigating these "repetitions" and "leavings of the site" in Ravikovitch's work, I wish to explore the traumatic experience expressed in her writing and to focus on the specific poetic language and structure of its articulation.

A caveat: in pointing to the state of orphanhood as a key to understanding the Ravikovitch oeuvre, I do not claim it to be the only key. Moreover, the psychoanalytical arguments I make aim to illuminate Ravikovitch's writing, not to make assumptions about her private life. Although Ravikovitch discussed some of her biographical experiences in interviews, this study is based only on her literary work. My aim is to identify a "poetics of orphanhood" and to explore the effects of bereavement within Ravikovitch's poetics.

A Legacy of Psychosis

On the road at night there stands the man
who once upon a time was my father.
And I must come to the place where he stands
because I was his eldest daughter.

And night after night he stands alone on the road
and I must go down to that place and stand there.
And I want to ask the man how long will I have to.
And I know, even as I ask, I will always have to.

In the place where he stands there is a fear of danger
like the day he was walking along and a car ran him over.
And that's how I knew him, and I found ways to remember
that this very man was once my father.

And he doesn't tell me one word of love
though once upon a time he was my father.
And even though I was his eldest daughter
he cannot tell me one word of love.

(CP, 19; BB, 3; cf. BK 55)

This poem expresses and embodies a deep understanding of the speaker's psychotic mechanism and obsessive behavior. The reader is informed that "in the place where he [the man, the father] stands"—that is, in the middle of the road—"there is a fear of danger." By forcing "his eldest daughter" to stand with him in the same place night after night, the father puts her at risk too. In this sense, the poem does not deal simply with the trauma of the father's death, but also with the state of perpetual psychotic risk in which the speaker lives: she cannot stop going "down to that place and stand[ing] there" night after night and, in so doing, exposing herself to the danger.

What's more, the daughter does not really know her father. She has to mark him in order to recognize him: "And that's how I knew him, and I found ways to remember/that this very man was once my father." This is even more evident in Hebrew: *shezeh haish atzmo hayah paam aba sheli/vehikarti oto ve-natati bo simanim* ("and that's how I knew him, and I made signs so that I could always recognize that this man was my father"). The expression *natati bo simanim*, literally "I gave him identifying signs," alludes to a law discussed in Mishnah *Baba metzia* 2:5–7. According to this Talmudic discussion, a per-

son who loses something in the public domain must provide *simanim*, identifying signs, in order to reclaim it.[5] But the only way in which the speaker can identify her father is through his crazy act of standing in the middle of the road in the dark. She can recognize him neither by his appearance nor by his voice. Rather, what enables her to recognize him is something she feels within herself, the notion that he *has* to take the risk (otherwise, he could have prevented his own death), and that she, likewise, *has* to follow. The father is thus the one in a position of power who forces the daughter into danger.

What stands at the center of the poem is not orphanhood per se, but the speaker's psychosis, which she inherits from her dead father. If orphanhood plays a role here, it is in the etiological connection the speaker makes between her orphanhood and the risk of psychosis that lies constantly in wait for her. In this way, the poem is not "fantastic," as it might appear at first glance. Rather, it is a poem of insight and self-analysis whose central image of standing in the road at night allows the speaker to investigate the origin of the power that repeatedly forces her to take a variety of psychotic risks.

Poetics of Trauma Symbolic Order and Repetition

One of the most notable elements of Ravikovitch's "On the road at night" poem is its structure. On the surface, it seems to adhere to a strict (symbolic) order: it has four stanzas of four lines each, and it is syntactically conventional. The poem also suggests a standard causality: "And I must come to the place where he stands/because I was his eldest daughter. . . . And even though I was his eldest daughter/he cannot tell me one word of love." At the same time, however, these features are entwined with a wild fantasy, one based on the irrational compulsion to visit the dead father "night after night."

According to Jacques Lacan, the symbolic order is a structure encompassing human existence, the sociocultural world of language and signifiers. Entering into language and accepting the rules and dictates of society is a fundamental part of humanity's social construction. Thus, the symbolic order is entwined with an acceptance of the Name-of-the-Father and its laws and restrictions, which contribute to the formation of both individuals and cultures.[6] In other words, the symbolic order is the law (the father's law), the hegemonic discourse, and everything within the confines of social censure. A movement of repetition and fixation, by contrast, arises from repressed desires, articulated in a metaphoric and metonymic language that does not yield to the rules of hegemonic censure. Accordingly, the repetition, fixation, and obsession expressed in Ravikovitch's poem are traumatic features that disconnect the poem from the language of logic and its rules, even as the compulsive repetition is articulated by using the very conventions of the hegemonic discourse. The poem thus maintains the symbolic order in its structure and language, but its fixation on the dead father actually deviates from both social and psychological norms, thus undermining the symbolic order's foundations.

A similar device is used in the poem "Clockwork Doll" (Bubah memukenet) to describe psychological collapse, a lack of control, and an attempt to escape estrangement:

CLOCKWORK DOLL

That night, I was a clockwork doll
and I whirled around, this way and that,
and I fell on my face and shattered to bits
and they tried to fix me with all their skill.

Then I was a proper doll once again
and I did what they told me, poised and polite.
But I was a doll of a different sort,
an injured twig that dangles from a stem.

And then I went to dance at the ball,
but they left me alone with the dogs and cats
though my steps were measured and rhythmical.

And I had blue eyes and golden hair
and a dress all the colors of garden flowers,
and a trimming of cherries on my straw hat.

(CP, 27; BB, 7; cf. BK 63)

The image of a clockwork doll that is broken and then fixed could refer to an emotional state, a gendered position, or to social estrangement. The poem presents a central tension between uncontrolled movement—"and I whirled around, this way and that" (in Hebrew: *vepaniti yeminah usmolah, lekhol haavarim*, literally "and I turned right and left, to all sides")—and reasonable, obedient behavior, "and I did what they told me, poised and polite" (in Hebrew: *vekhol minhagi hayah shakul vetzayyetani*, literally "and my behavior was levelheaded and obedient"). In the emotional space created within this

Manuscript of "Clockwork Doll," reproduced from Ravikovitch's unpublished bequest by kind permission of Ido Kalir.

tension, the speaker expresses her wavering back and forth between different wishes, capacities, and attributes that contribute to her experience.

The nature of the relationship between the traumatic event and the speaker's behavior is not clear. Is it a poem about the taming of the shrew—a psychotic breach ultimately brought under control by hegemony—or does it describe a unique event in the speaker's life, an event that by its very exceptionality in fact emphasizes her normative existence? Does the poem address an inherent gap between the speaker and her surroundings, or does it deal with the speaker's difficulty in assimilating herself anew into a society to which she believes she belongs?

The sonnet-like form suggests an internalization of the symbolic order as well as the speaker's consent to law. The poem articulates the heavy price paid by the subject for returning to normative behavior after the psychotic eruption, evident only in the description "and I whirled around, this way and that,/and I fell on my face and shattered to bits." Silencing the uncontrolled breach—accepting the symbolic order—entails obedience, self-correction, and facing up to the failure of reassimilation. Such a reading of the poem assumes a disparity between the symbolic order, which enforces its norms, and a psychotic or deviant personality, for which whirling around (disrupting the symbolic order) is an "authentic" form of behavior.[7]

Another reading, however, reveals an alternative interpretation of the relations between self, psychotic breakdown, and symbolic order. The poem opens with the declaration that the events described occurred on a specific night ("that night," *balaylah hazeh*, a phrase taken from the Passover Haggadah), when the speaker was a clockwork doll that whirled around until she fell and shattered to pieces. From this, one might infer that the speaker does not ordinarily resemble a clockwork doll, but is a woman fully aware and in control of her actions and their consequences, whose steps are "measured and rhythmical" (as they will be again later in the poem). Perhaps the breach did not stem from within her at all, but was caused by an aggressive and destructive activation of the doll. It is not the symbolic order but the crisis itself that has been forced upon her. She experiences and understands her psychosis not as an immanent part of her personality, but as an external force exerted upon her on a specific night.

There is another translation issue at stake here. Chana and Ariel Bloch render the third line of the second stanza "But I was a doll of *a different sort*." In Hebrew, however, Ravikovitch writes: *ulam az kevar hayiti bubah misug sheni*, literally "But then I was a doll of *a second sort*," a vernacular usage referring to something that is reduced, decreased, second-rate; "damaged goods," to use the Chana Bloch and Chana Kronfeld translation.[8] In essence, the doll is the same before and after the psychotic breach; afterwards, however, she is ridiculed and has declined in value. The poem thus traces not an inner transformation but an external crisis, which neither stems from the speaker's personality nor changes it dramatically.

These two readings do not allow a clear-cut separation between external and internal experience, which are encountered simultaneously and alongside the subject's awareness of her situation, establishing a complex hybridity inside the poem's rigid form. The subversive poetic expression of this duality and the interfusion of internal and external experience allows for the construction of a deviant subjectivity in a repressive environment. It is a lyrical manifestation of the mental Möbius strip of being simultaneously an object and a subject, a process implying a moving chain of relations and rhythms alien to any binary or dichotomous order.

To her surprise and disappointment, the speaker in "Clockwork Doll" is left "alone with the dogs and cats," an image that expresses her inability to integrate, even though her "steps were measured and rhythmical." This image of a "proper doll" sitting among dogs and cats embodies a central element in Ravikovitch's poetics. Even though the dogs and cats represent nonhuman existence, they are actually domesticated animals—just like the "proper doll." Cats, however, are typically independent and untamable. The dogs' presence in the poem hints at an even more complex existence. In the Talmud (in which Ravikovitch was well versed) reference is made to "a bad dog" (*kelev ra*)—a vicious creature that must be kept tied up, although in frontier communities, where there was a threat of marauders, it might have been unchained at night for protection.[9] Thus, dogs and cats are both animals with a dual character: although they appear to be sweet and domesticated, underneath they are of an uncontrolled and disobedient nature. This duality shows Ravikovitch's tendency to at once sustain and destroy the symbolic order.

Just as the poem's strict form expresses anxiety and the decomposition of the subject, so, too, most of Ravikovitch's work presents a paradoxical strategy of subversion from within the boundaries of formal rules. In the first review ever written on Ravikovitch, Baruch Kurzweil indicated that "a weird, interesting, and unrestrained combination" characterizes her book *The Love of an Orange*. While praising her poetry and illuminating its uniqueness, he argues that "Dahlia's intellect-will gets hold of her imagination."[10] Indeed, from this first book of poetry to her final book of short stories, *Come and*

Gone (2005), one of the most distinctive features of Ravikovitch's writing is the coexistence of a strict, rational language alongside motifs and logical disruptions (in the form of fantasies, obsessions, and fixations) that disconnect the content of her writing from rationality.

Ravikovitch is often compared to Leah Goldberg (1911–1970) and Yona Wallach (1944–1985),[11] yet neither of these major poets depicts the relationship between the symbolic order and its subversion with the same complexity as Ravikovitch. Wallach, Ravikovitch's near contemporary, shared with her the treatment of such themes as madness and estrangement, but unlike Ravikovitch, who expresses her subversive experiences in the language of the symbolic order, Wallach articulates them by means of fractured language, irregular syntax, and uncommon phrases. Goldberg, who preceded Ravikovitch by a generation, uses an intact language and rhythm that influenced Ravikovitch, but she does not use this metrical language to express unusual or "abnormal" content.

Ravikovitch thus offers a body of work unique in the Israeli context, one that disrupts the symbolic order without necessarily disrupting language. But why does the speaker of "Clockwork Doll" need to articulate her reenactment in the language of the symbolic order? Why does Ravikovitch express political and ideological subversion by adhering to the symbolic order and sustaining a traditional style, both linguistically and formally? Why does the Ravikovitch speaker maintain this ongoing duality of relaying tumultuous and disorderly experience through language that remains broadly lucid and conventional? What kind of psychological aspect of her poetic persona is revealed by this approach? What sort of emotional mechanism does it preserve?

Days of Mourning, Years without End[12] The State of Doom

Of the many possible answers to these questions, one critical explanation lies in the imprisonment of the Ravikovitch speaker in her orphanhood. All of the poems and short stories dedicated to the traumatic experience of her father's death refer to the state of orphanhood as an essence and an identity, and as a state of doom that destines the speaker to feelings of injustice, longing, need, deprivation, and helplessness.

The story "I Am Joseph" (Ani yosef) tells of the life and downfall of a man called Ehud,[13] whose depressive character and dysfunctional behavior are presented as the result of having lost his father in early childhood. The absent father is incessantly present in his life. Inspired by the biblical story of Joseph's reunion with his father, Jacob, after many years, during which Jacob believed his son was dead (Gen. 46:29–30), Ehud, as a child, fantasizes about the return of his dead father. In the Bible, Joseph says to his brothers, "I am Joseph," and asks, "Is my father still alive?" (Gen. 45:3). Although the narrator in Ravikovitch's story emphasizes, "I am Joseph, but Ehud is not Joseph and his father is not alive," Ehud, as an adult, continues to identify with the biblical story (*Winnie Mandela's*, 49). As long as his own story does not come to its "original" wishful conclusion—the reunion between father and son after being parted for so long—the distress of this modern Joseph cannot be relieved. His cathartic fantasy prevents Ehud from functioning on any other level and, as a result, his orphanhood becomes his main characteristic. His brothers have "made it, they [are] no longer two orphan babies . . . , but rather fathers," (56) but Ehud still cries out for his father. As opposed to the biblical Joseph, who, in Ehud's interpretation, "was rescued from prison because of his father's love," Ehud, deprived of that love, stays imprisoned in his orphanhood, unable to grow (59).

This eternal orphanhood is presented in the story as the main reason for Ehud's lack of vitality, which is manifested in his depression, his inability to function, and in all the "bad times" that "appeared every year, and were just endless" (57). The fatal and destructive potential that lies in Ehud's dysfunction is hinted at in the story's epigraph: "Three brothers we were" (48). This is a fragmentary quote from Nathan Alterman's "Poem of the Three Brothers," where the entire line reads: "Three/brothers/we were,/and lo two we stayed."[14] In Alterman's poem, the brother who dies is the one whose life is symbolized by the maiden, the poems, and the road, whereas the two brothers who survive are symbolized by the carters who travel on freight cars in the cities and the woods. The analogy to Ehud and his two brothers in "I Am Joseph" is clear: the story contrasts the brothers' normative development (army, college, family, financial establishment) with Ehud's downfall as the artist who cannot settle down. As the story's epigraph makes clear, Ehud's condition represents a chronicle of orphanhood, disconnection, and disruption—a chronicle of a death foretold.

Ehud's character represents a typical position in Ravikovitch: the paralysis of orphanhood, a disability from which there is no recovery. Orphanhood is not a condition to be overcome, but a fundamental experience and an ongoing emotional state of mind that establishes the character's subjectivity.

Among other engagements with the Bible,[15] Ravikovitch uses its psychological poetics, or "spiral movement," as Yael Feldman described the simultaneously cyclical and linear nature of biblical repetition-in-variation.[16] For Freud, explains Feldman, "the compulsion to repeat is associated with the death drive—the impulse to resist change, progress, and life. . . . In biblical narrative, on the other hand, it is through recall and recurrence that change is slowly brought about."[17] It is this spiral movement that motivates the speaker in Ravikovitch's to recall her father in order to let go of his haunting presence. Nevertheless, she falls over and over into the Freudian cycle, which resists adjustment and amendment. The speaker is thus, like Ehud, imprisoned in her orphanhood. She is fated to a continual rewriting of the past that leaves no space for a transformative present.

The story "A Death in the Family" (Mavet bamishpahah) which deals with the funeral of Miriam's uncle, seems to express a different approach to the state of orphanhood than that present in "I Am Joseph." Even though Miriam's memory of her father's death is a central experience in her life, the experience seems to lead to a feeling of vitality—as if only by being aware of life's potential can she respect the dead and go through the proper work of mourning. While Miriam is waiting in the cemetery for her uncle's funeral to begin, the reader is given access to her thoughts:

> "I have to see a river. I need to see mountains . . . I need to see everything. Otherwise, I will not be able to properly mourn my uncle."
>
> She became sad. "When my father died. . ." This horrible cave re-opened wide. Suddenly she decided, "My father died long ago." And she continued, "After the river I want to see the icebergs of Arkhangelsk and the frozen boxes in the winter port. I have to hear if the Bering Strait is really so loud. (Winnie Mandela's, 135)

What looks like a vital ambition—Miriam's wish to visit various exotic places—actually expresses her yearning for a fantastic and alternative world. Miriam's fantasies thus detach her from her reality as an orphan. Her uncle's death, the association of her father's death, as well as her anxiety about desistence and nullity, prompt fantasies about unreachable places like the glaciers and icebergs of Arkhangelsk and the Bering Strait. In other words, her anxiety about death arouses an exaggerated, almost grotesque desire. This is the same repertoire of fantasies and delusions that characterizes Ravikovitch's work in general, and these places, which are not actual locations on any geographic map, express a sense of partitioning and denial: I am not here, this event did not happen to me. Miriam deludes herself—and for a while also the reader—into thinking that she has managed to deal with her father's death, as though, unlike Ehud in "I Am Joseph," her orphanhood were not paralyzing. Yet eventually she realizes that she cannot escape the fact of her orphanhood, which girdles her behavior and understanding of the world.

At the end of the story Miriam's family gathers in the cemetery. On one level, this gathering for her uncle's funeral is a temporal affair, but on another, symbolic level, it is connected to Miriam's orphanhood and to Ravikovitch's depiction of orphanhood as a fundamental and permanent state. Michel Foucault defines the cemetery as a "heterotopic" space, which, from the beginning of the nineteenth century, constitutes not the sacred and immortal heart of the city, but rather "'the other city,' where each family possesses its dark resting place."[18] Heterotopias (literally "other places") are spaces that are "something like counter-sites, a kind of effectively enacted utopia in which the real sites . . . are simultaneously represented, contested, and inverted" (Foucault, "Of Other Spaces," 24). Miriam, then, does not merely visit the cemetery as a one-time event, but rather makes this heterotopic space a way of living; for her, it is not "the other city" any more, but the one and only city in which she can exist emotionally. Ravikovitch's work thus presents the death of the father[19] as a "horrible cave re-opened wide," to use Miriam's words; it is an enormous emotional void into which the father is swallowed up.

Ravikovitch's Psycho-Poetic Voice and the Missing Link

According to Slavoj Žižek, symbolic rewriting is related to the "missing link," the gap that disrupts the diachronic chain of causality. The "missing link" establishes an identity that lacks a present and experiences its future through its past:

> The time of the subject is never "present"—the subject never "is," it only "will have been": we never are free, it is only afterwards that we discover how we have been free. This is the ultimate meaning of the "missing link": it is never missing "now"—"now," in present time, the chain is always completed; it is only afterwards, when we endeavour to reconstruct the chain, that we discover how "something is missing."[20]

Correspondingly, the works of Ravikovitch dedicated to her father's death do not deal with past events in and of themselves; rather; they focus on how those events integrate into the present (or rather, the future perfect tense) and create synchronic fields of significance. As Zizek claims, precisely because the linear chain of causality is always a broken one—since language as a synchronic order is captured in a destructive circle—the rewriting of the past attempts to recapture the missing link through a retroactive reorganization of the past; that is, through the reconstruction and reestablishment of its foundations in a backward motion.[21] In other words, the constant rewiring of the past indicates the presence of a gap, of an alien and traumatic kernel that the emotional system tries to reintegrate post-factum—after the "event" or the "fact." If the movement from the "genesis" to the "structure" were continuous, there would be no inversion of the causal direction. It is the missing link that opens the space for the reorganization of the past.

The "proper" course is for the missing link to create streams of reconstruction and recovery, but in Ravikovitch's work in general, and in "On the road at night" in particular, this curative stream does not exist. It is replaced by a mechanism that preserves and duplicates the trauma that originally established the missing link. In other words, orphanhood leaves no space in which the past can be rewritten and restructured; instead, it constantly duplicates the missing link, preventing any possibility of escape or recovery from it. The symbolic entrenchment that surrounds the ever-erupting repetition expresses this imprisonment. The retroactive causality, which embodies the symbolic order—that is to say, the organized and causally poetic structure—duplicates itself in a way that prohibits the dismantling of the missing link necessary for change. The missing link stays on in the orphan's world, even when she tries to free herself by symbolic entrenchments. Paradoxically, the symbolic order and its representations actually maintain and establish the traumatic repetition, recurrence, and fixation that destabilize them.

In the case of Ravikovitch, the gap to which Zizek refers—the wound of orphanhood and the secret that does not heal—is responsible for some major deviant and aberrant breaches in her poetic articulation and functions as a significant psychological foundation for that articulation. Her use of and writing through the symbolic order express recurrent attempts to heal the injury that refuses to heal and to escape the chain of traumatic repetition in which the speaker is caught.[22] This repeated retelling of the disruption, the "chronicle of suffering foretold," working simultaneously with the illusion of reformation, underlies the relationship between the symbolic order and the emotional deviation in the Ravikovitch oeuvre. This duality may help explain the distinctive organization and structure of the poems, which bind the symbolic order and its constant disruption (obsessive repetition, uninhibited eruptions, and psychotic breaches) to each other. The rigid and rational structure, syntax, and argumentation of Ravikovitch's poetry are—in many cases—

the speaker's way of controlling or covering up her obsessive, impulsive personality. Other features of her poetic style, such as her tendency toward symmetric utterances, the absence of enjambement, and her intense use of syllogisms even in places where they are not necessary, are a result of this emotional need to conceal her proclivity to anxiety. Ravikovitch's poetic style is finally the *result* of the speaker's phobic anxiety and traumatized subjectivity, not a *contradiction* of them.[23]

"I Have a Little Secret, Nothing Shocking"[24]
The Secret, the Phantom, and the Crypt

Even with an understanding of Ravikovitch's characteristic poetic language, the fundamental question still remains: Why—to use her own words in the poem "Six Hundred Thirteen Commandments Plus One" (Taryag mitzvot veahat)—do "days of mourning" become "years without end" (cp, 16)? Or, to put it another way, what does it mean to be forever beholden? Why does the speaker "always have to"? What emotional mechanism creates this sense of doom?

One possible answer to these questions lies in the relationship between abandonment and the impossibility of experiencing the certitude of death. A fundamental element in Ravikovitch is the speaker's inability to assign the clearly defined boundary of death to the father's absence: "Did Dahlia's father die, or did he simply pass from the world without dying?" asks the narrator in the story "The Father of —" (Aba shel —).[25] In the autobiographical story "Twenty-five Years" (Esrim vechamesh shanah), the narrator recalls:

> That evening my father did not return home, but due to the general nervousness surrounding me I gave it little thought. During the following days I was told that he'd been hurt and was now recovering from his wounds. On my birthday, two months later, I was given a pouch and a pencil as a present, and was told by my uncle that the present was sent by my father.
>
> I never saw my father after that day and its events, which were etched upon me in a fragmented and misleading manner. An understandable occurrence, since his funeral was held the next day. Only ten years later was I informed that my father was killed by a British army driver.
>
> . . . Even today, twenty-five years after his death, [my father] exists for me as an indelible reality. (*Winnie Mandela's*, 196–97)

This experience, in which death is at once present and concealed, provides the psychological basis not just for those poems and stories explicitly concerned with orphanhood, but for the Ravikovitch oeuvre as a whole.

In their fierce efforts to confirm the father's death, what many of these texts actually end up exposing is the impossibility of ever doing so. Since the death is never definite or distinctly marked, a paradoxical duplication occurs: the father is both present and absent, dead and alive, victimizer and victim, a father and a deserter. On the one hand, there is no mourning process; on the other, mourning becomes the daughter's inescapable existential position. The attitude toward death and orphanhood in Ravikovitch can thus be read as expressing her poetic persona's self-imprisonment, and the impossibility of her disengagement from the emotional mechanism that binds her.

Three concepts in the psychoanalytic work of Nicolas Abraham and Maria Torok are useful for understanding this psychological mechanism: the secret, the crypt, and the phantom. The secrets that ensue from a traumatic event of loss are not something hidden by one person from another, but rather a mechanism of self-silencing activated by the subject in relation to herself. The "secret" is an inner experience; it represents an emotional split between one mental level that recognizes the existence of the hidden, traumatic event, and another that denies it, and therefore experiences the secret. The presence of an unspoken secret is passed to the child through an intermediary "phantom," which transmits not concrete information but gaps. The impossibility of dealing directly with the secret (not merely on account of its intensity, but because it is never articulated) triggers a reaction within the child who has experienced the loss: she buries the vague presence of the secret in an emotional "crypt." There is no release for the child from this inner crypt, and the unprocessed secret that is contained within it thereby becomes a pervasive presence, which dictates the subject's way of being in the world.[26]

The testimony in "Twenty-five Years," as in other works by Ravikovitch, exposes the existence of the secret, phantom, and crypt within her poetic persona. The father's absence and the speaker's denial of this absence merge in her vain attempts to break out of the crypt while continuously retelling the unarticulated secret. The incomprehensible and unspoken event/secret retains its hold on the speaker, preventing escape. As Ravikovitch writes in the poem "Three or Four Cyclamens" (Shalosh arba rakafot): "and I have a little secret, nothing shocking,/that seeps down into the vein of the palm/and colors my blood a lustrous red" (CP, 272; BK, 242).

The main problem of the crypt arises from the way that it exists on the borderline between the conscious and the unconscious. The crypt does not parallel the "unconscious," for if it did, it could be managed by the various defense mechanisms that the conscious mind uses against everything that has previously been unconscious. Abraham and Torok stress that the crypt is not to be confused with either the unconscious or the ego; rather it is an enclave between the two, a kind of artificial unconscious located in the ego.[27] This complicated location of the crypt establishes the past experience as an ongoing present; it is a "block of reality" that sustains refusal and denial. It is a reality that cannot disappear or expire, but also cannot renew itself and live.

This paradigm may explain the intensity of the emotional internment in "On the road at night" (Omed al hakhevish). The daughter's memory is located in the place where the accident occurred, because that is where the secret was established. It is this that she has always known, and to which she is forever beholden. Likewise, the need to recognize the father and to find "ways to remember" him may be understood in relation to the phantom. The speaker recognizes her father by marking him: "And that's how I knew him, and I found ways to remember/that this very man was once my father." The unspoken absence of the father makes it necessary to supplement the gaps in the untold story. The speaker makes a desperate effort to commit his image to memory, though the encrypted memory is characterized by absence and deficiency. "Only when the face is blotted out/can you remember anything fully," writes Ravikovitch in the poem "Pure Memory" (Zikaron tamim, in CP, 127; BB, 52).

Ravikovitch returned to her father's death in a later autobiographical story, "A Brief History of Michal" (Kitzur toledot mikhal):

> [The father's] love was not decreased with time until a car hit him in Jabotinsky Street in Ramat Gan, next to the synagogue, and he was killed immediately. When Grandpa David heard about it he fainted. The Six-Year-Old arrived home and thought that Grandpa was hurt by a car. She knew nothing about her father for two years. They told her that he went abroad to be healed. (*Come and Gone*, 15)

Unlike "Twenty-Five Years," this story emphasizes the place of the accident—the place where the secret was established. The phrase "she knew nothing about her father," in which "father" is used to signify the father's death, reveals the emotional mechanism of Ravikovitch's orphan character:

For the daughter, the father's death is also the moment of his birth. The phantom requires an attribution of signs to the (dead) father, because his death was never marked or articulated. After his death, the daughter does not go through a proper process of mourning that might have enabled her to take leave of him. Rather, she deals with the phantom and fills the gap of his absence with his imagined presence. Likewise, in the story "The Father of ——" (Aba shel ——), Ravikovitch writes: "Who knows Dahlia's father? Who remembers Dahlia's father? . . . Even Dahlia remembers just her memories. . . . All that was left of him is that he is Dahlia's father" (20). These painfully realistic words dramatize the moment in which she recognizes the gap between the actual dead father and the image she has created of him in her mind.

The construction of memories, the process of recollection, and the bridging of gaps are all endless projects that can never satisfy the orphan girl. Moreover, they constantly bond the attribution of signs to the father with the daughter's identity. At Grandma Bilha's funeral in the story "The Firstborn Grandchild" (Hanekhed habekhor), Amnon forces his wife Tami to watch her mother's burial because he believes she must "look in order to understand that it is final" (37). The narrator in "A Brief History of Michal," however, notes that although "all of his [the father's] exterior organs were intact . . . they did not allow the Six-Year-Old to look at him after he died" (16). Contrary to the proper work of mourning, which enables the bereaved to recognize the dead as such, the lack of visual or verbal evidence of the father's death keeps the orphan daughter in the permanent position of the Six-Year-Old (the age of the daughter when her father dies in "Twenty-Five Years" and also the daughter's nickname—bat hashesh—throughout "A Brief History of Michal," even as an adult).[28] This everlasting state constitutes the foundation of her existence, as attested by the narrator in "A Brief History of Michal": "The Six-Year-Old who shall step forth once more and will occasionally rise within the story, doing so against our will or hers" (10).

And so, Ravikovitch writes "words that cannot be uttered, . . . scenes that cannot be recalled, [and] tears that cannot be shed."[29] All of these have been assimilated along with the trauma that led to the loss, thereby establishing the tragic inner reality: "I always knew, I was forever beholden."

Chapter Two

"She Has Damaged the Little Girl"

Orphanhood and Motherhood

"Most of the mothers stopped taking care of their kids," says the narrator of the story "Tirtza in the Snow" (Tirtzah basheleg, in *Winnie Mandela's*, 178), a remark that distills the behavior of the orphan characters in Ravikovitch once they have become mothers. In stories by Ravikovitch told from the perspective of struggling orphan-mothers, dysfunctional motherhood creates, as it were, a *de facto orphanhood*. Other stories portray an orphan girl, presenting the experience of dysfunctional motherhood from the daughter's point of view. In these cases the mother is not necessarily an orphan, but she is experienced by her daughter as having the characteristics of an orphan (weakness, helplessness, etc.). The daughter thus experiences herself as "unmothered." The fatal Gordian knot that ties together orphanhood and dysfunctional motherhood in Ravikovitch's stories stands at the center of this chapter.

Although this chapter focuses on Ravikovitch's stories, the experience of motherhood is represented also in her book of poetry True Love (Ahavah amitit), in the section "Artistic Embroidery" (Rikmah meduyeket). This section contains five poems about the speaker's son, Ido, who was born in 1978. The poems, dated from March 1979 to June 1983, all contain various elements from Ravikovitch's personal life. Although they present a normative image of a mother who is amazed and elated by her newborn baby, it is interesting to notice that in the poem "In the Line to the Show" (Bator lahatzagah)—the only poem in which the baby is a little older and that takes place in a public space—the mother is unable to function and seems just as lost as her son. In this regard, the basic experience in the poems does not contradict the general image of motherhood in Ravikovitch's stories.[2]

Dysfunctional Motherhood, de facto Orphanhood

The story "Tirtza in the Snow" is about Tirtza and her three children during a storm (a storm probably imagined by Tirtza). Tirtza is depicted throughout the story as dysfunctional, unable to make the transition from the status of a child to that of a mother. As a result, Tirtza effectively raises her three children as orphans; all of them display the weakness that is characteristic of orphanhood in the Ravikovitch oeuvre. This is made painfully clear in the scene in which Tirtza denies her daughter: "Tirtza quickly opened the kitchen door and picked up the little girl from the floor. . . . Tirtza wanted to hit her and then she burst out laughing. 'Nice to meet you,' she thought and maliciously smiled with her eyes. 'What a pleasure that this child is not mine'" (*Winnie Mandela's*, 178).

In what appears to be a motherly gesture, Tirtza picks up her daughter. Even this, however, is performed without any feeling for her parental responsibility. The physical and emotional violence expressed in the way Tirtza touches her daughter drains the action of any recognizably parental quality. What might have been a sign, however minor, of Tirtza's commitment to her role as a mother becomes one more act of emotional abandonment.

Tirtza insists on preserving her pre-motherhood identity, refusing to adjust to her new role. Despite her daughter's intense desire for attention, for example, Tirtza neglects her and instead writes a letter to her own parents: "The little one [Tirtza's daughter] stood at the doorway and kicked with her feet on the door. She beat, and beat, beat and beat. Her eyes and nose were red from crying, and Tirtza locked the kitchen's doors so she could quietly write a letter to her parents" (177).

Tirtza tries to create for herself a closed sphere (the room, the letter) that will both delineate the space in which she is still a daughter and prevent the invasion of the space in which she is already a mother. This attempt fails twice: she cannot return to the (physical and emotional) space in which she holds the role of a daughter, and in attempting to do so she makes of her own daughter a de facto orphan.

Tirtza is also the name of a protagonist orphaned by her mother in the acclaimed novella *In the Prime of Her Life* by Shmuel Yosef Agnon,[3] the first Hebrew writer to be awarded the Nobel Prize for Literature (together with Nelly Sachs) in 1966. Tirtza in Agnon's novella is also the daughter of a dysfunctional mother. Her mother, who "died in the prime of her life,"[4] is described by her daughter in her sickness and her longing for Akaviah Mazal, her first and only love, though never as a mother. The Tirtza in Agnon's novella, just like Tirtza's daughter in Ravikovitch's story, cannot get her mother's attention despite desperate attempts. In her touching struggle for attention she pretends to be Akaviah Mazal, the person her mother is longing for. She understands that her only way to enter her mother's (emotional and concrete) spectrum is by pretending not to be her daughter. Thus, whereas Tirtza in Agnon's novella is the daughter who denies her own subjectivity in order to gain her mother's affection, Tirtza in Ravikovitch's story is the mother who struggles with her own subjectivity, and loses her children emotionally as a result.

A more developed variation of maladjusted motherhood can be found in Ravikovitch's "The Lights of Spring" (Orot haaviv). This story, in which the main character adopts a girl who had been orphaned by her mother, describes a situation that seems more like the protagonist's fantasy than any literary reality. The identity of the adopted girl is unknown: "I don't know whose girl she was, but she was not mine" (Winnie Mandela's, 138). Yet the relationship between the unloved girl and the protagonist—who becomes a mother almost against her will—is very similar in essence to the one in "Tirtza in the Snow." Just like "the little one" in the latter story, so too the girl in "The Lights of Spring,"

> despised her father and wanted me [the protagonist]. . . . the little one did not want to be lost and she wanted me. Not that she knew anything about me, and if she knew, she confused the fact because of her young age. I was not sure that I could hide from her the fact that I don't love her. . . . Maybe I was unfair with her, and maybe I was allowed to act as I wish, because every person—including me—is a person for himself. I wanted very much to be a woman for myself. (138)

Anxious about the permeable borders of the self, the protagonist worries that children may pose a threat to her own subjectivity. In Ravikovitch's stories, children must be (at least emotionally) abandoned at an early age and are thus condemned to an experience of semi-orphanhood. It is a painful cycle: the orphaned character who experienced her father's death (and abandonment) and her mother's helplessness (something I will discuss later), reproduces a similar experience, but this time as a deliberate withdrawal from her own children. The character's relationship with her children thus becomes an arena in which she has to fight for her subjectivity. This ongoing battle has a destructive effect both on her and her surroundings.

Tirtza and the protagonist of "The Lights of Spring" worry that their subjectivity will be lost as a result of motherhood. Feminist cultural theorist Luce Irigaray refers to a similar concern and presents the experience of motherhood and of being a daughter as a symbiotic experience that simultaneously establishes the self and puts it at risk:

> With your milk, Mother, you fed me ice. And if I leave, you lose the reflection of life, of your life. And if I remain, am I not the guarantor of your death? Each of us lacks her own image; her own face, the animation of her own body is missing. And the one mourns the other. My paralysis signifying your abduction in the mirror. . . .
>
> And the one doesn't stir without the other. But we do not move together. When the one of us comes into the world, the other goes underground. When the one carries life, the other dies. And what I wanted from you, Mother, was this: that in giving me life, you still remain alive.[5]

Even though Irigaray speaks from the daughter's perspective,[6] we can use her description to better understand the emotional process of the two women in Ravikovitch's stories. Both try to break open the symbiotic connection with their children in order to regain some sense of an independent existence, and in Tirtza's case, also to return to the child's sense of being taken care of and supported by her parents. Tirtza and the protagonist of "The Lights of Spring" actually look for a subjectivity that will not be defined solely by their role as mothers, but rather that will be defined by itself—"a desire to live self from within," to use Hélène Cixous's words.[7] As a daughter, the character in Ravikovitch's work is "the guarantor of [the mother's] death," and as a mother, she internalizes an anxiety about "going underground" and about an emotional death as a result of becoming a mother.

Antinomytic Womanhood

We might, then, understand the stories "Tirtza in the Snow" and "The Lights of Spring" as extreme (almost pathological) variants of the experience of "normative" motherhood: the emotional disownment of the daughter is total; the daughter is considered orphaned by her mother, and the mother—as long as she fulfills her role as a mother—is regarded as a non-existing woman.

The protagonist of "The Lights of Spring" finds an original way to deal with this destructive fate. The relationship with her daughter, which from her viewpoint is experienced as a forced relationship, can become valid if it is based on mutual volition: that is, if the mother chooses her daughter and vice versa, thereby overriding the enforced natural bond between them. To put it differently, given the dysfunction of the enforced biological relationship, the only way to proceed is by deconstructing the attachment itself. In this way, the basis of the relationship between the mother and her daughter is no longer natural or physiological, but wholly emotional. In her imagination, the protagonist touchingly plays with the emotional and theoretical possibility that motherhood is not biologically determined. By so doing, she loosens women's "biology chains," to use Simone de Beauvoir's notion.[8] The protagonist has to give birth anew to her daughter in an emotional-social birth as if it were free of any physiological aspect; she has to untie the physical bond that is culturally loaded, and replace it with a different and unique relationship.

This effort joins a larger discourse about what has been called antinomytic womanhood. The term "antinomy" comes from the Greek, and literally means "against the law." The violation of the "law" that connects the experience of motherhood with biological motherhood parallels the stories of Demeter and the Shunem Woman. Demeter, the Greek goddess whose daughter Persephone was abducted by Hades, and the Shunem Woman, whose son, born as a result of Elisha's miracle, dies (2 Kings: 4), both deny their children's death sentence and demand they return to life. Ravikovitch's character, in her refusal to unite the biological and emotional aspects of motherhood, tries to break its normative, hegemonic, patriarchal, and industrial law, and by so doing, actually fulfills a kind of antinomy that "breaks the permanent and eternal status of the superior law, and puts a possible limit to it."[9]

Adrienne Rich distinguishes between "the potential relationship of any woman to her powers of reproduction and to children"[10] and institutionalized motherhood, that is, all the social and cultural connotations that stem from the physiological experience and that establish the notion of motherhood according to patriarchal needs.[11] In adopting this distinction, by an extreme and fantastic erasure of the biological aspect of motherhood, Ravikovitch focuses on motherhood as a problematic, demanding, and violent institution that sometimes leaves no way out.

The mothers, writes Rich, "if we could look into their fantasies—their daydreams and imaginary experiences—we would see the embodiment of rage, of tragedy, of the over-charged energy of love, of inventive desperation, we would see the machinery of institutional violence wrenching at the experience of motherhood" (Of Woman Born, 280). Ravikovitch's motherhood stories offer a painful glimpse into such fantasies. The difficult feelings that her mother characters experience stem, at least partially, from the impossible expectations surrounding the institution of motherhood. The main representations of the prescriptions and the conditions that define proper motherhood are of an always-available-mother, a constantly-nurturing-mother, a woman who is willing to make no end of sacrifice for her children. In other words, the mother is a subject who lacks subjectivity, a being with no needs, who perceives her main role as supplier of her children's needs.[12] The misery of Ravikovitch's character thus stems from a fundamental sociocultural pitfall for women in a masculine society: women's entrapment in motherhood (and femininity) created by the patriarchy. Ultimately, the pitfall of being a mother and the pitfall of being a daughter is one and the same.

The story "Winnie Mandela's Football Team" (Kvutzat hakhaduregel shel wini mandelah) is about Rama's defeat in her legal battle against her exhusband, Dr. Litman, for the custody of their daughter Nitza. The judge Yehuda Chai Poraz decides that "Nitza Litman will remain under the custody of her father," because "the mother did not take care of her and did not enable separation and individuation of the child" (*Winnie Mandela's*, 26–27). Rama defines this verdict as a revocation of her license for motherhood (27). With this statement she exposes the institutionalized aspect of motherhood that, as Rich states, "aims at ensuring that the potential [for reproduction]—and all women—shall remain under male control."[13] Even though there is no doubt that Rama is Nitza's mother, her "license" is revoked because she does not conform to the court's definition of a proper mother.

Her frustration and helplessness are expressed on the one hand in the violent anger toward her ex-husband, the court, and the judge, and on the other in a range of symptoms of "female disease," such as insomnia and an obsessive cleaning of the house. "Female diseases," such as anorexia, hysteria, agoraphobia, amnesia, and aphasia, are caused mainly by patriarchal socialization, that is, by the problematic encounter between women and patriarchal dictates.[14] Rama's "female diseases" thus embody her inability to deal with patriarchal expectations about motherhood.[15]

On a conscious level, Rama's frustration and anger are directed at her exhusband and the court, but on another (namely, the level of her "female diseases"), these feelings are also turned against herself. Similar feelings of rage and dissatisfaction are part of Tirtza's world as a mother ("Tirtza in the Snow"), but in her case these feelings also turn against her children. Tirtza's sense that she has to choose between subjectivity and motherhood prevents her from functioning, and this leads her to unlikely and unrealistic solutions, such as the denial of her daughter. The climax of this destructive process is her desertion (whether real or fantasized, concrete or emotional) at the end of the story: Tirtza goes to the cinema, but not before giving her "bed blankets to the sleeping children" (*Winnie Mandela's*, 182), as though she feels she will not be back. It seems that from the moment she decides to go to the cinema, the option of returning home (i.e., of sanity, of functioning in any normative way) is blocked. She hallucinates that people around her are eating snails and that the road is blocked with snow. Under the spell of this delusional logic, Tirza sends an imaginary telegram to the president: "I cannot reach you. I am waiting for you to come." Never mind reality; even in her fantasy life she is unable to act.

Wildly Unmothered

The tension between subjectivity and motherhood, and the pressure of motherhood defined by patriarchal norms, which are part of the experience of motherhood in Western culture, are "solved" in Ravikovitch's stories by disownment, abandonment, or dysfunctionality. These are the accessible "solutions" and behaviors for a woman whose primary model of parenthood was that of abandonment and whose identity has been formed by the experience of orphanhood. In fact, Ravikovitch's orphan character cannot act in any other way, since motherhood demands the ability to detach (at least partially) from the status of a daughter. This task is impossible for the orphan who is trapped in her orphanhood and who is forever beholden to the status of being "his eldest daughter."

This doom also prevents the orphan girl from experiencing her mother as a supporting and protective figure; indeed, she feels "wildly unmothered." The term "unmothered," coined by Rich,[16] refers to an emotional state of mind in which the daughter feels herself as an orphan, not necessarily owing to a real death, but because she feels her mother—whether through work, depression, madness, addiction, or any other consuming state—has deserted her.

Nurit from the story "The Summer Vacation Tribunal" (Hatribunal shel hachofesh hagadol) regards herself as "unmothered." Her mother Devora's main characteristic is her absence, an absence that stands out especially in light of the suffering and humiliation Nurit experiences in the kibbutz (communal settlement). Even though Devora's absence is only temporal and has a practical explanation, Nurit experiences it as almost total abandonment:

"Devora went to academic seminars at Mount Scopus and Nurit was alone everywhere" (*Winnie Mandela's*, 105). During a major crisis in Nurit's life, when her mother tries to help to the best of her abilities, Nurit still feels lonely and afraid (111). From Nurit's point of view, her mother is a psychologically absent figure who fails to fulfill her child's needs. Critically, the information that exposes the mother's attempt to protect her daughter is not revealed until the end of the story: "She did not know that her mother went to Chaim [the person responsible for Nurit's humiliation and crisis] to beg him not to harass her anymore, but she didn't gain a thing. She did not know that her mother locked herself in her room and cried" (117).

At the same time that the daughter feels "wildly unmothered," the mother acts and suffers too. Just like Rama from "Winnie Mandela's Football Team," who struggles against the judge Yehuda Chai Poraz and is eventually rebuked as a flighty little girl, so too does Devora fail in her struggle against Chaim Gerstan, the judge at the tribunal. In these two trials, the inferiority of women, both mothers and daughters, is exposed: Rama and Devora appear as helpless begging orphans, lacking support, just like Nurit. Even more significantly, in her suffering and helplessness, Devora, the mother, becomes a duplicate of Nitza, her daughter. To be more precise, Nurit projects her own orphanhood (as well as its by-product, weakness and helplessness) onto her mother's behavior, thereby experiencing her mother as powerless and unable to help, and herself as unmothered. It is as though, because of the initial experience of the father's death, the daughter can feel nothing but a repeated abandonment. The emotional deficit of the orphan daughter does not allow her to receive and internalize the presence of her protective and nurturing mother; the emotional wound is so deep that it prevents the wounded daughter from recognizing the existing support in her life, to such an extent that the mother, though present, is regarded by her as nonexistent. In this sense, the mother is swallowed up in the orphan's "horrible cave."

The dysfunctional motherhood in Ravikovitch's stories is either a result of the weakness that comes from being an orphan, and its state of doom (i.e., the orphan girl is fated to "be his daughter," thereby preventing her from becoming somebody else's mother), or a result of a projection of the orphan child that can experience nothing but abandonment. In any case, this motherhood creates both de facto orphans, or "unmothered" children, and discouraged mothers, whose emotional states preclude the possibility of redemption. To put it differently, the state of orphanhood in Ravikovitch's stories creates an ongoing loop of either orphan mothers who deny their children, or orphan children who deny their mothers. The stories maintain a multilayered circle of orphanhood and motherhood: orphanhood becomes the essence of the girl who loses her father, thus wounding her subjectivity. The daughter who longs for her father's love ("he cannot tell me one word of love") cannot function as a mother to her children, and turns them into de facto orphans, who in turn yearn for her nurturing and affection. But the de facto orphan character does not merely create a "second generation" of semi-orphanhood. In some cases she also experiences her mother as an orphan, as a woman who shares similar characteristics that are the result of orphanhood (helplessness, loneliness, estrangement, unsatisfied desire for love). The orphan daughter projects her orphanhood onto her mother and, in so doing, creates an endless and unresolved circle of orphanhood.

Chapter Three

"His Eldest Daughter"[1]

Women's Symbolic Orphanhood

As a symbolic position, orphanhood can be seen as representing femininity in its social, cultural, and emotional formation. In Western society, which assigns power according to proximity to the father (to the totem, the law, the logos, the phallus), women are always both orphaned and excluded. In this chapter I explore the gendered aspect of the relationship between the symbolic order and deviant experience. To do this, I will return to "On the road at night" (Omed al hakhevish)—a poem that does not distinguish between orphanhood and womanhood—but this time I will focus on orphanhood not as a concrete experience of bereavement but rather as symbolic of the female position in a patriarchal society.

As was argued in chapter 1, "On the road at night" simultaneously makes use of and subverts the symbolic order. Notice that the poem's speaker, whose obsessive experience is articulated in the language of the symbolic order (the Name of the Father), is female. Thus, in the poem as in society at large, this style, which creates a space for an alternative voice that disrupts the symbolic order without disrupting language itself, has a significant gendered aspect.

One of the most sophisticated ways in which Ravikovitch makes her gendered position clear is through the poetic dialogue that she conducts with other major Hebrew writers. "On the road at night" is an outstanding example of this dialogue. The 2000 Israel Prize laureate, Meir Wieseltier (b. 1941, Moscow)—a central figure in Israeli poetry during the 1960s and a member of the group known as the Tel Aviv Poets—was the first to point out the connection between this poem and Nathan Alterman's writing, especially his well-known notion of the living dead. Wieseltier suggests replacing the speaker's biographical father in Ravikovitch's poem with the poetic father, namely, Alterman himself, who, along with Avraham Shlonsky and Leah Goldberg, is considered one of the greatest Hebrew symbolist poets of the 1930s and 1940s. Alterman established himself as the leading poet of the

1940s and 1950s, and together with Shlonsky was considered the unchallenged dean of modern Hebrew poetry—a position that made him the main "target" of the next generation's aesthetic revolution. In this sense, Wieseltier's suggestion to read the biographical father as Alterman can be seen as a recommendation to view Ravikovitch in the context of her generation's rebellion against the aesthetic school of Alterman and Shlonsky.[2]

Tamar Hess focuses and genders Wieseltier's claim and shows that Ravikovitch's poem refers specifically to Alterman's poem "Boulevards in the Rain" (Sderot bageshem) from 1938:

BOULEVARDS IN THE RAIN

The city is combed with light and rain.
Profoundly pretty, she is forever shy.
I will go out today, with my laughing daughter,
Among all of those things that have been reborn.

Here is the glass, her name is clearer than ours
And who shall trespass on her icy reflection?
On her threshold, as on the verge of our souls,
Sound departs from light.

Here is the iron, the idol and slave,
The blacksmith of days who shoulders their weight.
Here, my child, is our sister the stone,
She who never weeps.

In our time fire and water have risen.
We pass through gates and through mirrors,
It seems the night, too, is the river of both days,
Upon whose coasts entire lands alight.

It seems we, too, shall arrive by morning
At the last house upon that spacious road
Where the heavens are still standing alone
Where a small boy throws a ball at their feet.

The boulevard is combed with light and rain.
Speak, oh green one, roar!
Look, my lord, with my laughing daughter
I am strolling down your main road.

My undone city fastens her dress.
The smile of iron and stone still floats above.
All of these do not forget the grace
Of one single word of love.[3]

The connection between Ravikovitch and Alterman's poems is noticeable both in their poetic settings—in Alterman's, a father is walking with his daughter; in Ravikovitch's, a daughter comes "to visit" her father—and in the inverted quotation of Alterman's last two lines in Ravikovitch's poem: "he cannot tell me one word of love."[4]

The father in Alterman's poem strolls with his daughter in a world that contains the possibility of change and development "among all of those things that have been reborn." The daughter in Ravikovitch's poem, on the other hand, is doomed to an endless psychological incarceration. Ravikovitch could thus be said to duplicate the position of the daughter who is unable to escape the patriarchal structure whereby a woman can be nothing more than an accompanist. At the same time, by internalizing the speaker's doom, and by turning her poetic spotlight from father to daughter, Ravikovitch rebels against the place traditionally assigned to women (in the world, in genealogical relationships, in poetry). In Alterman's poem the daughter's voice is absent; in Ravikovitch's poem the daughter is the speaker (Hess, "Poetica," 39–40).

The poem, however, does not simply give voice to the daughter; it insists on changing the power dynamic between father and daughter. Alterman's poem displays a clear assumption about the father's ownership of the daughter. In the Ravikovitch poem, where the speaker must mark the father in order to recognize him, this relationship is reconceived: "And that's how I knew him, and I found ways to remember/that this very man was once my father." Now it is not the father who defines the daughter (by being the person responsible for her birth), but the daughter who, as it were, invents the father as her necessary fantasy and in some way creates him. This inversion empowers the daughter and enables her to bluntly accuse the father at the end of the poem. Although the accusation does not allow her to escape her emotional imprisonment, it repositions her within her mental captivity. The laughing daughter in Alterman's poem learns to express some of her misery and anger in Ravikovitch's poem.

Hess suggests "On the road at night" be read as a declaration of poetic independence from the poetic heritage of the previous generation in general and of Alterman in particular. To my mind, however, the poem asserts its autonomy not by rejecting Alterman's poetics (in terms of structure, rhythm, and language, there is a great deal of continuity between the two writers) but by the way in which it offers us a gendered lens through which to look at the world.

Ravikovitch's poetic dialogue with Alterman reveals the profound difference between the feminine and masculine experience of reality. Because daughterhood is an "empty space" in the psychoanalytic definition of social development, Ravikovitch insists on articulating a feminine voice that is defined as "his . . . daughter" (and not, for example, as the independent voice of an adult woman). The daughter's voice preserves the symbolic frame that establishes the father's experience, and creates a different voice within that same frame. In this way Ravikovitch stresses that feminine experience, though occurring within the same symbolic order, is different.

What's more, the father and the daughter—in the poem and as symbolic entities—are the two most asymmetrical figures in terms of gender, authority, and cultural privilege. While the father is, by definition, present, his daughter—any daughter of the Father, the origin and cause of logos—is always absent.[5] Ravikovitch depicts these power dynamics and emphasizes this very absence within the confines of the symbolic order.

Replacing the father's voice with that of the daughter is thus not a symbolic patricide in the Freudian sense. First, because it preserves the figure of the father, and second, and much more significantly, because it emphasizes not a poetic-generational relation but the *location* of each of them in regard to the position of power (the symbolic order): the father—both in the poems and in the culture at large—possesses power; the daughter doesn't. The father speaks the language of the symbolic order, and walks within it safely, whereas the daughter is either silent (in Alterman's poem) or imprisoned by it (in Ravikovitch's poem). To put it differently, to understand Ravikovitch's subversive statement—outlined by the poetic dialogue with Alterman—it is important to understand that she uses the father-daughter relationship as an indicator not of generational or autobiographical difference but of gender difference. Both of them are "the father" and "the daughter" of the symbolic order; both are signifiers of a gendered position of power and weakness in the world and a delineation of masculine superiority and feminine inferiority in regards to centers of power and language.

In the poem "On the road at night," as well as in many other poems such as "The Love of an Orange" (Ahavat tapuach hazahav, in CP, 11–12; BB, 49–50), "Clockwork Doll" (Bubah memukenet, in CP, 27; BB, 7), "The Dove"

(Hayonah, in CP, 32; BK, 66), and "A Small Woman" (Isha ktanah, in CP 34; BK, 68), Ravikovitch deals with feminine subjectivity. The subversive aspect of her process lies in her poetic conceptualization of feminine subjectivity as socially and culturally different from masculine subjectivity. Ravikovitch's work resists the allegedly universal experience posited by Alterman and genders the relations between hegemony and alternative, marginal forces. Ravikovitch's work, in its establishment of feminine subjectivity, reveals an awareness of the culturally constructed gaps related to a gendered power structure, and reads through these gaps the fundamental disparity between femininity and the symbolic order.

Ravikovitch's style—which maintains the symbolic order as a formal organizational framework for expression while simultaneously disturbing it through breaches of deviant (at times psychotic) energies—can thus be seen as representing the feminine position in the world. The insistence on articulating the daughter's voice (and in other poems, that of the doll, the dove, or the beloved woman) is a subversive act that underlines the social mechanism whereby masculinity creates language and functions as its subject, while femininity serves as language's voiceless consumer. As a result of this power structure, women speak a language from which they are excluded. The "father" and the "daughter," men and women, appear to be speaking the same language, but the position they hold within that language is different and unequal: the father exists as a subject within language, while the daughter's presence within that same language is purely nominal. Ravikovitch's innovation is to create a deviant, aberrant, victimized feminine voice that does not deny the symbolic order, but which is not identical to it.

In light of this, it will come as no surprise that, as Hess claims, "On the road at night" is conceptually much closer to Leah Goldberg's 1955 poem "The Chant of the Faraway Star" (Pizmon hakhokhav harachok) than to Alterman's poem.[6] Unlike the masculine experience in Alterman's poem that ends with a moment of grace, Ravikovitch and Goldberg body forth a feminine experience of doom and imprisonment, that is distinguished by a sense of discrimination, abandonment, and the absence of love. Although Alterman is not overtly conscious of this fact, his position can be seen as distinctively masculine, which is to say, hegemonic and power-wielding

"On the Road at Night" also brings to mind Leah Goldberg's cycle of poems "Night and Last Days" (Layla veyamim achronim), first published in 1940.[7] The speaker in Goldberg's poem, who lost his little sister in childhood and his friend in battle, is awake at night, haunted by the memory of the dead. What stands at the center of both Goldberg's and Ravikovitch's poems is the power of traumatic loss over the one who survived, and the survivor's inability to escape from the memory of his or her loved ones. The relationship between Ravikovitch and Goldberg thus brings together the two meanings of orphanhood discussed above: literal orphanhood, which can lead to a haunted and entrapped subjectivity, and symbolic orphanhood, which represents the position of women in a patriarchal society. These are two different yet related types of inferiority, and two fundamental elements in the (impossible) project—one that I will address presently—of voicing an alienated and traumatized female subjectivity.

Part Two

Estrangement

The Project of
Female Subjectivity

Chapter Four

Estrangement and the Collision of Perspectives

"I look at my reality and see that it differs from conventional reality," Ravikovitch once said in conversation with the journalist Saar Dayan.[1] This feeling of aberration that Ravikovitch recognizes in her life is central to both her poetry and prose, and to the manner in which her poetic persona perceives her own subjectivity.

This chapter discusses Ravikovitch's character's sense of estrangement, which is one of the central elements in the establishment of her identity. I use the term "estrangement" as a translation for the Hebrew *harigut*, a word, it should be noted, that contains multiple meanings: otherness, difference, aberration, outsider-ness, minority, and dissidence. The character's estrangement at once reflects and constructs her position in the world. The shaping and preservation of her estrangement become the enterprise of self-production, a mission regarded by the character as an essential component of her self-image and, moreover, as an act of emotional survival.

In an interview with the newspaper *Haaretz*, Ravikovitch expressed her disappointment with the movie adaptation of a novel she admired:

> She [Muriel Spark] wrote the novel *The Prime of Miss Jean Brodie*, the almost insulting adaptation of which was screened at the Tel-Aviv movie theater. This is not the first time I have watched a novel ruined by its movie adaptation. It is very upsetting. The movie vulgarized the novel. The book is a tragedy of a woman whose naïve and romantic nature led her to take up fascism. It took up a very small part of her personality. She was not a bloodthirsty woman in any way. Fascism was one of the most negligible, naïve aspects of Miss Brodie. The movie's emphasis of fascism

could either be a result of the director's limitation or his assumption that he was addressing an audience suffering from similar limitations.[2]

Such divergent interpretations of Miss Brodie's involvement with fascism reveal a fundamental rift between, on the one hand, the normative understanding of the director and his audience, and, on the other, Ravikovitch's own idiosyncratic understanding, which is unbound by external norms and frameworks. This distinction, which is also a distinction between external and internal perspectives, establishes the reality of Ravikovitch's female character.

The director views fascism as a significant part of Miss Brodie's personality and attaches symbolic significance to her involvement with it. In so doing, he conforms to a sociopolitical order, whereby people are classified according to political-ideological categories, which can never be viewed as anything less than central to an individual's personality. Ravikovitch offers an analysis of far greater complexity: she reads the character's behavior as manifesting the gap between her inner and outer lives. That is, Miss Brodie's interiority is naïve and romantic, but society's external viewpoint classifies her as an out-and-out fascist. The two interpretations—the internal and the external—are both present in Miss Brodie's representation; her self-production expresses and represents one understanding of the circumstances, while the external view of her expresses a different understanding.

This recurring deviation from societal norms is a fundamental aspect of Ravikovitch's character's subjectivity. Moreover, the character, both in the poems and in the stories, repeatedly fails to understand the deviation or simply cannot deal with its consequences. Ravikovitch's interpretation of Miss Brodie assumes that a woman can become a fascist out of naïveté and romanticism, and that fascism needn't be a major aspect of her life. Ravikovitch rejects the director's interpretation, which posits the impossibility of being anything less than an out-and-out fascist, an interpretation apparently based on fascism's devastating historical results. Thus the process of self-production attributed to Miss Brodie by Ravikovitch allows for a "partial" fascism by refusing to conform to an external view of the protagonist, and the external perspective exists alongside the character's inner interpretation of herself, without any connection between the two perspectives.

The character in Ravikovitch's oeuvre establishes herself in a similar manner, constantly experiencing a rift between the internal and the external. Generally speaking, this rift applies to any action carried out by any subject. Both the internal and the external perspectives "read" the action, signify it symbolically, and infuse it with meaning—each according to its language and set of governing rules. The subject and its action become an interpretive battleground. Unlike this generally normative process, however, Ravikovitch's character experiences the rift as a battle on two distant and mutually incomprehensible fronts. As a result, this struggle, an existential struggle shared by all subjects, becomes a violent and uncompromising collision for Ravikovitch's character.

Inside-out and Outside-in
Elizabeth Grosz and the Möbius Strip

The feminist philosopher Elizabeth Grosz offers a theory about the establishment of subjectivity, focusing on the collision between the external and internal interpretative perspectives.[3] Her model is particularly relevant to the understanding of the character in Ravikovitch's work, whose existence is based on this very collision. Grosz's theory of subject-construction views the subject as part of a broad sociocultural structure that exceeds the subject's boundaries but continuously influences it, creating situations in which a significant difference is revealed between the subject's self-perception as a personal subjective experience and the self's definition by society's external view.

Grosz uses terms that refer to the corporeal aspects of the subject's existence, and by so doing she unsettles the binary dichotomy between body and mind: "The objective of the inverse . . . is to displace the centrality of mind, the psyche, interior, or consciousness (and even the unconscious) in conceptions of the subject through a reconfiguration of the body."[4] Grosz's basic argument is that the body image contains and constructs, by its very nature, both the external perspective (outside-in) and the internal perspective (inside-out), thus abolishing the traditional distinction between body and mind: "The body image is as much a function of the subject's psychology and sociohistorical context as of anatomy. The limits or borders of the body image are not fixed by nature or confined to the anatomical 'container,' the skin. The body image is extremely fluid and dynamic; its borders, edges, and contours are 'osmotic'—they have the remarkable power of incorporating and expelling outside and inside in an ongoing interchange" (*Volatile Bodies*, 79).

The innovation of Grosz's argument lies in her claim that rather than being constructed by the process of adapting to the differences between body and mind, the subject is in fact constructed by a process of assimilating herself to the gaps between external and internal perspectives, both of which contain imagery of body and mind. Grosz claims, therefore, that analysis of the process of subject-construction should not focus on the distinction between the representations of the physical-biological body and its psychological representations, but rather on the distinction between the external and internal perspectives, each of which contains representations of both anatomy and psychology. The subject is constructed, then, not through her struggle with the relationship between body and mind, but through the interplay between the external and internal perspectives, both of which are intertwined in her representations. The unfeasibility of clearly distinguishing between the two perspectives makes it necessary to continuously examine their interconnecting, dynamic relations and their reciprocal effect on the subject's construction and representations.

To demonstrate the uniqueness of her argument regarding the complex and immanent relationship between body and mind and between the internal and external perspectives, Grosz uses the notion (suggested by Lacan to describe the subject) of the Möbius strip, a metaphor that is crucial to her understanding of the non-binary aspect of the distinction between the outside-in and inside-out perspectives:

> Body and mind are not two distinct substances or two kinds of attributes of a single substance but somewhere in between these two alternatives. The Mobius strip has the advantage of showing the inflection of mind into body and body into mind, the ways in which, through a kind of twisting or inversion, one side becomes another. This model also provides a way of problematizing and rethinking the relations between the inside and the outside of the subject, its psychical interior and its corporeal exterior, by showing not their fundamental identity or reducibility but the torsion of the one into the other, the passage, vector, or uncontrollable drift of the inside into the outside and the outside into the inside. (xii)

The concept offered by Grosz sheds light on the complexity of the process Ravikovitch's character undergoes in establishing her identity and subjectivity. Far from experiencing a "proper" process of socialization, in which the relationship established between the inside-out and the outside-in allows the subject to live in peace with herself and to adapt to her environment, the character in Ravikovitch's poems and stories never strikes the desired balance between the two. Grosz's Möbius-strip self is therefore subject, in Ravikovitch's work, to a series of never-ending disturbances that result in a permanent state of estrangement and aberration.

The Tribunal

The collision of interpretations found in the arena of self-definition, particularly between the outside-in and the inside-out, is most clearly evident in various trial scenes in Ravikovitch's writings. Actions occurring in the court setting, viewed on both the real and symbolic levels, reveal the matrix of conflicting forces and the gaps between them. Michel Foucault recognizes that legal proceedings are dominated by an aggressive apparatus (power) that influences both social structures and individuals' self-construction: "Whether one attributes to it the form of the prince who formulates rights, of the father who forbids, of the censor who enforces silence, or of the master who states the law, in any case one schematizes power in a juridical form, and one defines its effects as obedience. Confronted by a power that is law, the subject who is constituted as subject—who is "subject"—is he who obeys."[5]

The opening of the story "Winnie Mandela's Football Team" (Kvutzat hakhaduregel shel wini mandelah) enables a close tracking of the two perspectives that occupy almost parallel planes during the trial proceedings conducted by Rama, the protagonist, and Dr. Litman, her ex-husband, for custody of their daughter. Rama attempts to conform to the court's norms by dressing appropriately. Careful to choose clothes that will neither emphasize her young age nor appear to the court as bold, she is conscious that "the judge should not think that she is an arousing woman, but he should not be repulsed by her physical appearance either" (*Winnie Mandela's*, 24).

Nevertheless, the story's opening scene clearly shows the gaps between the language of the court and Rama's own private language, as well as her failure to appreciate the difference between the two:

> "I ask, your honor, that we hold this trial without attorneys," said Rama in a language she believed would appeal to the judge, "our case is human and not legal."
>
> His honor Yehuda Chai Poraz said, "The case is legal and not emotional, the attorneys will participate in the hearing."
>
> Was my voice weak or is the judge hard of hearing, Rama asked herself. (23)

Her request to hold a trial without the presence of lawyers ironically bears witness to Rama's inability to comprehend the motives of those in power who set the tone of the situation she faces. This naïveté precludes any possible chance of Rama's victory. Hannah Naveh points out the existential nature of Rama's question, a question that in fact expresses "a summary of the pitfalls of female representation, . . . an impossible [situation] of a woman entrapped in femininity created by the patriarchy."[6]

The contrast between Rama's voice and the judge's perception stems from the culturally constructed gaps of a gendered power structure, whereby masculinity forms language, while femininity voicelessly consumes it; hence women speak a language from which they are excluded. Rama and the judge appear to be speaking the same language, but the position they hold within that language is unequal: the judge exists as a volitional subject within language, Rama as a passive, excluded object. In her discussion of women's inability to be present as subjects within language, Luce Irigaray argues that the only place intended for the female is in relation to male subjectivity and that language reinforces their traditional roles as wives and mothers, as objects of desire.[7] In accordance with this, Rama's voice, in the courtroom, will always fall on deaf ears: the court only allows for a direct channel of communication between those who are present within the language—the male lawyers and the judge.

Rama's voice—a feminine, deviant voice striving for a different type of self-production—invades a patriarchal space, whose symbolic order she threatens to destabilize, and is therefore excluded and silenced: "[Rama's] attorney looked at her in disappointment. Not only was the judge hostile, he had *a mad woman* for a client"; "[Judge Poraz] had a reputation for being an experienced and reasonable judge. *Not only did he not listen to Rama, he did not even lift his gaze to look at her*" (*Winnie Mandela's*, 26, 24, my italics). The silencing of her "mad," feminine voice is necessary to maintain order in the courtroom, a place in which only that which has been translated into its own language—the language of the logocentric symbolic order—is acceptable.

As the symbolic order's overseer, the court is one of the clearest representations of the order and its functions. The conflict between the officers of the court (professional males) and Rama thus reflects not only the obvious legal struggle but also a latent struggle between the symbolic order and Rama's attempt to create a space for an alternative mode of being. In accordance with the hierarchy of power in the story, Rama's subversive alternative must be harnessed and appropriately channeled for social cohesion and regulation. Despite the seemingly powerful nature of her deviant act, it is therefore important to note its suppression by the court, which underscores Rama's weakness. Although Rama's speech threatens the order of the legal proceeding, the court is intractable: it maintains its position of power and represses her disruptions. Like many feminine, deviant, or psychotic eruptions, Rama's attempt fails to affect the superiority of either the court or the order that established it, and fails to liberate Rama from her weakness.

In Ravikovitch's work, then, the empowering influence and the weakening effect of subversion exist simultaneously. On the one hand, deviation is an expression of the character's self-establishment and is therefore an act of inner strength that subverts the symbolic order. On the other, not only do these deviations fail to have any concrete effect on the symbolic order, they also fail to salvage the character from, and oftentimes even intensify, her weakness.

Rama's weakness is brought home by the court's decision to leave her daughter in the father's custody, their rationale being that Rama has failed in her role as a mother. In other words, the court is authorized, as a representative of the symbolic order, to define what constitutes proper motherhood. In the struggle between interpretations regarding "proper" motherhood, Rama remains powerless. Excluded from the symbolic order, she is relegated to one in which fantasy prevails, as she imagines harming Dr. Litman and the judge and daydreams about Winnie Mandela. Such fantasizing is clearly portrayed as the result of her inability to handle patriarchal dictates about motherhood.

Rama first becomes acquainted with Winnie Mandela through a newspaper photograph (*Winnie Mandela's*, 30). According to Lacan, the gaze is intersubjective: I do not only look, I am also being looked at. Through the other's gaze, a person comprehends his or her role as an object of desire.[8] When Rama's trial is over, she chooses Winnie Mandela's gaze and by so doing transforms herself from an object constructed through the gaze of the legal system into a subject created by the viewpoint of Winnie Mandela. Although Mandela is an actual historical figure, in the story she functions as a fictional character. As it is Rama who provides the reader with all the information about Mandela and her view, Mandela's gaze set upon Rama is not merely imagined by Rama, but functions as her own gaze upon herself. This shift of the constructing view is significant and enables a turn in the logic of events. The first part of the story occurs in a courtroom and is driven by the male authority's voice and gaze. At the trial's conclusion, Winnie Mandela's presence is summoned by Rama's imagination so that Mandela may invade the judicial arena and subordinate it to her gaze (which is, in fact, Rama's gaze), a shift that leads to a reorganization of the narrative sequence. The intersection between Mandela's gaze and Rama's gaze allows for the appropriation of Rama's eyes from the confining contemplation of the court's authorities. This dynamic of identification thus reshapes the organizing logic of the remaining narrative, shifting, for example, the location from the courtroom arena to a domestic sphere, mainly Rama's own.

Winnie Mandela's character functions as a means for Rama's self-construction. She serves as a new signifier for Rama's self, offering Rama the opportunity to reflect on herself from outside her boundaries, with the purpose of creating herself as a signifier that will allow a functional self-world relationship. Such interrelations are exemplified by Lacan's mirror stage, which, while essentially defining the self also defines the world. By providing a distinction between the world and the self, it enables a self-world dynamic.

In this context, where subjectivity and the process of identity construction are regarded as a battle of gazes, Rama's poetic wish to blind the judge as a means of revenge is easily understood. Irigaray claims (mostly regarding Freud's work) that:

> Woman's castration is defined as her having nothing you can see, as her having nothing. In her *having* nothing penile, in seeing that she has No Thing. Nothing *like* man. That is to say, no *sex/organ* that can be seen in a form capable of founding its reality, reproducing its truth. *Nothing to be seen is equivalent to having no thing.* No thing and no truth. The contract, the collusion, between one sex/organ and the victory won by visual dominance therefore leaves woman with her sexual void, with an "actual castration" carried out in actual fact.[9]

Rama, whose relegation to a non-reflexive visibility and exclusion is based on "what cannot be viewed," is thus empowered and granted presence by the fantasy of harming the eye that excludes and cannot see her, an action that allows a different view to exist, and an invisible and non-existing subject to become present. By blinding the possessor of the phallus, Rama negates the construction of her world on the foundation of the phallogocentric view, and she is thus able to judge and construct herself.

Rama must construct herself, and the relationship with her daughter, as a subject who does not depend on a view inherently destructive to her—a view that, for example, regards her solely in terms of the discourse about proper motherhood. Rama's plight, in common with all Ravikovitch's characters, stems from the fact that the removal of the destructive view can only occur within the realm of fantasy.

The story "The Summer Vacation Tribunal" (Hatribunal shel hachofesh hagadol, in *Winnie Mandela's,* 87–117) depicts kibbutz life as degrading and miserable for those who do not fit in. At the end of the story, the school's student body and Chaim Gerstan, who is responsible for the children's group, put the protagonist, Nurit, on trial, after she escapes from her job following harassment by her classmates. Nurit's trial can be seen as an exaggerated counterpart to the trial scene in "Winnie Mandela's Football Team," and in what might be considered a dramatized portrayal of the story's central metaphor, embodying the exclusion of women and their absence from the judicial sphere, Nurit herself does not participate in the trial.

Her defense team is made up entirely of the misfits of the kibbutz society. In a fashion similar to Rama's trial, Nurit's trial is conducted by a power structure that seeks to instill, verify, and reinforce the desired hegemonic norms and patterns of behavior. The trial becomes an educational and indoctrinating event that reserves the right to punish the undisciplined "heretics," the powerless, those who have been rejected. Far from being an arena where justice is served, the courtroom functions as a space in which lawmakers and the law's adherents take care to serve their own power and the established order. The court cannot provide a fair hearing; prosecution and defense are never equal adversaries. The bearer of both power and knowledge puts the defenseless on trial, while the latter is neither proficient in nor familiar with the language of the law.

In this manner, the court scenes in these stories depict the female character in Ravikovitch's writing as inferiors within a supposedly equal society (be it a democratic welfare state, a kibbutz, a family, a group of children, etc.). The character's inferiority is "transparent," veiled, non-verbalized, and has no apparent legal status. This is, in fact, the general condition of women in many patriarchal societies: inferiority veiled as equality, oppression disguised as freedom.

Both Nurit's and Rama's trial scenes reflect the unequal power relations that exist under the guise of equality. The center creates a trial setting, and only a non-hegemonic spotlight can succeed in uncovering its underlying ideology and motives, namely, hegemony's unyielding need to construct itself, preserve its existence, and destroy any threatening forces. The marginal's presence in the trial proceeding is either a result of a survival mechanism (Rama) and/or a product of coercion (Nurit). The marginal and powerless subjects cannot make use of the trial proceedings; their presence in these proceedings will be invoked only when the central body so requires and chooses. In Rama's trial, "Judge Poraz lifted his gaze and saw Rama as though it was only at that moment that she appeared before him" (*Winnie Mandela's*, 26), and Nurit's only presence in her trial is as an idea intended to uphold and defend the kibbutz's ideology. The court views Rama and Nurit solely through its own eyes, a "male mirror view"[10] that fails to contain their voices. In fact, the court uses them for its own needs. Because laws are applied and interpreted during the trial, the trial becomes another opportunity for educating women (and other marginalized groups) and for launching truths into the public space. The actual application (the legal proceedings, verdict, and sentence) thus becomes an opportunity to teach, learn, and relearn the "paternal law," to reconfirm the hegemonic and symbolic order. This is particularly critical because the symbolic order, by signifying the subject from the outside, actually transforms it into an object and thereby affects the reality of these individuals, defines (within the law) their practice, and fixes their inferior position in the world.

A Short Delay

The nameless female protagonist of the story "A Short Delay" (Ichur katan, in *Winnie Mandela's*, 79–86) is an eighteen-year-old soldier, whose estrangement is expressed in her tendency to wear a pinkish-gray robe at her military base. From the beginning of the story, the robe is regarded by those around her as extremely odd. After she is sexually harassed by her superior, Major Rosenblum, the protagonist undergoes an internal shift and adopts the army's code of conduct.

Her initial fashion choice can be read as an act of subversion aimed at the military system. It is worth noting, however, that the protagonist substitutes the military uniform, which signifies that she holds the lowest rank in the military hierarchy, for a traditional item of female clothing, a robe, which signifies a low place in the social hierarchy. In other words, it is possible to see the robe not as a subversive gesture but as one that betrays her internalization of her inferior status. Whatever the case may be, it is clear that her choice is not accidental: the protagonist's protest is not aimed solely at the specific institution of the military but is a much broader attempt at self-definition. The starting point of this effort is a general sense of gender inferiority, which is certainly reinforced by the military system. Wearing the robe on the base—like making a forbidden call to her mother and breaking the rules by listening to the radio—is therefore a subversive act born of a desperate attempt to salvage her individual subjectivity from the homogenizing forces surrounding her.

This act, however, loses its subversive power when Major Rosenblum sexually harasses the protagonist. The robe, which might have allowed for a non-sequestered female existence in a patriarchal society, is interpreted from a male perspective as a garment of seduction, and so fails to protect the private female space within a larger public masculine space. The robe thus places the protagonist in an even more inferior position to the uniformed officer and she fails to maintain her subversive stance, instead adopting Major Rosenblum's perspective when she reflects that "the pinkish-gray robe was so inappropriate" (84).

This development is painfully ironic. In her attempt to resist the anonymity and conformity conferred by the military uniform, the protagonist ends up adopting another uniform, one that both undermines her individualism and deepens her inferiority. Despite the fact that it was chosen as a symbol of resistance to the military uniform and all it represents, the robe not only generates the same set of signifiers within the military structure, it also absorbs what in the protagonist's view is unique and individual into the military structure's established, normalizing language. Wearing the robe enhances her eccentricity, aberration, estrangement, and social inferiority, and signifies her inability to conform to the field of socialization. The pursuit of uniqueness causes the protagonist to fall into a trap of typicality.

The invasion of the Major's perspective and his authority to define, common to all bearers of power in the story, conceptualizes the protagonist's expressions and language of individuality as eccentricity and weirdness, and in other cases as an expression of madness and insanity. The character thus loses the right to her own interpretation; no room is left for her in the symbolic order. Just like Rama in "Winnie Mandela's Football Team" and Nurit in "The Summer Vacation Tribunal" the female soldier is relegated to another conceptual order, one ruled by fantasy and delusion: "in a short while I'll inherit the best in life. . . . I'll get double of whatever I wish for. . . . only a short delay, I laughed. . . . Double of everything, I thought. I'm sure of it. Everything will come at just a short delay" (86). She comforts herself with the belief that her permanent deviation is only temporary and will be corrected. She is unaware of the categorical, unbridgeable difference between the inside-out and outside-in perspectives, between the idiosyncratic nature of her behavior and the symbolic order, between insanity and normality.

In spite of the protagonist's attempt at a subversive form of protest, and although the story's central scene (the incident of sexual harassment) presents her as holding her own ground, "A Short Delay" ends with the protagonist's helpless fantasies of a better future. The story provides an account of the character's struggle for her own subjectivity and for an individual existence, a clash of perspectives regarding her actions, and, above all, her failure that only feeds her dreams of doing better in the future. The story's title, "A Short Delay," can thus be read as a common symptom of the Ravikovitch character. It expresses an inherent structural pitfall the character encounters, a permanent split between dream and reality (what I will later refer to as a split between "here" and "over there"), and an existence that is being constantly misunderstood by others.

The collision between the outside perspective, which defines and interprets the character's behavior, and the internal perspective, which drives this same behavior, is fundamental to the character's experience of the world and plays a central role in the way in which the character establishes her subjectivity. All of the stories and many of the poems include information about the character's unusual and aberrant behavior; we encounter negligent mothers, careless teachers, rebellious and undisciplined soldiers. Both the people surrounding the character and the reader regard her behavior as a deviation from the norm but, just as Miss Brodie's view of fascism does not correspond to the external view of her political affiliation, this is not the manner in which the character perceives herself.

This ongoing collision of perspectives reveals not just the gap between how one is perceived and how one perceives herself but also the victimhood inherent in a subjectivity constructed within the "contact zones" of conflicting perspectives. The term "contact zone" originally referred to concrete territories on the globe in which different nations and cultures live but has also been used to name a mental location, where various cultural elements within the self meet.[11] Mary Louise Pratt defines the term as "social spaces where disparate cultures meet, clash, and grapple with each other, often in highly asymmetrical relations of domination and subordination."[12] Using the term 'contact zone' to name a particular facet of an individual's emotional experience emphasizes the complex relationship between the internal and external gazes. It should be stressed that these are not simply polar perspectives, which place the subject in diametrically opposed positions; rather, the subject is placed in dynamic and variable positions, as though at different points on a Möbius strip. As Shoshanna Felman says: "The cultural situation it implies in effect involves a *conflict* between codes; the confrontation of the different context is thus not a spectacle but a dynamic, an inter-*action* which displaces both domains and decenters them with respect to each other. What is at stake is not simple exchange, but a movement of *ex-centering*."[13]

This clash of perspectives, so evident in the trial scenes, creates a permanent structure of conflicting forces within which Ravikovitch's character occupies an inferior position. These power relations affect different aspects of the character's life. Observing her various decisions (both conscious and unconscious) within this power structure, it becomes apparent that the character fully understands the hierarchy and her position within it. Nevertheless, she refuses or fails both to deduce conclusions that might improve her situation or to operate from a position that accepts the power's authority. The character experiences the power structure as an ongoing struggle, regarding any adaptation or concession to those in power as an act of self-negation. She therefore attempts to preserve the internal perspective in the face of the challenge posed by the external. As a result, and in order to retain her identity, the character adopts a deviant and detached persona that is at odds with the symbolic order.

The Ravikovitch oeuvre addresses the personal struggle for the right to the construction and interpretation of one's own subjectivity, the right to determine the nature and value of one's own actions and opinions; and the right to conceptualize and interpret the world. Yet these rights are also seemingly denied the character in Ravikovitch, who again and again is sentenced to remain in an aberrant and jarring space and to be regarded by others as estranged and psychotic.

Chapter Five

"Imaginary Geography"

The Gap between "Here" and "Over There"

I simply create for myself an imaginary geography, lands I will never get to which are pleasing to think of. These countries like Zanzibar, Madagascar, and all the rest are very vibrant to me, and I dream of them endlessly.

Ravikovitch[1]

There did I know a delight beyond all delight

Ravikovitch[2]

Ravikovitch says of her first book, *The Love of an Orange*, that it "is written in eloquent language. I devoted myself to exalted situations."[3] These words articulate one of the fundamental qualities of her writing, namely, it's acute awareness of the gap between the flawed nature of lived experience and the perfection that we can imagine but never realize.[4] The experience of this discrepancy between what might be termed "here" and "over there" is manifested in her poetic engagement with the conflicts of life and death, truth and falsehood, justice and iniquity, passivity and action.

The "over there" in Ravikovitch's work is located in exotic and fantastic geographic locations: the rivers of Damascus, the land of the setting sun, beneath the sea. It is also to be found above roofs, in the sky, in the Mediterranean sea and the Atlantic and Pacific oceans, in China and Madagascar and Scandinavia, and on the beaches of Norway and the deserts of Australia. These exotic areas all have connotations of material affluence and biblical history. They constitue a rich trove of fantasies and delusions rather than points on a real geographic map. In Ravikovitch's words, hers is "an imaginary geography, lands I will never get to which are pleasing to think of."[5] Yet although some of the expressions of "over there" present a reality beyond time, others present a reality that, however imaginary, is grounded in recognizable historical fact.

In any event, "over there" is a space of desire and wish-fulfillment, as expressed in the poem "Delight" (Chemdah): "There did I know a delight beyond all delight" (CP, 35; BK, 69). The speaker's "over there," an alternate time and space, contains her yearning for peace and for something unnamable: "many days from now/I will find what yet my soul sought" ("In Praise of Peacefulness" [Beshivchai hashalvah], in CP, 29). The poem "The Land of the Setting Sun" (Eretz mevo hashemesh) addresses the gap between "here" and "over there," and presents an epistemological drama:

THE LAND OF THE SETTING SUN

And he took away the horses that the kings of Judah had given to the sun . . . and burned the chariots of the sun with fire.

I heard there is a way to the land
of the setting sun,
but nobody ever said it's a land
where I could go.

I had no friend to come with me
so I set out alone
for the land where the setting sun
rides a chariot of gold.

And they told me: kings without equal,
magnificent kings,
ruled over the land of the setting sun
long, long ago.

And I told myself: when I come to the land
of the setting sun,
they'll give me a robe of purple,
a throne of gold.

And in that land I will find peace
for ever and ever.

—That tale I made up myself.
That tale I was never told.

(CP, 20; BB, 12; cf. BK 57)

At the center of this poem stands the disparity between "here" and "over there." While the description of "there" and the speaker's desire for it are everywhere apparent, the "here" is suggested only by its absence. The "here" is characterized by a sense of loneliness, discrimination, and deficiency. The "over there," on the other hand, the land of the setting sun, is a rich and fantastic place of well-being, presented through biblical language and imagery.

A linguistic muddling of the motto from II Kings 23: 11—using the modern Hebrew word *Mevo*, which means entrance, instead of the biblical word *Mibo*, which means "[preventing from] entering"—frames the description of the "over there." The speaker fuses her own imaginary land with the biblical image of the burning of the chariots of the sun as part of Josiah's purification of the temple. What was destroyed with instinctive and colorful violence in the biblical text here ignites the speaker's fantasies. Biblical layers join the speaker's associative contours. She uses, for instance, the phrase "at the entering (the setting) of the sun" (Mevo hashemesh), which appears both in the blessing given to the Hebrew people in Deuteronomy 11: 30 and in the promise of the land in Joshua 1: 4 and 23:4. Such biblical authority is adopted in order to express truths about the speaker's land of the setting sun: the exaggeration and intensity of these texts serves the sense of the definite and absolute that characterizes the "over there." In this land there will also be "peace for ever and ever." In other words, the desire for ultimate tranquility and an escape from time will be realized. This moment in the poem is the apex of the desire to escape from the "here," the desire for annihilation and redemption.

Two details in the poem warrant particular attention: the phrase "And I told myself" (fourth stanza), and the statement "That tale I made up myself" (fifth stanza). Here the speaker explicitly declares her awareness of the fictive nature of the land she is describing. Furthermore, these phrases reveal her mental mechanism, the establishment of the narrative that characterizes most of Ravikovitch's work. The separation between the "here" and the "over there," and the illusion that "over there" is a place one might actually reach, function as narratives through which the speaker in this poem, and Ravikovitch's character in general, establishes her own subjectivity. The stories that she tells herself over and over again, though expressed in different ways, actually comprise the fundamental story without which the character would be unable to function in the world. The Ravikovitch character thus vacillates between sustaining a normative reality and abandoning it altogether. Generally speaking, the ability to recognize the distance between "here" (reality) and "over there" (utopia) is considered a requirement for belonging to the symbolic order. The abolition of this distance—by means of mentally leaping between the edges of "here" and "over there"—exceeds the symbolic order and thus threatens to undermine it. These sentences ("And I told myself," "That tale I made up myself") express the dominance of the symbolic order over the deviant experience, but they do not revoke the power of the symbolic. In other words, the speaker immerses herself in an imagined world so thoroughly it begins to seem like reality.

"The Land of the Setting Sun" is a fascinating poem because of the way in which it explores this duality: on the one hand, it reflects the mechanism of the "here" and "over there," while on the other, it exposes this mechanism as a fiction: "That tale I made up myself./That tale I was never told." Even though the illusion exists in the speaker's mind, the poem ends with the speaker recognizing that the ultimate peace promised by the land of the setting sun, the "over there," is not achievable in reality. In a paradoxical way, this awareness reveals the logic of the fantasizing mechanism. The "over there" becomes the illusory redemption of the tortured soul.

"But That Which Was Ordained for Them/Shall Not Be Ordained for Them by My Lord"[6] Idiosyncratic Justice

The concept of "here" and "over there" as a protective mechanism brings to mind the notion of the psychic dissociation caused by a traumatic event. Pierre Janet (1907) was the first to show how dissociation is a direct psychological defense against overwhelming traumatic experiences and to describe the dynamic of traumatic memory splitting off from the rest of consciousness.[7] In Ravikovitch, however, the separation between the "here" and the "over there" creates not a dissociation of the psyche but a new order of morality and justice. Unlike the state of dissociation in which certain emotions, thoughts, and memories are separated from the rest of the psyche, the separation that takes place in Ravikovitch's works does not neglect the unpleasant aspects of the character's reality, but rather suggests a new context in which they might be understood. In this way, for example, Nurit from the story "The Summer Vacation Tribunal," does not dissociate herself from a humiliating incident, but rather interprets it according to her idiosyncratic sense of justice and waits patiently for God's intervention, which she believes will not simply bring revenge but also reveal her own superiority to everyone she knows.

Similarly, the fact that the speaker's arrival in the land of the setting sun also involves her enthronement is not accidental: it expresses both her sense of personal election and the unique conception of justice she believes will be realized in the "over there." As in the poems "Seats for Trial" (Khisot lemishpat, in CP, 26) and "The Sorrow of Night" (Tzaar halaylah, in CP; BK, 65–66), this sense of justice does not exist in the "here," but only in the future, in the "over there": "many days from now/. . ./there shall be erected a house of measure for me" ("In Praise of Peacefulness" [Beshivchai hashalvah], in CP, 29). Because the character is convinced of her own uniqueness, she creates an imaginative hierarchy that differs from conventional social hierarchies. In her conception of justice, there is no doubt as to her superior status and the promise of a better future. She believes that, thanks to "God's eye," which will impose her own brand of justice, she will overcome her estrangement, weakness, and vulnerability: "but that which was ordained for them/shall not be ordained for them by my lord" ("Seats for Trial").

The speaker's longed-for peacefulness—something that can only be reached in the imaginary "over there"—is derived from a painful, threatening, and violent interaction with the people of the real world: "I will move away from people's fury/poison of snakes and scorpions" ("In Praise of Peacefulness"). The idiosyncratic conception of justice in Ravikovitch thus stems from (and to some degree also shapes) her character's sense of deprivation and iniquity, which are all part of her reality, her "here and now." There is therefore a strong connection between the character's estrangement and the unique brand of justice she conceives.

Martin Heidegger asserts that the experience of the human being (*Dasein*) is characterized by the experience of *being-with-others*. The individual experiences different kinds of relationships with the moral order and is enveloped in social and cultural systems of meaning that define his subjectivity. The experience of *being-with* takes various forms and can be harmonious and fulfilling or antagonistic and hostile. For Ravikovitch's character, however, *being-with* might better be replaced with *being-against*. The psychoanalyst Carlo Strenger explains that individuals who feel themselves in opposition to normative forces experience "the moral order of society as a field of force that is antagonistic and a source of pain to them. They do not feel linked to society by way of community and belonging, but that the moral order has injured them irretrievably."[8]

Strenger adds that these individuals "protest against this injury by denying that the social order is itself morally justified" (124), and this is to some extent what Ravikovitch's character achieves by creating her own idiosyncratic justice. By conceiving of this new justice, she effectively denies the social-moral order from which she feels excommunicated.

Consider the story "The Summer Vacation Tribunal," which ends with the protagonist's fantasy about the fulfillment of her idiosyncratic justice: "He [God] will destroy the kibbutz. . . . she [Nurit] will be in the city . . . She trusted that God will do everything for her, and he will do it fairly" (*Winnie Mandela's*, 117). The story describes Nurit's life of misery and isolation leading up to this moment of fantasy. At the apex of her humiliation and despair Nurit "was certain that God was with her and that he examines everything that is happening to her, and that he refers to the things exactly as she does. Until now he stood aside, but from now on he will start intervening" (116–17). It is precisely in her weakest moment that Nurit is most convinced of her own righteousness and the existence of a superior justice that will one day be put into effect by God's destruction of the kibbutz.

A similar approach can be found in the story "Clouds" (Ananim) (60–75), which describes Nurit's heartbreak after she has fallen in love with Ilan: "Nurit always felt that she relied on the mercy of natural forces and celestial bodies" (63). It appears that her connection to the divine has been damaged when she compares herself to the broken tools that God creates (75). This duality, however, is part of the same conception: the ideal world exists, but only in the future. Although the character suffers and feels outcast in the present, in the future, she believes, her superiority will be revealed to all when God takes revenge on her behalf. That she should compare herself to one of God's broken tools suggests that she sees herself as part of a divine plan that will one day be revealed.

The two tenses, present and future, are variations on the spatial opposition in Ravikovitch's work between the "here" and the "over there." In Levo-Vardinon's words, it is the variance between "the lift-off and the falling."[9] In the present, Nurit works and suffers in the kibbutz, but in the future "she will have a house full of couches, and she will move from couch to couch like a cat" (*Winnie Mandela's*, 107). The protagonist of "A Short Delay" (Ichur katan) spends her life preparing for a momentous change she believes will one day occur: "this is how I prepare my life, and later on life will arrive" (86). In "The Wild Geese" (Avazey habar) Nurit walks on the streets and feels that everything she sees contains some hidden essence (120). In "Clouds" Nurit is "destined for greatness," and her imagination "lifted her sometimes above the clouds . . . Only the fall was always a collapse" (64). Thus, we can see that in the characters' emotional reality the different spaces mesh with different temporal zones.

Ehud, the protagonist of "I Am Joseph" (Ani yosef, in *Winnie Mandela's*, 48–59), also moves back and forth between a disappointing present and a promising future, between reality and fantasy, between a sense of neglect and one of election. The story describes Ehud's life and eventual downfall, beginning in childhood with his father's death, on through the family's move to the kibbutz, and reaching its climax in his adolescence, when he stays in bed and is unable to function. The reference to the biblical Joseph ironically suggests that Ehud, a modern Joseph, is destined for greatness and that his sufferings will ultimately lead to and be justified by a "happy ending."

Thus far Ehud has experienced only the few first steps of the biblical narrative (the closeness to the mother and the separation from the father), but through his identification with Joseph hopes that he himself will one day enjoy the dreamer's eventual happiness and reconciliation. It is through this identification that Ehud is able to survive the ordeals he encounters. The biblical story serves as the otherness in time and space that he needs in order to endure the misery of the "here and now." Ehud's conception of justice can thus be seen as stemming from his suffering and alienation.

To achieve some sense of autonomy and control, those people whose desires have been frustrated by reality often reinvent themselves in such a way as to escape society's censure. In Ravikovitch, this project of self-creation often involves an attempt to recreate some aspects of the characters' (internal and external) reality. Since these characters are too ineffectual to have any palpable influence on the world or even chart the course of their own destiny, this reinvention is usually limited to the realm of fantasy.

The idiosyncratic justice created by the Ravikovitch character legitimizes her estrangement. The character needs this approval because her estrangement is not simply the result of an external reality but of her subjectivity itself. Any moderation of this estrangement would thus be experienced as a compromise undermining her sense of self. The Ravikovitch character has developed a seemingly paradoxical approach: as her relationships with her environment become more destructive, her individuality and subjectivity are further reinforced and protected. The preservation of her estrangement is thus synonymous with the preservation of her very identity. Ironically, perhaps tragically, her project of self-creation, in other words, deepens her socially marginalized status.

People who deal with pain through self-reinvention are often characterized by a combination of individualism and emotional vulnerability. Their tenacity does not allow them to sacrifice any of their central desires without feeling that they have been compromised as individuals (Strenger, 82). Such emotional complexity needs a protective mechanism to enable the subject to exist in a hostile environment. The sense of absolute justice in Ravikovitch's characters can be viewed as just such a protective mechanism, as it leaves them no doubts about their chosen status. They consequently understand every instance of adversity (such as humiliations in the kibbutz, maltreatment in school, harassment in the army, and injustice in the custody trial) as merely temporary. They face these hardships secure in the knowledge that their righteousness and nobility will ultimately be recognized and rewarded ("over there"). The characters deny the moral order they recognize in the "here," from which they feel estranged, and construct their own moral order in its place.

In fact, Ravikovitch converts the estrangement and aberration into a sign of distinction. This combination of ultimate justice and chosenness represents a Christian model. The greater the suffering, the greater the holiness. Ravikovitch's work portrays a subject with a paralyzing sensitivity who simultaneously functions as a victim and as the one who unveils the suffering of others. Her character's estrangement stems from (and creates) a subjectivity that empathizes with the downtrodden and seeks to help them. This acute sensitivity increases both her estrangement and her existential suffering. Her idiosyncratic sense of justice, then, combines both the notion of the stigmata—bodily marks that correspond to Christ's crucifixion wounds—and that of the Agnus Dei (lamb of god), the ultimate victim whose sacrifice atones for the sins of humanity. By creating her own order and understanding of the world, the Ravikovitch character celebrates the triumph of the suffering Other (the woman, the orphan, the excluded, the mad), transforms this Other into a chosen one, and leads him or her to the messiah's arrival:

a throng of the blind and lame and stammering,
a gate shall be placed and we shall come forth celebrating.

Sin has not captured me, and a snare shall tempt me,
a gathering of counts refraining from law
The day you will lift with your love before me
a flag fixed in your halls.

("Seats for Trial" [Khisot lemishpat], CP, 26)

Part Three

"She Tried to Escape and Lost Her Senses"[1]

Mania, Depression, and Madness

What's madness but nobility of soul
At odds with circumstance? The day's on fire!
I know the purity of pure despair,
My shadow pinned against a sweating wall.
That place among the rocks—is it a cave,
Or winding path? The edge is what I have.
  Theodore Roethke, "In a Dark Time"[2]

chapter six

The Manic-Depressive Mode

Poetics of *Mobilité*

Dorit, the protagonist of Ravikovitch's story "The Natural Laws" (Chukey hateva) testifies about herself that "I'm tired of distinguishing between darkness and light, red and green. I don't understand what is happening to me. I don't understand the natural laws any more" (*Come and Gone*, 189). With these words she describes a fundamental sense of detachment, confusion, and estrangement. In the world of the typical Ravikovitch character, these kinds of feelings come to be categorized as not merely estrangement but outright madness. Dorit's case is especially interesting because it takes place after her release from a psychiatric ward, a release that she had not wanted. In Ravikovitch's work, psychiatric hospitals operate both as an oppressive space ruled by hegemonic norms and as a liberating space where eccentricity can be freely expressed. This duality has the potential to subvert the strict differentiation between the "mad" psychiatric space and the "normal" world outside of it. Accordingly, we might wonder about the poetic meanings and consequences of Ravikovitch's so called "madness": does Ravikovitch describe a symbolic entrance into and departure from madness, or is her description itself an instance of entering and departing from madness? By focusing on Ravikovitch's unique voice, which blurs the binary differentiation between *speech about madness* and *mad speech* (as well as that between mania and depression), I will explore in this part of the book the ways in which Ravikovitch's oeuvre presents a unique perspective on madness and otherness.

In the imaginary space between estrangement and madness, neither in it, nor outside of it, we again come across Dorit's life. The story "A Small House at the 'Ganim' Neighborhood" (Bait katan bishkhunat ganim, in *Come and*

Gone, 47-49) describes her cyclical routine: from times of passivity during which she lies in bed for long stretches staring at the ceiling, to periods in which she feels strong, writes, socializes with friends, and goes on impulsive shopping sprees. This routine illustrates the behavior of a woman suffering from bipolar disorder, also known as manic-depressive illness, a condition that "encompasses a wide range of mood disorders and temperaments. These vary in severity from cyclothymia—characterized by pronounced but not totally debilitating changes in mood, behavior, thinking, sleep, and energy level—to extremely severe, life threatening, and psychotic forms of the disease."[1]

Before I discuss the treatment of madness in Ravikovitch's writing, I want to dwell for a moment on the nature of this condition. Unlike the story "A Small House at the 'Ganim' Neighborhood," published late in her career, which deals with the symptoms of bipolar disorder directly, most of Ravikovitch's work presents fragmented glimpses and representations of different aspects of cyclothymic temperament and manic-depressive experience. Without getting into the psychiatric terminology, Ravikovitch describes a condition (which, in reality, outside of her imaginative world, is a mental illness) involving episodes of serious mania and depression. The speaker's mood usually swings from overly "high" and irritable to sad and hopeless, and then back again, with periods of a "normal" mood in between. The cyclical nature of the changes in mood and thought brought on by mania and depression is the major characteristic of Ravikovitch's treatment of this theme, and this cyclical nature is articulated by the use of vocabulary, images, and metaphors related to the periodicities of the natural world, the seasonal patterns, and the intensity of nature, as can be seen, for example, in the titles of several poems: "The Sorrow of Night" (Tzaar halaylah, in CP, 31; BK, 65-66), "Like the Rolling Dust before the Whirlwind" (Kegalgal lifnai sufah, in CP, 46; BK, 76-77), "A Hard Winter" (Horef kasheh, in CP, 66; BK, 96), "Faraway Land" (Eretz rechokah, in CP, 51; BK, 82-83), "Hills of Salt" (Gvaot melach, in CP, 53; BK, 84), "Waning and Waxing" (Gorea vezoreach, in CP, 98; BK, 117-18), "In the Right Wind" (Baruach hanekhonah, in CP, 100-101; BK, 120-21).

My discussion will focus mainly on the fluidity inherent in Ravikovitch's representations of manic-depressive temperaments, the way these supposedly opposite moods and energies are interlaced, and the poetic braiding of these contrasting experiences. The manic-depressive, or cyclothymic, temperament, "responds to the world with a wide range of emotional, perceptual, intellectual, behavioral, and energy changes, and it creates around itself both the possibilities and chaos afforded by altered experiences and fluctuating tempos."[2] Thus, the rapidity and fluidity of moves across and into such contrasting experiences creates in Ravikovitch's case a poetics of *mobilité*, that is, of intense (and usually circular) mobility and movement between emotions, rhythms, times, and spaces. The titles "Around Jerusalem" (Saviv liyrushalaim, in CP, 44; BB, 15), "Day unto Day Uttereth Speech" (Yom leyom yabia omer, in CP, 133; BK, 143), and "From Day to Night" (Min hayom el halaylah, in CP, 143; BB, 81) are just some of the manifestations of this mobilité, which expresses both the manic feeling ("At night there's a train/That goes round/And around Jerusalem.//Mountains circle round about her,/ Winds make moan from the ruins inside her./Birds are screeching in the calm air/And when night falls, owl eyes glimmer" ["Around Jerusalem"]) and the depressive mood ("I pass from day to day/from day to night/like a feather the bird doesn't feel/when it drops" ["From Day to Night"]).

"What does this frantic search for motion conceal? Why is stasis so terrifying and yet, in the end, so sought after?" asks Marina van Zuylen of obsessive behavior, and answers: "Because by definition, the idyllic moment is always doomed to turn into something less intoxicating, while the bliss of passion produces a strange amnesia capable of dissipating the anxiety of being oneself."[3] Adapting these questions to Ravikovitch's movement between mania and depression, as well as to her passages inside and outside madness, suggests a different answer, focused not on the anxiety of being oneself, but rather on the *inability to not be oneself*. Ravikovitch's poetics of mobilité can thus be seen as part of her ongoing struggle for self-determination according to a tenacious conception of her own subjectivity.

The Manic-Depressive Temperament and the Wish for Annihilation

> I could not love except where Death
> Was mingling his with Beauty's breath—
>> Edgar Allan Poe, "Romance"[4]

> We all want to be a character, to be Mister Somebody (monsieur quelqu'un) *rather than Mister Nobody* (Monsieur Personne)
>> Pierre Janet

> The most important thing in love is not love, but emotions and above all novelty
>> Simone[5]

TWO GARDEN SONGS (SHNEI SHIREI GINAH)

GIANTS

Some ants found half a carcass of a fly
and what a time they had
hauling it out of the grass.
Their little hips nearly split with the labor.
And of all things, suddenly the grass
swelled and made sheaves like a barley field.
Isn't it crazy for grass to think it's a barley field.
I knew that ants would come to a bitter end—
all that hard work and an early death.
A few husky insects strutted about in the grass,
whistling at those foolish ants.
Each flower grew to the best of its ability,
the roses more showy than in years past.
And then I wept.
All of them around me had become such giants.

ALL OF THEM GROWING

A swarm of gnats seethes every day at six.
It's growing hunchback, my pathetic grass.
Each day again there's something I desire.
The sun no longer resembles a ball of fire,
On the inside, the sun is seething.
No air to breath, there is only pleading.
I tell you, if this summer should finally pass,
everything will be restored:
the flower to the plant, the wing to the bird,
the sand that wandered away to the shore.
With a few stalks of corn and some aphis-stricken leaves
it's impossible to live.
I tell you it's impossible to live.
So many just grow and grow, and hardly anyone is in bloom.

(CP, 91–92; BK, 112–13)

The speaker in this poem identifies with the ant's exhaustion and smallness. Her sense of smallness is not existential but arises from the manic at-

mosphere around her: "suddenly the grass/swelled and made sheaves like a barley field." In the poem "The Blue West" (Hamaarav hakhachol) the sun symbolizes the passionate vitality of the manic experience—"I want to ascend to the fringes of the sun/And not fall prey to the fire"—and its intensity: "A sun will shine for us blue as the sea,/A sun will shine for us warm as an eye,/Will wait for us till we ascend/As it heads for the blue west" (CP, 56–57; BK, 87–88). But the same image of the sun that motivates the manic feelings in "The Blue West" (as well as in other poems such as "Faraway Land" [Eretz rechokah], in CP, 51; BK, 82–83) and "Murmurings" (Milmulim, in CP, 52; BK, 83–84)) creates a feeling of depression in "Two Garden Songs": "The sun no longer resembles a ball of fire,/On the inside, the sun is seething./No air to breathe, there is only pleading." The speaker feels she has been swallowed up by all the growth surrounding her; her sense that "all of them around me had become such giants" reflects her feelings of helplessness and suffocation, and above all, her emotional diminution, which leads to feelings of worthlessness and meaninglessness. This process is not a one-time event, but rather an ongoing and repetitive process, as we can see from the poem "Waning and Waxing" (Gorea vezoreach):

Now the moon's on the wane,
now the moon drops.
Look at him, love, come look:
He always comes back.

(CP, 98; BK, 117–18)

The use of ants and giants to describe difficulty and despair brings to mind the well-known poem "I Have Only Known How to Tell of Myself" [Rak al atzmi lesaper yadaati] by Rachel Bluwstein Sela.[6] As Dan Miron asserts, Rachel develops the image of the ant in a way that actually empowers the image of the speaker (the ant goes to "the top of the tree"—a symbol and metonym of greatness).[7] Ravikovitch, on the other hand, focuses on the ants' pathetic and useless struggle: "Their little hips nearly split with the labor./. . ./I knew that ants would come to a bitter end—/all that hard work and an early death." Additionally, while Rachel's image leads to disappointment and doubt— "Distant beacons, you have deceived me./Why did you beckon, miraculous land?"[8]—Ravikovitch's poem ends with the awareness of despair: "I tell you it's impossible to live./So many just grow and grow, and hardly anyone is in bloom." The speaker's sense of worthlessness, as well as her emotional diminution, has reached its nadir. The poem ends with the speaker expressing that she lacks any special characteristics that would give her life some distinction and that she has missed her opportunity to bloom.

This sense of despair, which can also be understood as existential anxiety about a conventional and banal life, is central to Ravikovitch's work, and it stands out especially in light of the fact that Ravikovitch's oeuvre in general does not express any other anxieties. The main fear in her work is that of being ordinary, of letting "the sun set at its own pleasure," ignoring its "infinite treasure" ("Surely You Remember" [Ata bevadai zokher], in CP, 89–90; BK, 111). We can thus understand Ravikovitch's inner motivation for the poetics of mobilité as the speaker's need to escape a prosaic existence—to escape the destiny of those who grow but do not bloom. Haunted by the fear of a mundane life, Ravikovitch's poetic persona, like the characters in her stories, pledges her life to a project of uniqueness and distinction. The prosaic outside world is doomed always to disappoint and can never live up to the utopian fantasy of perpetual meaning and greatness. Such an existence, however, explains Van Zuylen (discussing the artistic monomanic temperament), "leaves nobody unscathed; while lavishing on its perpetrators a grandiose sense of purpose, it turns everyday necessities into trivial burdens and injects into ordinary emotions a bored sense of déjà vu."[9] As a result of this emotional mechanism, the poetic speaker is trapped in a cyclical movement between, on the one hand, (realistic) depression and a sense of a diminished existence among "such giants" and, on the other, a (utopian) manic desire "to break out of the depths of the earth" ("The Blue West" [Hamaarav hakhachol], CP, 56; BK, 87).

The character's obsession with being different and with the anxiety of ordinary life might be understood as a protective mechanism, as a way of blocking out the world's dangers and of escaping its cluster of dreads and worries that are part of the human condition. Negating other people and reality is of course a way of not engaging with them. Thus, being directed by something bigger than life, by an idée fixe of a utopian existence, rescues her not just from the emptiness of the everyday, but from all its inner anxieties. According to Van Zuylen (in relation to Pierre Janet's understanding of obsessive disorders), the attachment to what is not present, to what will lead the subject deeper into unreality, "points to the dangerous desire *not to understand* what is directly around us, favoring instead an ideational region."[10] In this manner, the idée fixe in Ravikovitch's work functions as an emotional tool that turns the chaotic fears of the speaker into a stable certainty, and by so doing enables her to deal with the tyranny of the everyday. Since perfection is intolerant of reality, and reality always holds fears, Ravikovitch's characters skirt these two threatening elements by embodying an absolute mastery of the idiosyncratic idée fixe in their reality. This idée fixe has a comforting virtue not simply because it provides reliable and predictable boundaries, but also because it gives the subject a sense of agency.[11] Thus, given that "being held hostage by an idée fixe (whatever its nature) makes one vulnerable to the particular idea but immune to one's own personal torments,"[12] the characters' anxieties about leading a conformist life, and the idée fixe that both establishes this anxiety and results from it, dominates their lives on the one hand and protects them on the other.

Whether the anxiety of ordinary life is a protective mechanism or a unique existence lacking common anxieties, it is articulated through a clear movement between (realistic) depression and (utopian) mania. I wish to suggest a reading of the statement "it's impossible to live" in the poem "Two Garden Songs" (Shnei shirei ginah) in light of this cyclical mechanism. "It's impossible to live" expresses the speaker's rejection of life and her desire for self-annihilation, both of which are symptoms of her depression and anxiety. It is an expression, furthermore, of her frustration with an existence lacking glamour and meaning. Yet Ravikovitch's larger corpus of work seems to present another aspect of this "impossibility to live." The speaker's desire to self-obliterate is also a by-product of her manic desires; it is a gloomy expression of an impossible ongoing desire to reach the unreachable, to "ascend to the fringes of the sun" ("The Blue West") and to "find peace/for ever and ever" ("The Land of the Setting Sun" [Eretz mevo hashemesh], in CP, 20; BB, 12). In this sense, her desire to self-annihilate is not *a result* of the failure to bloom and to reach the desirable "over there," but rather the ultimate way of *being* "over there."

The speaker in the poem "The Blue West" says she "want[s] to ascend to the fringes of the sun/And not fall prey to the fire." With these words, she expresses both her vivid ambitions and her awareness of the danger contained in these ambitions. Consequently, this poem affirms her determination to remain safe. The caution expressed in this poem, however, is uncharacteristic of the Ravikovitch oeuvre more broadly, which usually represents a different desire, a destructive desire to be "eaten by fire."

Earlier, I discussed the gap between the poetic persona's morbid view of her reality (her "here") and the perfection of a utopia reachable only "over there." At this point I would like to focus on the speaker's desire for self-annihilation, which is derived from this discrepancy and which shapes the representations of depression in Ravikovitch's writing. The gulf between the "here" and the "over there" prevents the speaker from having any intermediate existence. In "The Land of the Setting Sun" the speaker fantasizes that she will find definitive peacefulness: "And in that land I will find peace/for ever and ever." The yearning for this peacefulness, which disconnects her from the regularity of time and existence in reality, expresses her deep desire to escape from "here." In other words, the desire is for a self-annihilation that would result in an ultimate redemption.

The desire to break away from the "here" and to get closer to the "over there" is colossal, even anarchic, as is evident, for example, in the poem "Royal Gifts" (Matnot melachim): "And by degrees my desire hath grown/Insatiable, my desire grew bold/Partaking six and sevenfold/I want to head stone/To stroke the head stone" (CP, 24–25; BK, 60–62); in the poem "On the road at night" (Omed al hakhevish): "And I must come to the place where he stands" (CP, 19; BB, 3); and in the poem "The Love of an Orange" (Ahavat tapuach hazahav): "Orange/loved the one who devours/Loved with every fiber/the one who abuses" (CP, 11). Succumbing to this desire is dangerous, as the speaker is all too aware: "My desire shall yet be my ruin./Behold, the day of my death is upon me" ("Royal Gifts," CP, 24–25; BK, 60–62); "In the place where he stands there is a fear of danger" ("On the road at night," CP, 19; BB, 3); "Orange/consumed by the one who devours/Beneath its skin/even in its flesh" ("The Love of an Orange," CP, 11). It seems that the speaker takes pleasure in the threat of danger or in fantasizing about it: "I sank in a cloud of pleasure,/I sank,/I melted away" ("The Roar of the Waters" [Sheon hamayim] CP, 65; BK 95; BB, 30).

The speaker's emotional make-up does not allow her to recognize the possibility of continuity between her concrete "here" and her fantasized "over there." The only desirable existence is "over there," a place without compromises. Thus, the urge to be dragged into extreme and dangerous situations is actually an expression of the need for a greater existence. In many of Ravikovitch's writings, and especially in her first book, *The Love of an Orange*, the fulfillment of this desire actually means self-annihilation. The speaker desires an emotion that will take full possession of her being. Freud's statement that "the aim of life is death"[13] is central to the obsessive, manic, and depressive temperament. In Ravikovitch's poetry, it is a yearning to be swallowed up, to arrive at an end.

This paradox—or seeming paradox—of the apex of vitality that can be fulfilled only through destroying life frustrates some scholars. Few of them

Manuscript of "The Love of an Orange," reproduced from Ravikovitch's unpublished bequest by kind permission of Ido Kalir.

try to "correct" this paradox, namely to arrive at a reading that neutralizes the speaker's desire for self-obliteration and converts it into a desire for life. Miri Baruch, for example, claims that in the poem "The Love of an Orange," the death of the orange is voluntary, "since with his death he actually starts to really live."[14] Juliette Hassin argues that this same poem has a mystical meaning, that it is not about loss and destruction, but rather about an appropriate absorption in order to "be materialized anew in a more truthful way."[15]

I believe that every attempt to "rescue" the poems of *The Love of an Orange* from the desire for self-destruction that is presented in them in fact distorts the unique emotional mechanism that characterizes this book, as well as much of Ravikovitch's work. It is not without reason that the phrase "The Love of an Orange" serves as the title of Ravikovitch's first book, as well as its opening poem (and indeed, the opening of her entire oeuvre): the title contains a fundamental statement about her writing, namely, her state of doom and her incapacity to escape the basic mental condition of an inner division between the loathsome "here" and the desirable "over there."[16] The orange in Ravikovitch's poem loves its consumer in the same way that the slave-for-life from Exodus 21: 6 supposedly loves his master.[17] It is a non-egalitarian "love," constructed under coercive circumstances that prevent the possibility of meaningful choice. Moreover, the question of choice and the potential for willful agency are not applicable to this psychological mechanism, as it is an emotional—and in the slave's case, also practical—necessity. It is a mental quality that establishes the manic (obsessive and repetitive) mechanism of the speaker in Ravikovitch's work. The book *The Love of an Orange*, then, does not simply represent "the motif of love for the destructive lover" or of the motif of "the yearning for the dead father," as Baruch Kurtzweil indicates.[18] Rather, in various ways and by dealing with different themes, the book exposes a complex mental disposition of deterministic mania and obsessiveness. This disposition inherently contains a desire for self-annihilation. The book thus deals not with love (for a man, for the dead father, for life, for creativity, or for wisdom) as a volitional act or as the result of free will, but rather with *the impossibility of not desiring the "over there."* It is a book about the dissatisfaction, deficiency, and craving that result in a self bent on its own destruction.[19]

"Like the Rolling Dust before the Whirlwind"[20]
Fluidity of Mania and Depression

And by strange alchemy of brain
His pleasures always turn'd to pain—
His naivete to wild desire—
His wit to love—his wine to fire—

Edgar Allan Poe, "Romance"[21]

Ravikovitch's poem "Like the Rolling Dust before the Whirlwind" (Kegalgal lifnai sufah) expresses a manic state on the verge of restlessness and irritability:

LIKE THE ROLLING DUST BEFORE THE WHIRLWIND

Kislev and Nisan, like horses twain,
Gallop around the zodiac wheel.
In the moon of Tammuz the wind roars,
Flogging the tree with knotted whips.
No longer do lions scold in the night,
No angels sing their chants at night.
Like a seething cauldron the wind roars.
There's a god hiding behind the rain.

Deep in the mountain embers flare;
Like the sides of a pot the night is charred.
In the month to come, you will waft us aloft
In a swift and beautiful sailing craft
On the Great Sea from shore to shore.
The radiant face of the sea will flood
And in its cunning, the stricken tree
Will flower at dawn in a burst of red.
How bitter it is when the wind roars!

In the moon of Tammuz the tree moans
When the wind flogs it with knotted whips.
The moon of Nisan slips away like a thief,
The moon of Kislev like chaff in the wind.
Like a seething cauldron the wind roars.
There's a god hiding behind the rain.

(CP, 46; BK, 76–77)

The manic experience in this poem is articulated both from an inside-out and from an outside-in perspective. The speaker is outside the manic experience, and she maintains a certain distance from it. Thus the poem does not present an in medias res description from within mania but rather describes it in retrospect. At the same time, the poem also presents the speaker's voice from the "inner" intimate experience of being in a manic situation.[22] This combined speech is manifested in the title of the poem: "Like the Rolling Dust before the Whirlwind," which can be read in two ways. The first and most common reading focuses on the biblical meaning (Isaiah 17:13), which refers to the state of whirling dust *during* a storm, and which expresses the intense, restless, unfettered state of mind during the mania. The second reading is literal and focuses on the whirling dust *before* the storm has started. In this sense the title of the poem foreshadows the title of Ravikovitch's last book of poetry, *Half an Hour before the Monsoon* (1998). This latter meaning focuses on the moment before the storm, on the expectation of the intensity, and on the awareness of what is yet to come. Thus the retrospective voice that is familiar with and attentive to bipolar disorder—which involves episodes of both mania and depression—exposes the cyclical and repetitive nature of the manic-depressive state, and the fact that the manic experience is a continuous ride of mental ups and downs.

Articulating an emotional experience from different perspectives is not unique to Ravikovitch's writing. What is interesting in her case, however, is that blurring the differences between the outer and inner perspectives enables her to challenge one major dichotomy that stands at the center of the standard conception of bipolar disorder: mania vs. depression. Without ignoring the differences between the manic and depressive states, Ravikovitch's writing emphasizes the oscillation into, out of, and within these diverse states. This oscillation, as Kay R. Jamison notes in her research about the correlation between manic depression and the artistic temperament, "is, in its own right, a hallmark of manic-depressive illness. Manic and depressive symptom patterns clearly have a polar quality, but the overlapping transitional, and fluctuating aspects are enormously important in describing and understanding the illness as a whole."[23]

In the poem "Like the Rolling Dust before the Whirlwind," Ravikovitch articulates this aspect of the bipolar condition by choosing the month Tammuz, with all its symbols and meanings, as a frame for the manic experience. The images and associations that create the description of mania in the poem—such as the "seething cauldron," "embers flare," and the charred night—are inspired by the commentary of Rabbi Shlomo Yitzhaqi (better known by the acronym Rashi) about the worship of the Akkadian god Tammuz, mentioned in Ezekiel 8:14: "Then he brought me to the door of the gate of the Lord's house which faces north; and, behold, there sat women weeping for Tammuz." According to Rashi's commentary, the way to worship Tammuz was by heating his statue from within. The lead inside would melt and the idol would look as if it were crying. Ravikovitch takes these images of fire and heat to describe the intensity and agitation of the manic experience, a powerful vitality that stems from within and takes control of body and mind.

These same images of fire and flame, however, also have destructive connotations. Rashi's image is actually that of a crying idol. The manic energies, just like the burning inside of Tammuz, are not a sign of power and fruitful vitality, but are destructive forces that lead to sadness and powerlessness. The image of the burning and weeping Tammuz thus contains both the manic energies and the latent depression that are simultaneously present and yet to come. These dual images, with their contradictory connotations, allow the poem at once to segregate manic experience from depression and to challenge this very separation.

And the poem goes further in challenging this division. The manic episode in the poem takes place in Tammuz, a summer month in the Hebrew calendar, which normally falls around June or July. It is interesting to note that Tammuz is a month in which no Jewish holiday is celebrated, except for the Fast of the Seventeenth of Tammuz, which commemorates the breaching of the walls of Jerusalem by Nebuchadnezzar (586 BCE) and Titus (70 CE). The manic experience can thus be seen as containing a destructive aspect. In this way, too, the manic experience in Ravikovitch's writings is not directly opposed to the experience of depression. The moods in the bipolar experience are instead part of a spectrum, which enables the speaker to experience them as separate, as working simultaneously, or as part of continuous range.

Ravikovitch's decision to situate the poem's manic experience in the month of Tammuz also limits it, temporally. The mania is not experienced as an endless condition, but rather as a temporary (though repetitive) event in the annual periodicity, which already contains—even if only as unfulfilled potential—the next depressive stage. Moreover, the fast of the Seventeenth of Tammuz ushers in the *Bein hamtzarim* (literally "between the straits"), the three-week period of mourning over the destruction of Jerusalem. Accordingly, it is not merely that the manic state is *followed* by a period of mourning (i.e., sadness and dejection), but rather that these latent feelings exist *during* the manic condition, that a melancholic element lies always somewhere in the background of the manic state.

This idea of a constant undulation of emotions is also noticeable in another aspect of Tammuz, who as the Akkadian vegetation-god is the counterpart of the Sumerian Damuzi and the symbol of death and rebirth in nature. As described in the Sumerian myth of Inanna's descent into the netherworld (which is also extant in an Akkadian version), each year Tammuz dies in the hot summer (in the month of Tammuz), and his soul is taken by the Gallu demons to the underworld. Woe and desolation fall upon the earth, and Ishtar leads the world in lamentation. She then descends to the netherworld and, after many trials, succeeds in bringing him back, as a result of which fertility and joy return to the earth.[24] Tammuz's cycle of death and resurrection maintains the force that differentiates life and death from one another (as well as fertility and infertility, abundance and scarcity, etc.) and, in so doing, engenders fundamental binary oppositions. At the same time, however, by the very act of moving back and forth between the supposedly separate states, the cycle subverts the trenchant separation underpinning the binary. In a similar way, even though the separation between mania and depression exists in Ravikovitch's writings, her poems express the experience in which one aspect of the binary is fused to the other. Like Tammuz, who travels between the two worlds but retains a part of each, the speaker in Ravikovitch's poems cannot experience the mania as an opposite emption to depression, for feelings of depression already flow into her manic state, creating a manifold transformation. As Thomas Willis wrote in 1683, presaging Ravikovitch's tendency to blend the two different emotional states: "these two, like smoke and flame, mutually receive and give place one to another."[25]

chapter seven

"Therefore I Invented Conversation"[1]

Speech about Madness,
and Mad Speech

After Ehud, the protagonist of the story "I Am Joseph" (Ani yosef), learns that "for years it has been written in the school reports that you are hated by the rest of the students" (*Winnie Mandela's*, 53), his school principle advises him to seek psychological treatment. In another story, "Winnie Mandela's Football Team" (Kvutzat hakhaduregel shel wini mandelah), psychological counseling becomes an incriminating document in the trial of Rama, the story's protagonist (23–31). This recurring motif of marking individuals as psychologically unsound arrives at its dramatic conclusion in the hospitalization of various characters (Leah, Ricky, Ruth, Orli) in the story "Prepare for the Messiah's Arrival" (Hikhonu lebiat hamashiach) (32–47). Indeed, the movement from estrangement to insanity characterizes a process of exclusion that many of Ravikovitch's characters undergo. The gap between society and the individual grows steadily wider, causing the web of external definition to tighten around her until she can no longer escape the signification of madness. As long as society perceives estrangement as normative (unstable but not harmful), characters are allowed to continue existing within the symbolic order. The character's estrangement, however, comes increasingly to be shaped and confined within patterns that define it as insanity.[2] Once a character's feelings and behavior are defined as insane, she has to be excluded from the space of normal life and imprisoned in a separate, isolated location.

To put it another way, the typical character's movement from estrangement to madness in Ravikovitch's work may be explained as part of a "chronicle of increasing repression." This Foucaultian concept refers to the history of containment, exclusion, and classification, as well as to a chronicle of silencing voices that are regarded as alien and eccentric.[3] In her writing, Ravikovitch presents madness as something with its roots in estrangement and repression. The detachment between characters and their surroundings grows as outside notions of madness close in on them, leaving no possibility for disentanglement. This oppression reaches its climax when they are categorized not merely as abnormal but "mad."

Taking Foucault's ideas as her starting point, Joan Busfield argues that "the phenomena of mental disorder occupy a bounded, highly contested and changing terrain that falls between physical illness, deviance and normality."[4] Since Ravikovitch only rarely hints at the physical aspect of madness, my discussion focuses on the axis of deviance and normality. It is not by chance that Ravikovitch centers on those aspects of madness. As Sander L. Gilman shows (especially in the chapter "The Mad as Artist"), in the late nineteenth century, madness was perceived as an alteration of mind rather than of emotion ("mind illness is brain illness," to use the words of Wilhelm Griesinger, dean of nineteenth-century biological psychiatrists[5]). By the fin de siècle, with the influential studies of Jean Martin Charcot (1825–1893), the founder of modern neurology, and Sigmund Freud (1856–1939), the basic definition of mental illness had begun to focus on emotions, neuroses, instincts, and drives. The twentieth-century discourse about madness—influenced by the writings of Wilhelm Reich, Michel Foucault, Gilles Deleuze, Felix Guattari, and Ronald David Laing—generally linked personal psychic repression with social repression.

In *History of Madness* (1961), Foucault argues that madness is culturally and socially determined and that in Western culture there is a structure of power that situates madness in opposition to reason, and in so doing, contributes to the construction of Western society as a rational society. Foucault thus places madness within a normative system of power relations and defines it as an element of the regulating discourse. The classification of insanity (an exclusion from the "normal" to the confinement of "insanity") is a political, ideological, and manipulative tool, which enables society to transform the rebellious subject into an unthreatening object.

In her book *Writing and Madness (Literature/Philosophy/Psychoanalysis)*, Shoshanna Felman notes a growing preoccupation in the twentieth century with insanity in various disciplines and areas of research. Felman focuses on a basic distinction inherent to most modern discussions of insanity, particularly after Foucault's discourse in *History of Madness*, namely, the distinction between speaking about madness and mad speech—that is, "to say madness": "to give madness a voice, to restore its language: a language *of* madness and not *about* it."[6] Speaking about madness identifies it from the outside by relying on institutions or individuals who are in positions of power that enable them to name insanity. In other words, speech about madness is external: madness is identified from without by those with power enough to name it and thereby separate themselves from the one who is mad. This privilege of definition, of course, belongs to those in power, those who dominate the language. Mad speech, on the other hand, is self-reflective and internal; it allows insanity to speak itself from within. The boundary is erased, the voice of madness breaks through, unmediated, free of a need for an outside object (view, perspective, focus) to define it as insane and keep it at a safe distance.

Despite the methodical, conceptual, and political importance of the separation between speaking about madness and speaking madness, it is important to note that this separation is not always dichotomous, neither in theory nor in Ravikovitch's work. Rather, the cultural discourse about madness and mad speech maintain a complex interplay between inner and outer: the mad person and the social world (and their respective languages) mirror each other in a reciprocal relationship of doubles. Furthermore, self-interpretation does not always stand in opposition to the social mechanism of classification and exclusion (and not only in cases in which the subject a priori internalizes the societal definition of madness), and cultural definitions of madness are not necessarily disconnected from personal experience. Since conceptions of madness are often entwined with mad speech and maintain mutual dialogue with it, madness can be externally defined and constrained, and at the same time be also a site of self-production. Thus, the meanings of madness are formed and inhabited simultaneously outside of, prior to, and inside of formal, cultural, and personal discourse about madness. In Dwight Fee's words (that originally refer to depression), madness "is not a circumscribed label or a preset sick role as much as it is an increasingly pervasive yet fluctuating point of cultural and personal awareness—a mutable conceptual framework used to read into self and experience."[7]

Nevertheless, referring to the separation between speaking about madness and mad speech, Felman raises an important question that offers an innovative way of thinking about and interpreting insanity: "Do we really understand the significance of writing about madness (as opposed to writing madness)? Since there is no metalanguage, could it not be that writing madness and writing about it, speaking madness and speaking *of* it, would eventually converge—somewhere where they least expect to meet? And might it not be at that meeting place that one could situate, precisely, *writing*?"[8]

Ravikovitch's work provides a fascinating opportunity to examine the type of writing Felman postulates. Ravikovitch examines representations of insanity both from an external viewpoint (the external symptoms of insanity exhibited in the story "I Am Joseph," for instance, or the behavior of the women committed to the psychiatric ward in the story "Prepare for the Messiah's Arrival" [Hikhonu lebiat hamashiach]) and from a viewpoint that attempts to *write madness* and its language (found, for example, in the nonlinear organization of the story "The Lights of Spring" [Orot haaviv]). In fact, Felman's distinction between speech about madness and mad speech enables a methodical classification of Ravikovitch's representations of madness into two groups: those speaking about insanity from a self-proclaimed position of sanity, and those allowing madness to speak directly, free from mediation. Even though this separation is not clear-cut, but rather works as a kind of Möbius strip, it still contains two different discursive, or narrative, positions. The narrator of Ravikovitch's stories, like the speaker in her poems, moves in and out of madness.

Insofar as madness is a disruption of the law[9] and "a violation of residual rules,"[10] any attempt to read it latches onto the same places in which language (normative language, determined by the symbolic order) is disrupted: in syntax, internal organization, references, structure, etc. The attempt to solicit madness to speak itself (mad speech)—particularly in a literary text—would be artificial. This is not only because madness as a communicative act (all the more so in an artistic medium such as literature) is being mediated, but because this attempt faces the well-known paradox regarding the inherent limitations of language: it is seemingly impossible to break loose from the symbolic order when all of the participants in such an attempt (proponents and opponents) are captives of the same linguistic mechanism. Thus how can madness be spoken in the same language that constructed and excluded it? Paradoxically, as Foucault argues, "the ultimate language of madness is that of reason";[11] therefore any attempt to read or write madness is limited not to erasing language, but to locating its disruptions: "[the language of reason] forming outside the totality of images and the universality of discourse a singular, erroneous organization, whose dogged particularity makes up madness." Locating the disruption is a step toward uncovering the manner in which madness speaks itself.

The story "I Am Joseph" provides an account of Ehud's illness, a disease described by a friend as "a women's disease, not men's,"[12] which is characterized by lying in bed for prolonged periods of time and by a feeling described as "sinking":

> Ehud Tzur-Chaim lies in his bed. . . . He has long stopped thinking of the kibbutz, but still his hands won't respond and dull waves of disgrace flow out of the top of his head, urgently moving down to the different parts of his body, reaching the tips of his fingers before returning to his incessantly blinking eye. Light, rapid spasms distort his upper lip. He feels a flaming fire burning between his stomach and chest. Not an actual fire, a burning sense of disgrace. Time is standing still. It's as if seven atmospheres weight down his arms and his brain. His legs change their position under each other. The sheet is stale, and the wall by the bed exhibits a slight crack fitting in the shape of the underlying blocks. It is difficult for him to complete a thought in order. He is wordless and restless. In half an hour he will be allowed another cup of sedative syrup, and in the meantime, the best he can do is to count the minutes. One, two, three. Even the second hand isn't sweeping rapidly enough for Ehud. Now only twenty-seven minutes were left till the sedative syrup. In spite of the disgrace destroying his thoughts he completes a sentence: "and still, time isn't standing still." (*Winnie Mandela's*, 51)

This passage gives a painful glimpse into the daily routine of a character living out his estrangement as "a dreadful commentary on the ends of power,"[13] someone for whom aberration is by no means a choice, a daring struggle, or something within his power to control. And althought the passage gives us insight into the world of madness, it is not conducted solely from the outside. The world of insanity is self-produced and reveals itself almost without mediation signifying, organizing, or operating it. The described voice is approximate to madness speaking itself, an effect enabled through the use of combined discourse that produces a relationship of distance and proximity between narrator, character, and reader. This voice brings to mind Rivka Feldhay's definition (discussing Amalia Kahana-Carmon's prose): "Doubting the narrating I's concepts of time, space, and meaning signifies insanity."[14] Ehud's experience of time is indeed disrupted. For him, time is no longer a consistent, continuous, uniform phenomenon, but something to which he cannot adapt. Ehud experiences a sense of time different than "usual" linear time: it is a time that fails to pass without stopping. Nor does he feel at ease in the space in which he exists: his body refuses to rest, his hands fail to respond to his will, he experiences spasms, and his legs move uncomfortably.

The disruption of meaning is particularly evident in the attempt to describe the physical sensation in his stomach: "He feels a flaming fire burning between his stomach and chest. Not an actual fire, a burning sense of disgrace." The physical sensation is emotionally interpreted, but this is not necessarily a mad expression, since, as Foucault explains, "body and soul communicate immediately in the symbolic value of shared qualities. . . . Body and soul are in a perpetual metaphorical relationship, where qualities do not need to be communicated because they are already shared, and where the facts of expression have no need to acquire a casual value, for the simple reason that body and soul are always the immediate expression of each other."[15] What hints at a possibility of mad speech is the personal-associative-emotional correlation Ravikovitch draws between "flame," "burns," and "disgrace." The formal logic of the symbolic order would regard this correlation as incorrect, perhaps meaningless. It appears Ehud's language of madness is most clearly expressed when he finds it difficult "to complete a thought in order" and "is wordless." Ehud, unable to act in accordance with the rules of logic, which are the basis of rational thought, finds it impossible to express himself in the language of reason: the passage from the story thus manifests disruption of or disconnection from language as that which constitutes madness.

However, although it may seem that we are faced here with a self-description of madness, it is impossible to avoid the fact that the description is simultaneously speaking *about* madness. The account of Ehud's disease can also be viewed as an almost systematic description originating from an external, containing perspective. The description abounds with expressions such as "he feels" and "it is difficult for him," all of which create a clear separation between the protagonist and the (mediating) narrator. At the same time, the description relies heavily on a combined discourse that portrays the insane person's experience of reality as though it were an objective account: "dull waves of disgrace flow out of the top of his head"; "he feels a flaming fire burning between his stomach and chest." Combined discourse thus enables Ravikovitch to articulate mad speech, on the one hand, and to express the narrator's identification with Ehud and her external observation of his situation, on the other. The view that speaks about madness and conceptualizes Ehud's behavior and situation as insanity participates in the signification and exclusion. The combined discourse is a means of creating fluidity between literary vantage points, setting up the meeting place Felman writes of, namely, a simultaneity of speech about madness and mad speech, which converge at "that meeting place that one could situate, precisely, [as] *writing*."[16]

"But I Can Also Escape"[17] Deviant Breaches

One of the most striking detachments from the language of reason occurs in the story "The Imaginary Hoop" (Hachishuk hadimyoni, in *Winnie Mandela's*, 76–78). This story relates a real or hallucinated incident in which a teacher puts her students to sleep during class and then falls asleep herself. During this sleep or hallucination, the rules of conventional reality break down: the teacher knows "that in sleep one ceases to age," and that during the slumber "her aching skin would quietly heal" (77). The strawberry tree outside the classroom enters the room, and as a result "the taste of strawberries entered her mouth and her eyes were shaded by the leaves," and "she was never closer to being an angel." If not for its ending, the story could be read as surreal (something suggested by Gabriel Moked),[18] with the central scene a hallucination that frees the protagonist's imagination. At the end, however, the teacher's friend arrives and wakes her. At this point, "the children slowly lifted their heads. The imaginary hoop vanished" (78). Read one way, this awakening can be considered the delineation of a clear border between the real and the imagined, as well as a value judgment ensuring that the teacher is rightly returned from the fantastic dimension to reality. On the surface, it appears that order is restored; rationality celebrates its triumph; the symbolic order reasserts itself after the interruption.

A significant detail, however, renders this interpretation problematic: "the teacher took pity on the two little ones and left them sleeping on the mattress all night, even when the other children left school" (78). This information extends past the dimension of reality and leaves the narrator within the boundaries of the irrational. The story's ending forces us to recognize the residue left by the aberration; order's attempt to overcome the disruptive force is therefore unsuccessful. At this moment, what had been a proper form of imagination is transformed into an illegitimate phenomenon that has departed from the boundaries of reason. This is insanity. Foucault explains this transformation: "An image is not madness. Even if it is true to say that in the arbitrary world of the phantasm, alienation finds its first opening onto its vain liberty, madness itself only begins further on, at the moment when the mind binds itself to this arbitrary power, and becomes a prisoner of this apparent freedom. . . . Inside the image, trapped within it and incapable of escaping, madness is still more than the image, forming an act of secret constitution."[19]

The ending of "The Imaginary Hoop," which remains entangled in "this arbitrary power" of itself, thus prevents us from reading the story as a mere fantasy. Since this is the case, we might raise the question of whether the narrator tells us about madness, or whether madness speaks itself? It seems that this story intensifies the blurring between the two possibilities, something hinted at in "I Am Joseph."

Another way in which Felman's notion of the convergence of speaking about madness and speaking madness applies to Ravikovitch's stories is that the stories demonstrate how this convergence contains its own deconstruction. According to Felman, the relationship between the character who experiences madness and the narrator who reports it is grounded in an unresolved tension between two types of discourse and description: "The hero introduces a visionary, dream-like mode of discourse which constantly moves toward hyperbole or overstatement . . . By contrast, the narrator initiates a critical mode of discourse which constantly tends toward litotes, understatement, reduction, reserve."[20]

The use of combined discourse, which is evident in the story "The Imaginary Hoop" and others such as "I Am Joseph," "The Lights of Spring" (Orot haaviv), and "Tirtza in the Snow" (Tirtzah basheleg) blurs the distinction between the (rational, sane) narrator and the (crazy, delusional) character. Blurring the distinction in this manner deconstructs the prerequisites for the different types of discourse, thereby also deconstructing the differentiation between speech about madness and mad speech. Characters are given an opportunity for self-representation, as well as the right to self-interpretation, thus transforming them into subjects who bind the reading of the story to their consciousness. In Ravikovitch's stories the binary dichotomy between the two types of discourse becomes increasingly difficult to sustain as characters mature. Eventually, speaking about madness in its pure form ceases and is replaced by a voice in which the separation between speaking about madness and speaking it is blurred beyond recognition.

The story "The Lights of Spring" obscures this distinction by using a hidden narrator, represented by a first-person narrator-protagonist, and by poetically shaping the story in a manner rendering the delineation of any boundary between reality and imagination hopeless. The story, a puzzled monologue of "a confused woman" talking about an interview she had with a reporter who asked her to write for his magazine, includes lengthy digressions on topics ranging from a child the protagonist is emotionally forced to adopt to the arrest of a woman accused of collaborating with the Nazis. It is impossible to determine whether two of the three main themes of the story are reality, a distortion of reality, or a complete hallucination. Is the presence of the girl who was "tired of her father and wanted me" (*Winnie Mandela's*, 138) a personal interpretation of a certain biographical situation the protagonist has found herself in, or is it pure delusion? Is the background story concerning the prisoner and her attachment to the protagonist grounded in reality, or is it a personal fantasy? The unfeasibility of making any clear determination, a result of the intentional blurring of fantasy and reality that characterizes the entire story, is compounded by the protagonist's repeated testimonies about her unstable condition: "I tried to put her [the child] out of my thoughts until my mind resettled"; "I really wanted to master myself, but my jumbled thoughts are what prevent me from mastering myself"; "I met the reporter . . . and was a little confused as usual. . . . the reporter's suggestion irritated me, but also sparked my imagination. This is also usual" (139); "'I'll draw and I'll write,' I said, but I don't know how to draw" (140).

The manner in which the protagonist relates to the world becomes increasingly difficult, to the point that she does not know how to act: "I must do something I don't know." She thinks of imagination and fiction as the only possible route for survival: "so many things I had to do. Anything I didn't know I was forced to invent from imagination" (141). The narrator admits that she has made up the conversation with her friends and invented the newspaper article. Reading the story from a point of view that searches for symptoms and representations of insanity and its language can lead to the conclusion that the entire story is a figment of the protagonist's uncontrollable imagination, a testimony to insanity's disrupting presence, even if none of it is directly defined in these terms.

Madness is more clearly defined (and confined) in the story "Prepare for the Messiah's Arrival" (Hikhonu lebiat hamashiach), which takes place primarily in a psychiatric ward. In this story, which addresses madness directly, formulates it, and confines it physically, the characters continue to make a persistent effort to maintain their deviation and uniqueness within a framework that forces the symbolic order upon them. Insane behavior, explains Phyllis Chesler, "represents a socially powerless individual's attempt to unite body and feeling," namely to act in his or her own way, even if this behavior meets the resistance of the bearers of power. The action—i.e., the realization of thought and desire—would lead to hospitalization.[21]

Many feminist theorists, such as Barbara Ehrenreich and Deirdre English, Julia Kristeva, Carol Gilligan, Elaine Showalter, Shoshana Felman, and Jane Ussher,[22] confront the impact of institutionalized knowledge and its role in self-construction and discuss how women's subjectivities have been caught up and negotiated within psychiatric discourse.[23] Similarly, Chesler—who provided the pathbreaking study about the interconnection between gender and madness—views insanity as part of the repressive patriarchal structure directed against women. She claims that the classification of the "insane" and their institutionalization in psychiatric hospitals are punishment against femininity itself, and particularly against individualistic attempts to escape the male-defined view of femininity. Sanity is an acceptance of the behavioral norms attributed to the individual's sex (and gender), and insanity is a partial or complete refusal to undertake the stereotypical gender role. Women denying the roles of femininity or displaying ambiguity toward it are destined therefore to psychiatric classification.[24]

Ruth, one of the characters in the story "Prepare for the Messiah's Arrival" (Hikhonu lebiat hamashiach) was probably hospitalized, at least to some extent, following a course of events that is in accordance with Chesler's description. Despite (or perhaps because of) her powerless position, she attempts during her hospitalization to continue acting from the same powerless place, a place seeking to construct itself and make its power present. "I have twenty normal minutes a day," calculates Ruth, "I can fall asleep and wake up tomorrow morning to the same filth, but I can also escape" (*Winnie Mandela's*, 38). And indeed, Ruth uses the twenty minutes to leave the hospital.

Ruth flees to her home and there contemplates suicide, but decides to postpone it until morning. This decision reflects her unusual "rationale," which is incommensurate with the symbolic order (believing a suicide can be postponed for a few hours is similar to thinking that it is possible to be only a partial fascist or that a "human" rather than "legal" trial can be carried out in a courtroom—two examples I discussed in detail in chapter 4). Later she listens to a song on the radio that reflects her feelings ("help, somebody help") and sleeps. The hospital staff—who represent reason, order, and ethics (and, naturally, the "male mental health ethic," to use Chesler's words[25])—manage to convince her to return to the hospital. At this point, the closing scene of "The Imaginary Hoop" is duplicated. Order has seemingly been restored, the outburst restrained: "Ruth promised to return to the hospital by ten a.m." (*Winnie Mandela's*, 40). But the character does not fully succumb to the order forcing itself upon her, and traces of what has happened remain in the wake of the deviant outburst: "but she fell asleep and only returned in the afternoon." Maintaining estrangement is a dominant part of the construction of her subjectivity, despite the fact that complete estrangement remains impossible in the symbolic order. Holding on to a sign of personal singularity—as slight as allowing two pupils out of thirty to continue sleeping (in "The Imaginary Hoop"), wearing a pinkish-gray robe on a military base (in "A Short Delay" [Ichur katan]), or choosing tardiness over submission, escape or suicide (in "Prepare for the Messiah's Arrival")—is a matter of emotional survival and is, therefore, vital to the characters in Ravikovitch's work.

The powers that lead Ruth to return to the confinement of the hospital and leave her with no means of expression save arriving late are the same powers that drive Rama (from "Winnie Mandela's Football Team") into futile fantasies of revenge against the court, Tirtza (from "Tirtza in the Snow") into endless hallucination, and Nurit (from "The Summer Vacation Tribunal") to her idiosyncratic and self-aggrandizing conception of justice. Lateness becomes a syndrome of autonomy under siege. It is not a refusal or a concrete change, merely a delay. Thus, the "short delay" progresses toward its ultimate meaning: in "A Short Delay" it is portrayed as a postponement of the protagonist's bright future; in Ruth's case, it results in a late return to the psychiatric ward. In the mental hospital, while lateness is not totally devoid of meaning, it remains only a temporary evasion of the inevitable. So being late need not be read as a wish to change or as an option of escaping but becomes only a manner of surviving within the confines of power, the same power that has made the change necessary in the first place.

Like the protagonist's struggle in "A Short Delay" and those of the rest of the Ravikovitch characters, Ruth's struggle is an attempt to endure her own personal mental economy. Her peculiar, deviant outburst does not protect her from external forces, but it allows her personal needs to be fulfilled. As discussed in chapters 4 and 5, the process of identity-construction creates a structure of basic emotional rules and behavior that govern the typical Ravikovitch character's self-perception. Any deviation from these rules is perceived as self-ruin. The character's insistence on her aberration is a product of these basic rules, and she therefore believes that her behavior protects her from self-destruction. This touching persistence, however, also contains destructive elements evident in any interaction between the Ravikovitch character and her environment. Her deviant position will always be grounded in a place of weakness that attempts to burst into a stable, established, and powerful world. Therefore, the character's behavior is only meaningful and powerful (if an action stemming from a survival instinct can be viewed as possessing the privilege of power) in the framework of her self-construction: the character's inside-out perspective fails to affect or meaningfully change the outside-in perspective. Resisting, moreover, does not provide the character any sense of satisfaction. On the contrary, she experiences the full range of disciplinary mechanisms—from verbal and physical abuse ("The Summer Vacation Tribunal" [Hatribunal shel hachofesh hagadol]), through a denial of her right to self-definition, speech, choice, and motherhood on her own terms ("Winnie Mandela's Football Team"), and ending finally in a complete banishment to the realm of insanity ("Prepare for the Messiah's Arrival").

Although signifying aberration as madness and restricting it to the confines of the psychiatric ward allows it to erupt free of all restraints, censorship, or fear, Ruth refuses to conform even to this apparently ideal place. She declines to obey institutional protocol and continues to insist on conducting her outlandish outburst according to her own needs and preferences. In so doing, Ruth voices her objection to the space forced upon her and chooses an alternative space, within which the uncommon, aberrational action can be realized. The psychiatric ward is in fact the ultimate place for anyone wishing to freely express herself and her idiosyncratic conception of justice (the inside-out perspective). The critical and oppressive outside-in perspective is completely erased (although its traces remain in the presence of therapists, orderlies, and doctors), and the subject's Möbius strip may extend into a uniform continuum of absolute justice. Theoretically, this should have been the ideal space for the Ravikovitch character, as it allows the inside-out to function continuously, uninterrupted by the outside-in. Nevertheless, because the characters in Ravikovitch maintain a fundamental position of resistance to any norm (even if the norm is, paradoxically, non-normative) and constantly come into conflict with their environment, they insist on maintaining their estrangement even in an arena that has eliminated this possibility. Estrangement is thus no longer a reflection of the characters' difficult reality, but rather constructs their subjectivity both emotionally and practically. Ruth's estrangement becomes the ultimate expression of her permanent and absolute freedom. It is now the core of her identity.

Regarding the breach as a stage in the character's process of self-construction enables us to view Ruth as the embodiment of Ravikovitch's innovative approach to insanity. Ravikovitch's so-called "madness" subverts the hegemonic system by using it to constitute the mad Other as a subject within the very system that otherwise objectifies madness.[26] By blurring the boundaries of the distinction between speech about madness and mad speech, Ravikovitch's work establishes a poetic means of getting in and out of (as well as through) madness.

Ruth's decision to leave the psychiatric ward, a place that should be ideally suited to her, seems to position her outside madness, as if entering and leaving the psychiatric ward were a symbolic entrance and departure from insanity itself. Her existence outside the hospital, however, fails to position her outside madness, since the same mental economy that was at work inside the hospital continues to govern her once she has left. This depiction of Ruth's madness may be viewed as a fascinating literary reflection on the dynamics, patterns, and causes of insanity; rather than observing Ruth's action as an entrance and departure *from* insanity, her state should be regarded as madness documenting itself: *a madness of entering and departing from madness.* In a way, this is the deconstruction of the distinction between speaking about madness and speaking madness, suggested by Felman.[27]

Ravikovitch's blurring of this distinction reaches its peak in her portrayal of Ruth, a character who displays an interplay of all perspectives (speech about madness/mad speech; inside-out/outside-in), allowing a great variety of options on the insane/sane continuum, and destroying any differentiation that could allow narrator, characters, and readers to participate in the exclusionary practice of signifying and conceptualizing the displayed behavior as sane or insane.

"Then Shall the World Turn"[28] Summary

Ravikovitch portrays insanity as the result of a process of exclusion and repression, a process that begins with estrangement and reaches its most extreme expression in the state of madness. As the gap between characters and their surroundings steadily increases, so tightens the web defining them as insane. At the peak of the "chronicle of increasing repression"[29] the character's estrangement is defined as madness.

The stories' controlling structure is shaped by their attempt to differentiate between speech about madness and mad speech (and by so doing, to differentiate between the "mad" and the "sane"). At first pass, Ravikovitch's work seemingly conforms to this (rational, masculine) controlling structure, which excludes the "insane" subject, who is related to as an object, as the Other. Despite this apparent acceptance of the separation between "sane" and Other, however, the stories simultaneously blur this very separation and disrupt the stability of the dominant structure. The subversion and innovation of Ravikovitch's writing, then, are to be found in her use of this structure to grant presence to the "insane" Other by constructing her as a subject within the very structure that transformed her into an absent object. In other words, while seeming to operate within the boundaries of the distinction between speaking about madness and speaking madness, Ravikovitch's work ultimately reveals a blurring of this demarcation, which unsettles the dominant discourse.

Ehud from "I Am Joseph," the protagonists of "The Imaginary Hoop" and "The Lights of Spring," and Ruth from "Prepare for the Messiah's Arrival" all embody Ravikovitch's rejection of the binary approach to signifying madness. These stories use literary techniques characterized by their lack of distinctness: the hidden narrator, the combined discourse (which obscures the different identities of both narrator and character), and the poetic devices undermining any consistent organization of realistic time and space within the story, as opposed to the time-and-space dimensions of the characters' hallucinations. Furthermore, the subjectivity of the Other is evident in the way the characters are shaped to allow the reader a glimpse into their inner worlds. As though identifying with the characters' inside-out-related distress, the narrators attempt to mediate between the characters' inside-out and the reader's outside-in.

The combination of literary devices and voices in Ravikovitch's stories makes possible an exposition of her oeuvre's moral position, a position that does not quite hold true to Sandra M. Gilbert and Susan Gubar's suggestion that female insanity is portrayed in literature within the structure of male-female power relations, serving as a masculine mechanism for confining and excluding women and for handling difference, and as a feminine experience of gendered imprisonment and a mechanism allowing women an escape from a masculine home and text. It also differs from Chesler's view, according to which madness (actual, not literary) is to be understood as an "alienation to a gender role"[30] and as the act of a socially powerless female subject. Ravikovitch's position also refuses to fully comply with Foucault's interpretation of madness as a cultural construct serving as the basis for building a rational Western identity, or to accommodate Kristeva's theory, which regards the semiotic as an expression of insanity. Moreover, it is not a simple realization of Felman's theoretical suggestion regarding the interpretation of madness.[31]

Although Ravikovitch's writing combines all of the above, it is augmented by its demand that her readers undergo a process of emotional and intellectual self-reflection. Such a process forces readers to constantly move between experiencing madness from within and from an outside perspective, while exposing the inside-out and the outside-in perspectives and their points of collision and convergence. At the same time, the reader must also deal with Ravikovitch's constant blurring of these binary representations.

The unique poetics of Ravikovitch's writing thus challenges familiar approaches toward madness, while offering a fascinating alternative to the dynamics of madness and society's perception of it. This sophisticated method of seeming to accept the distinction between the mad and the sane while simultaneously deconstructing this separation is a subversive, layered act. The excluded character gains recognition in her subjectivity by using one of the major mechanisms responsible for her objectification. Ravikovitch in fact creates a complex means of enabling madness to articulate itself and to reject its categorization as Other.

In a more general way, Ravikovitch also resists the exclusionary aspect of madness. She recognizes not only its oppressive dimension but also the cultural, hierarchical, and social forces that draw strength from their power over individuals and weaker groups and deny them legitimate space within the framework of the cultural community. The blurring of the distinction between mad speech and speech about madness exposes the culturally constructed—which is to say, purely imaginary—nature of power relations. This blurring undermines the very existence of the system, which has long placed the females in a subjugated position.

What's more, Ravikovitch exposes the different participants in the act of literary creation—the narrator, the characters, and the readers—to their complicit roles within the structure of excluding and defining insanity and challenges their secure and detached position on this issue. The participants' surrender of their beliefs stands at the foundation of Ravikovitch's innovative suggestion, and enables them (and us) to succumb to the blurring and to allow movement within the space of madness and its representations. Readers, who cannot participate in the delineation of the otherness of madness and who experience both identification and estrangement with respect to it, also experience the collapse of the defense mechanisms that they have built for themselves as part of their social and cultural formation. One who can no longer mark the distinction with relation to madness will find it difficult to continue to define femininity, motherhood, and normal behavior with assurance. This collapse is one of the central subversive components in Ravikovitch's writing. Like any subversive act, this one is not about a sweeping change or a sociocultural revolution, but about undermining the existing order and paving the way for a different kind of thought.

Part Four

Unveiling Injustice

Testimony, Complicity, and National Identity

I think that the role of poetry is, somehow, to fortify human strength; to stand against all the inhumanity surrounding us. . . . Eventually I try, maybe, to unveil injustice or ugliness. I think that the role of all art is to offer human strength . . . I am taken by literature or deterred by it according to the writer's capacity to observe; according to his ability to unveil injustice where it exists.

Ravikovitch[1]

Chapter Eight

"Hovering at a Low Altitude"

Witnessing and Complicity

On June 6, 1982, the Israel Defense Forces (IDF) invaded southern Lebanon. As part of an attempt to diminish the military implications of this war, the Israeli government, media, and public first referred to it as "Operation Peace for Galilee" (Mivtza shlom hagalil). It later became known in Israel as the Lebanon War, and since the 2006 Lebanon War it is commonly called the First Lebanon War.

The First Lebanon War left a significant imprint on Israeli society. As Israel's first war of choice (that is, the first war it fought in which it was not responding to an enemy attack), it provoked widespread debate within the country. While some Israelis agreed with the army's more limited objective of destroying the Palestine Liberation Organization's power in southern Lebanon in order to protect Israel's northern population, others disagreed with the larger goals set forth by Ariel Sharon, then the IDF's defense minister, and Rafael Eitan, who was then its chief of staff. These larger, apparently imperialistic goals, opponents argued, had caused an unnecessarily high number of Israeli and Palestinian civilian casualties in Lebanon. For the first time in the history of the State of Israel, people took to the streets for anti-war demonstrations.

The public responded even more fiercely to the Sabra and Shatila Massacre, which took place between September 16 and 18, 1982. On September 14, Bashir Gemayel, leader and president-elect of the Lebanese phalanges, was assassinated. On September 16, without obtaining prior cabinet approval, Ariel Sharon and Rafael Eitan moved Israeli troops into West Beirut and permitted Christian phalangist forces to enter the Palestinian refugee camps of Sabra and Shatila with the purpose of routing out remaining PLO forces who had evaded evacuation. The Phalangist militias, however, massacred hundreds of Palestinian civilians.[2]

The news about the massacre provoked fury within Israel. On September 25, the Israeli NGO "Peace Now" (Shalom Akhshav) organized a demonstration in Tel Aviv, known in Israel as "The Four Hundred Thousand Protest." It attracted about 300,000 protestors, demanding a thorough investigation of Israel's involvement in the massacre. Dahlia Ravikovitch stood in front of the crowd at the demonstration and read Nathan Alterman's monumental poem "Where Will We Carry the Shame?"[3] Alterman's poem, published in 1941 in his book *The Joy of the Poor* (Simchat aniyim), responds to the events of the Second World War and expresses the poet's anxiety about the future of humanistic civilization and European culture, as well as about the fate of the Jewish people in particular. By reading Alterman's poem in the context of the First Lebanon War and the Sabra and Shatila Massacre, Ravikovitch not only gave new meaning to the powerful line "Where will we carry the shame?" but also located the political events of the time within a larger ethical and moral discourse. The implication was clear: these events were shameful and there was no way to justify them. Moreover, there was no place "to carry the shame," as it was a disgrace that cannot be removed. One could no longer conceive of day-to-day life, Ravikovitch was exhorting the crowd, without acknowledging one's own complicity in this crime.

There soon followed another event that proved an impetus for Ravikovitch's political expression. In December 1987, Palestinians in the West Bank and Gaza started a mass uprising against the Israeli occupation. This uprising, or Intifada (literally "shaking off," in Arabic), was a spontaneous explosion of popular resistance to the Israeli occupation. The intensity of the uprising drew international attention to the Palestinians' poor living conditions under Israeli occupation. The striking images of Palestinian children throwing stones at armed Israeli soldiers and of groups not previously viewed as resistance fighters, such as women and adolescents, gave rise to international sympathy for the Palestinian people and challenged the Israeli occupation as never before. Criticism of Israeli policy increased markedly, not just in the international arena, but also within Israel itself. Questions began to be raised about the necessity of the occupation, its morality, and the levels of brutality it entailed, as well as about the thin line between legitimate fighting and excessive violence.

One of the foremost critiques of the atrocities committed by Israeli soldiers during the First Intifada came from a young Jewish Israeli rock singer, Si Himan, who wrote and performed the song "Shooting and Crying" (Yorim uvokhim), denouncing the conventional image of the Israeli soldier as "a moral, humane occupier":

The street cleaner told me
that in his village everything has changed
and life seems different to me
in the shadow of the filth.
And in my house, the window is broken
Tel-Aviv is bursting in
even its smell has changed
I feel the danger.

Boys playing with lead
girls with steel dolls
life seems different to me
in the shadow of the filth.
And it does not matter to me at all
who will win now,
my world is gone now
and the big light was put out.

Shooting and crying
burning and laughing
when did we learn at all
to burry people alive?

Shooting and crying
burning and laughing
when did we forget
that our children were also killed?

On both sides, people only want to live
in this fear, it is impossible to see
looking for shelter, from the struggle
it does not matter to me, who—is the stronger.[4]

During the First Intifada, a Palestinian girl lost her eye after being injured by rubber bullets from an Israeli soldier. This event, published throughout the Israeli press, became a symbol of the uprising. The eminent singer Nurit Galron recorded her arresting song "Après Nous le Déluge" (Ahareynu ham-abul) about the incident and criticized the Israeli population for its indifference during the upheaval:

> There is a country of stones and petrol bombs
> And there is Tel Aviv burning with night clubs and whoring it around
> There is a country of insurrectionists where they bandage the wounded
> And there is Tel Aviv rejoicing in life, eating and drinking
> No, don't tell me about a girl who lost her eye
> It makes me feel bad, bad, bad
> It makes me feel bad[5]

These critiques were not met kindly by the Israeli populace. Both Himan's and Galron's songs were censored by the IDF radio station. Galron was condemned by some of the Israeli public and was verbally abused by some of her fans. Public reaction was so strong that it is possible that this episode discouraged other artists and public figures from writing provocative lyrics and expressing their political views publicly.

Ravikovitch contributed her revolutionary and subversive voice to this intense political environment, which as it happens produced very little Hebrew protest poetry overall. Since the First Lebanon War in 1982, Ravikovitch had been writing protest poetry, focusing primarily on the suffering of Palestinian Arabs. Most of these poems are collected in the books *True Love* (1987) and *Mother with a Child* (1992). Even though the focus of these two books is the First Lebanon War and the First Intifada, Ravikovitch does refer to other current events in the Middle East. Such is the case, for example, in the poem "Two Isles Hath New Zealand" (Shnei iyim lenew ziland), where she seems to refer to the Iran-Iraq War (1980–1988): "Asia—it would make your hair stand on end./Trapped in the mountains, trapped in the swamps./the human body can't bear it,/there are limits to the life force, after all" (CP, 209–10; BK, 198–99).

The protest poetry of Ravikovitch is characterized by the solidarity of the speaker with the victims. While addressing the political aspects of the war and the First Intifada and the suffering she witnessed, Ravikovitch also raises questions about the significance and implications of witnessing and testimony. For Ravikovitch, from the moment of being exposed to the injustice of the occupation, which she referred to as "The Wrong,"[6] silence and evasion do not exist as morally credible options. Her political writings manifest witnessing as a powerful act of criticism and protest and as an expression of responsibility. Ignoring this aspect of witnessing, it is implied, entails complicity with "the Wrong." In this chapter I focus on the poetic and moral position of Ravikovitch's witnessing, and examine the connection she draws between responsibility, guilt, immorality, and national identity.

Ravikovitch's subversive voice, politically and poetically, arises from her engagement with questions of national identity, testimony, and complicity. Her protest does not settle merely for emotional solidarity, but also provides intellectual criticism for the Israeli political mechanism responsible for the creation of evil. In other words, the exposure of suffering that characterizes this poetry is not a result of mimetically representing suffering, but rather stems from a process that unveils the existence of evil in political and social contexts. Evil in these contexts is to be understood not as immanent in the world but as a product of human acts, and therefore it is examined in its political and private, not theological or metaphysical, terms. The speaker's relation to suffering and victimhood is inextricable from her gaze, which identifies with the suffering and experiences it as if it were her own. Traditionally, the witness position inherently creates some kind of distance between the witness and the subject being witnessed. What is so distinctive about the witness position in Ravikovitch's writing is that the witness identifies intensely with her subject in spite of the distance. This unique perspective of "identifying witnessing" enables the speaker to be at once a comprehensive critic and a local viewer. Yet unlike the local viewer, the comprehensive critic locates the subject matter being analyzed in a causality context that is wider than the context that the participants themselves can recognize. The aim of the critic is thus to unveil the mechanisms of oppression in order to learn about the conditions that enable their existence.[7]

This combination of distance and identification—the combined position of the comprehensive critic and that of the local viewer—enables the speaker in Ravikovitch's political writing "to tell in details all about the Wrong, misery, oppression and insecurity."[8] In other words, Ravikovitch exposes the mechanism of evil, through both the private suffering of individuals it creates and its global and universal aspects.

Ravikovitch's political poetics are evident even in her exclusively personal early writings, as Hamutal Tsamir's insightful reading of the poem "The Messiah's Arrival" (Biat hamashiach) reveals.[9] By exposing political aspects in supposedly "personal poems," Tsamir challenges the strict distinction between "political poems" and "personal lyric poems" and shows that Ravikovitch's poetry combines the two supposedly separate categories.[10] In the light of this claim, I wish to emphasize that my use of the terms "political writing" or "protest poetry" throughout this chapter refers mainly to poems that deal directly with national-political issues, such as the First Lebanon War (1982) or the First Intifada (1987). This methodic choice does not duplicate the dichotomy between Ravikovitch's personal writing and her political one, but rather emphasizes the impossibility of separating the two—not simply because "everything is political," but mainly because Ravikovitch's political understanding stems from the same emotional mechanism that informs her personal writing. Thus, by focusing on the "identifying-witnessing" position, I wish to claim that Ravikovitch's sensitivity to the suffering of others is not detached from her own suffering. Ravikovitch's writing illuminates the victimhood of others and interprets the political through the experience of someone who has suffered greatly herself. Her speaker experiences suffering and exposes the suffering of others simultaneously, and by so doing dissolves the separation between the personal and the political.

"All this Trouble/Upon Me and my Head"[11]
Witnessing and Responsibility

> [While I am writing a poem] I feel more relaxed, as always happens when somebody expresses something that bothers him. It can be that nothing has changed, but he has said it, and I have also said it, and this is my status: the status of a watchman and of a witness.
> Ravikovitch[12]

The book *True Love*, especially the section "Issues in Contemporary Judaism" (Sugiyot beyahadut bat-zmaneynu), which contains seven protest poems, signals the beginning of Ravikovitch's political phase.[13] In an interview with Zukerman, Ravikovitch refers to her earlier political writing and to the difference between this and *True Love* and *Mother with a Child* as follows: "Many years ago I wrote a much more subtle protest. But I started writing it before the [First] Lebanon War, because the horrors started before the Lebanon War. Children were injured by shootings in the West Bank even before the Lebanon War, and it was very intense. These were the clouds before the Lebanon War."[14]

Even though the definition of contemporary Judaism is connected to current political issues (mainly the First Lebanon War), the emphasis in all the poems is not political in the narrow meaning of the term; rather, they emphasize the human and moral implications of political and military decisions.

Perhaps this is why Ravikovitch herself prefers not to describe this poetry as "political," but rather as "protest"[15] or "guilt" poetry.[16]

Ravikovitch's discussion of Jewish identity does not stem from theoretical issues of religion or secularism but rather from concrete historical events that shed light on the moral stature of Jewish society. As Ravikovitch claims, "The death [of Palestinian children] becomes an issue in contemporary Judaism only if we are involved in their deaths; only if our fault intervenes in the guilt of their death."[17] The encounter between Judaism and a different nation—mainly in the Israeli-Palestinian context—raises crucial moral questions. Israeli Judaism, expropriated from its narrow religious aspect, is called to an acute moral examination in view of Judaism's function on a wider stage, namely, as a culture devoted to humanistic values.

It is open to interpretation whether Ravikovitch's section title "Issues in Contemporary Judaism" is intended ironically, to suggest that wrongdoing and immorality are the last remnants of Jewish culture. It could be argued that the title calls instead for a self-examination in order to renew the discussion about different aspects of Judaism and their manifestation in the current political reality. Either way, the questions and the conflicts that Ravikovitch raises in her poems are never simply theoretical, but stem from and are connected to a concrete reality and to specific actions whose consequences cannot be erased or forgotten. While referring to political problems, the speaker cannot ignore the suffering and the Wrong she witnesses. Her testimony is in the spirit of "hovering at a low altitude" (Rechifah begovah namuch), to use the title of one of her poems, a title that suggests having neither a concrete presence at nor a lack of awareness about any given event. Furthermore, from the moment the speaker is exposed to such events, she can neither choose silence nor claim ignorance, since her witness position carries a political, moral, and poetic commitment.

True Love opens with "The Beginning of Silence" (Tchilat hasheket), a poem that situates the speaker—and the reader—inside a room: "Now the silence descends like a mighty hand/enfolding the room in a bolt of linen" (CP, 161; BK, 161). The silence leads the reader on a path and shows him or her how to read the book, and specifically how to understand its political nature. It also provides clues for understanding the protest poetry in Ravikovitch's subsequent book, *Mother with a Child*. This is not the conventional passive silence of rest or quiet but a silence that "shrieks inside me/and I shriek inside it"—an active and living silence involved in a symbiotic relationship with the speaker.

This unique and powerful silence establishes the speaker's gaze, as well as her poetic reaction, and in a more general sense characterizes many of Ravikovitch's writings, including her political ones. It is a position of simultaneous tranquility and agitation, stillness and anguish, identification and distance. Unlike the biblical Sodomites who were characterized by social unresponsiveness and "quiet ease" (Shalvat hasheket),[18] Ravikovitch forms a different kind of "quiet" and "ease" that require exactly the opposite of Sodom's egocentricity: "And I look up, and behold:/opening, revolving,/entire worlds within the room" ("The Beginning of Silence").

The poem "The Window" (Hachalon) positions both the speaker and the reader inside a house, and presents Ravikovitch's characteristic perspective: "Whatever was needed/I saw in that window" (CP, 175; BK, 171). As with most of the poems in *True Love*, here the point of view is not detached and all-encompassing but intimate, particular. It does not see the totality of the outside world, but rather creates a limited perspective. As the speaker of "They're Freezing up North" (Batzafon kofim) declares, "Most of the act/I didn't know and I haven't seen" (CP, 200–201; BK, 191–92, my translation). It is a fairly protected position, intermittently touching and pulling away, from which the speaker can witness (to some extent) without intervening. It also places a transparent but concrete limit on the artistic act; the window is the frame for Ravikovitch's work, and it serves as an aperture for her gaze, but not as a universal representation of enclosure in a room. The window does not obscure the gaze, but enables a personal perspective for observation. In Ravikovitch's words: "I wrote only about my personal perspective, as I always write. It was much easier for me to write poems about the Lebanon War. I wrote out of a sense of guilt; a sense that I am part of the iniquity."[19]

This position combines distance and caution throughout the poem "Hovering at a Low Altitude" (Rechifah begovah namuch), thus presenting the speaker's approach toward wrongdoing.

HOVERING AT A LOW ALTITUDE

I am not here.
I am on those craggy eastern hills
streaked with ice
where grass doesn't grow
and a sweeping shadow overruns the slope.
A little shepherd girl

with a herd of goats,
black goats,
emerges suddenly
from an unseen tent.
She won't live out the day, that girl,
in the pasture.

I am not here.
Inside the gaping mouth of mountain
a red globe flares,
not yet a sun.
A lesion of frost, flushed and sickly,
revolves in that maw.

And the little one rose so early
to go to the pasture.
She doesn't walk with neck outstretched
and wanton glances.
She doesn't paint her eyes with kohl.
She doesn't ask, Whence cometh my help.

I am not here
I've been in the mountains many days now.
The light will not scorch me. The frost cannot touch me.
Nothing can amaze me now.
I've seen worse things in my life.

I tuck my dress tight around my legs and hover
very close to the ground.
What ever was she thinking, that girl?
Wild to look at, unwashed.
For a moment she crouches down.
Her cheeks soft silk,
frostbite on the back of her hand.
She seems distracted, but no,
in fact she's alert.
She still has a few hours left.
But that's hardly the object of my meditations.
My thoughts, soft as down, cushion me comfortably.
I've found a very simple method,

not so much as a foot-breadth on land
and not flying, either—
Hovering at a low altitude.

But as day tends towards noon,
many hours
after sunrise,
that man makes his way up the mountain.
He looks innocent enough.
The girl is right there, near him,
Not another soul around.
And if she runs for cover, or cries out—
there's no place to hide in the mountains.

I am not here.
I'm above those savage mountain ranges
in the farthest reaches of the East.
No need to elaborate.
With a single hurling thrust one can hover
and whirl about with the speed of the wind.
Can make a getaway and persuade myself:
I haven't seen a thing.
And the little one, her eyes start from their sockets,
her palate is dry as a potsherd,
when a hard hand grasps her hair, gripping her
without a shred of pity.[20]

(CP, 179–81; BK, 174–76)

The poem opens with the speaker's assertion of her own detachment, "I am not here," and continues by emphasizing the safety that arises from it: "The light will not scorch me. The frost cannot touch me." The speaker is highly aware of her unique position. On the one hand, the fact that she describes what is happening means that she is witnessing the event (even if she does not take any action). On the other, she is not present in the event: "The girl is right there, near him,/Not another soul around." In this way, the poem does not define "*what is* the reality that the artist ought to see—a brutal act that has been done to an innocent young girl,"[21] but rather it defines *the way of seeing* that reality. Namely, the poem raises questions about the very meaning of testimony and its implications.

This point of view merges two contradictory aspects: an aesthetic distance from the discussed object/subject and a commitment to representing it. This approach is similar to the distance that characterizes Alberto Giacometti's art. As Jean-Paul Sartre says, for Giacometti "distance is not a willing isolation, not even a movement of retrogression. It is a requirement, a rite, a sense of difficulty, the product . . . of attraction and repulsion."[22] Barbara Mann claims that "Hovering at a Low Altitude" "has been admired as a great philosophical achievement because it simultaneously embraces both the distance of aesthetics and the passion of engagement."[23]

In more general terms, the "hovering at a low altitude" position expresses a central element in the relationship between any event and testimony about it. Ana Douglass suggests that the connection between trauma and testimony is not a relationship between the source and its observer—the trauma, in other words, is not the "original" that the witness observes—but that the testimony is both external to and inherent in the trauma. A sign and a symptom of the event thus lingers, a traumatic trace that challenges the standard assumption that testimony can be *about* an original event. Following Derrida's "logic of supplement," Douglass proposes thinking about the relationship between a testimony and an event as something that is at the same time foreign or supplemental to the event and a necessary essence of it.[24]

If we accept that testimony is both external and essential to trauma, we might understand the moment of exposure to the Wrong as a moment of collaboration with the establishment of the trauma. The testimony in the spirit of "Hovering at a Low Altitude"—that is, not a concrete presence but an awareness of the events—is therefore related in Ravikovitch's writing to taking responsibility for what is being seen. From the moment of exposure to the trauma, which is also the incident in which the trauma is created, it is not really an option for one to ignore the Wrong.[25] A similar idea is expressed in the poem "They're Freezing up North" (Batzafon kofim): "What do I need with all these,/to think about all these/to remember all these/. . ./all this trouble/upon me and upon my head" (CP, 200–201; BK, 191–92, my translation).

Nevertheless, in "Hovering at a Low Altitude," the speaker is also aware of the difficulty of such a position and of the emotional defense that enables the witness to ignore injustice:

She still has a few hours left.
But that's hardly the object of my meditations.
My thoughts, soft as down, cushion me comfortably.

I've found a very simple method,
not so much as a foot-breadth on land
and not flying, either—
Hovering at a low altitude.

This is neither a total evasion ("flying") nor an absolute identification; the speaker does not place herself in the victim's position and does not intercede on her behalf ("foot-breadth on land"); rather, she is in an in-between state, that of hovering at a low altitude. This hovering constitutes a recognition of the status of witnessing, a refusal of the option of escape:

With a single hurling thrust one can hover
and whirl about with the speed of the wind.
Can make a getaway and persuade myself:
I haven't seen a thing.

One might argue that this refusal contains an awareness of its own limitations and does not develop to become rebellion. The distinction between *a refusal* and *a rebellion* is significant. According to Adi Ophir, a rebellion must offer a political alternative and justify its preferences, whereas a refusal can consist of a general moral sensitivity.[26] We ought not to conclude from this distinction that the refusal is a minor or lesser act; the refusal stands at the center of all change, and of political writing in particular.[27] It seems that in *True Love* Ravikovitch moves between refusal and rebellion, but that she reaches total rebellion only in *Mother with a Child*.

Even as "Hovering at a Low Altitude" enables a choice between "a foot-breadth on land," "flying," and "hovering at a low altitude," the poem's figuration of seeing (the witnessing) as the "Archimedes's point" of the different possibilities (given that even the flying does not cancel the looking) explicitly does not enable the speaker to ignore the *awareness* of the Wrong. The position of witnessing—with its limitations, on the one hand, and the responsibility it carries, on the other—therefore does not allow a renunciation of the awareness. Neither does it allow erasure or ignorance of the event or for the denial of complicity in its creation.

In an earlier poem, "All Thy Breakers and Waves" (Kol mishbarekha vegale-kha), Ravikovitch comments on the nature of the witness position that will characterize most of her writing: "and I saw the tears of the oppressed/fade away on their cheeks" (CP, 139; BK 147–48, my translation). But what does it mean to see the tears fade away? Why does the speaker focus on the moment of fading away? Yochai Oppenheimer reads this line as a statement about the role of the political poet, about the poet's obligation to the victim's tears, about his duty to speak on behalf of their tears.[28] I would add, however, that by focusing on the tears fading away, Ravikovitch distinguishes between the people who experience the horror and the people who witness it. Ravikovitch's speaker does not look directly at the horror but at its victims. Lot's wife looked at the horror directly and became a pillar of salt (Genesis 19). In other words, she internalized the tears and was transformed into a representation of pain: crying. Ravikovitch, in her turn, does not look at Sodom, but at Lot's wife. She witnesses the iniquities, although her poems deal neither with them nor with the crying eye as a result of the iniquities. Rather, the poems focus on the very act of looking at the iniquities. To put it differently, Ravikovitch's political writing centers on the eye that sees the tears of the oppressed, its responsibility toward this tear, and the guilt that stems from this witnessing.

While never collapsing the embodied distinction between the one who experiences suffering and the witness to that suffering, Ravikovitch's observation nonetheless does not create the usual, or traditional, buffer between her world and that of the victim. The eyes that are directed inside, the eyes that are directed outside, and the eyes that bring her literature into being—these are all the same. It is as though Ravikovitch observes the world through the eyes of Narcissus, and it is this observation that serves as the basis for her writing, just as she writes in her poem "True Love Isn't What It Seems" (Haahavah haamitit einah kefi shehi niret): "Ourselves we love with great devotion,/attuned to ourselves with rapt attention" (CP, 197; BK, 188). I suggest we read Ravikovitch's political writing in light of this poetic declaration, as it does not allow for a separation between the internal layers and the external ones or between her private life and political events. This is not just because "the personal is political," but mainly because the way in which Ravikovitch deals with the external and the public stems from an intense self-attentiveness. The attentiveness to another's suffering is not disconnected from her own personal suffering; the public problem is also a personal problem, and any other's problem is also her own problem.[29] As Ravikovitch once said: "When the housing minister decided to confiscate lands from Arabs in Beith Zaphapha, I felt as if somebody had come to my place in order to confiscate part of my apartment."[30] This response neatly expresses one of the emotional reflexes that underpins her entire oeuvre, and of her political writing in particular: even though she is neither among the decision-makers nor the people affected by these decisions, she experiences the events from a position of almost total identification with the victims.

As discussed in chapter 4, the typical Ravikovitch character experiences herself via the gulf between the external and internal perspectives. Her identity is constituted as a maladjustment, creating a subject with acute and paralyzing sensitivity to the suffering and the victimization of others. Ravikovitch's political writing might therefore be read as an expression (or even as an acting-out) of this inner psychic mechanism. Reading her protest poetry in this way uncovers the inseparable conflation between her "private" identity and Israeli national identity. In other words, I suggest reading Ravikovitch's political writing not necessarily as a reaction to external events but rather as a reflection and projection of her characters' emotional world, as a symptom of a psyche whose self-definition is inextricably bound up with the sense of its own victimhood.

According to Emmanuel Levinas, it is possible to defend against evil only when each and every one of us accepts responsibility for others—by recognizing that "I" can be responsible for something "I" have not done, by adopting a misery which is not "mine."[31] We find a similar attitude in Ravikovtch's witness, who identifies with the subject being witnessed (her "identifying witnessing" position). This is related to the "transparent skin"—skin that doesn't protect the flesh,/not in the least", as she writes in her poem "We Had an Understanding" (Hayta beyneynu havanah, in CP, 189–90; BK, 181–82)—which creates a subject that functions simultaneously as a victim and as the one who unveils the victimhood of others.

This position is the basis for the protest in Ravikovitch's work. Seeing the suffering and being ceaselessly aware of it—in fact, being unable *not* to be aware of it—is what enables her to articulate the Wrong. In the poem "Hamlet, Supreme Commander" (Hamlet, matzbi elyon) Ravikovitch explicitly defines her protest, while referring to its moral necessity:

My protest is not in bitterness.
It is a cat's paw. At its tips are claws.
A puny complaint is naught but the whimper of a cooing infant,
drowned out in the din.
. . . .

for who would bear the whips and scorns of time,
. . . .

without growing—sedulous, in secret—
a nail sharp-whetted as a cat's paw
to wipe out with one swift swipe of the hand
that affront.

(CP, 212; BK, 199)

The two metaphors—the cat's paw and infant's coo—demonstrate the speaker's perspective: her protest is never violent, and the difficult matters she criticizes, maybe even her protest itself, are protected by her aesthetic detachment. From various remarks Ravikovitch herself has made, it is clear that she is well aware of the risk of not being heard as a result of this aesthetic choice: "The author and the artist have no role because they have no authority. You cannot measure or prove their influence. I express myself, and if somebody wishes to join me, he is welcome. . . . My influence is limited to those who read me, and my political writings answer only to my own need."[32] Nevertheless, an infant's coo is hard to ignore, and a cat's claw can scratch, especially when it is the sharpened claw of one who has been affronted.

More significantly, however, Ravikovitch's protest develops from within her own experience of suffering. It is the protest of the sufferer, a protest possible only from the "identifying-witness" position. Ravikovitch is aware of the ambivalence expressed in her work. The reader, like the speaker, finds herself in the situation described in the poem "Hovering at a Low Altitude": she "can make a getaway and persuade myself: I haven't seen a thing," but even so she will always be aware of the events, a witness to the Wrong. In Barbara Mann's words, "the space in which the poet is 'not here' is also the space in which the reader must acknowledge her own silence, and perhaps her own complicity, in the violence unfolding before her."[33] Again, even if Ravikovitch's poems do enable her readers to choose between "a foot-breadth on land," flying, and "hovering at a low altitude," the poems do not allow the reader to be silent or to hide her awareness of the Wrong by avoiding the act of seeing.

Biblical references in "Hovering at a Low Altitude" extend the discussion and further relate testimony and responsibility to questions of power, guilt, and complicity:

The girl is right there,
no one else around.
And if she runs for cover, or cries out—
there's no place to hide in the mountains.

The last two lines contain references both to biblical rape laws (Deuteronomy 22: 23–29) and to one of Jeremiah's destruction prophecies (Jeremiah 23: 24). Biblical law imposes some of the responsibility for a rape onto the victim: it finds her guilty if she does not cry out and innocent if she does. In Ravikovitch's poem the responsibility is imposed upon the witness, the person who hears the scream, and not upon the screamer. Ravikovitch exposes the blindness to the Wrong; for her, a horror that occurs in the "field," among "craggy eastern hills"—not "here" but "over there"—does not remain unheard and unseen. The act of witnessing rules out the option of willful ignorance. To fail to respond in some way is to be complicit.

The allusion to Jeremiah's prophecy links this guilt to a position of power expressed both in the direct reference to God's strength ("Can anyone hide himself in secret places, so I shall not see him? says the Lord," Jeremiah 23: 24) and in the specific content of the prophecy that deals with the punishment that will befall both leaders and false prophets who incite their people to diverge from the path of righteousness (Jeremiah 23: 1–2, 14). The prophecy emphasizes that it is these leaders and the prophets—and not the people—who will suffer most of the punishment. In other words, the blame lies mainly with those who have the power to influence the people. The power Ravikovitch's poem refers to is, thus, not just that of the man who hurts the girl, but also the power of the witness, a power that is embodied in her awareness of the event. In the Ravikovitch oeuvre, the witness occupies a position of power that entails responsibility.

The connection between testimony, power, and guilt is also made in the poem "On the Attitude toward Children in Times of War" (Al hayakhas li-yladim beitot milchamah). The poem was written, as we learn from an endnote, as "a variation on a poem by Nathan Zach that deals [satirically] with the question of whether there were exaggerations in the number of children reported killed in the [1982] Lebanon War" (CP, 208; BK, 197–98). Allegedly, both Nathan Zach's poem "On the Desire to Be Precise" (Al haratzon ledayek) and Ravikovitch's reaction to it deal with the role of language in shaping political reality. Zach's poem reads:

And then there was a major exaggeration in the body count:
There were some who counted about a hundred, and some counted
    several hundreds
And this one said, I counted thirty-six burnt women

And his friend said, You are wrong, because it was only eleven
And the error is deliberate and political, not accidental.[34]

A closer look at the poem, however, reveals that it is not referring to the sources that use language to obscure the reality of evil. Rather, it is directed at those who would engage with everything that surrounds the suffering but not with the suffering itself. With his signature irony, Zach describes utter indifference to and disaffection toward monstrous events and their victims: the exaggeration is in counting the corpses, not in the killing itself. In fact, the poem presents a very long list of killing techniques (shooting, crucifixion, burning, etc.) as a supposed distraction, and presents a world where what people should doubt is the reports about the events, not the events themselves.

According to Oppenheimer, "the indirect way in which Zach chooses to refer to the theme of war and death is expressed by his parodic style."[35] In my view, however, Zach's approach is not in the least indirect; it is a precise description of his (and Ravikovitch's) position. He is witnessing the events, even if he does not see them directly. He knows about them and is aware of their existence, and therefore, even though he was not present when they occurred, he has become a witness who cannot choose silence. Zach quotes the discourse about the war not simply in order to decipher and better understand the reality he refers to in his poem but to examine both his own position as a writer toward the events and the reality of other Israelis on the home front—a reality that only seems detached from the "close north" (i.e., Lebanon). If nothing else, the poem stresses how easily one can seem to detach oneself from the events of the Lebanon War, and drives home the fact that such detachment comes with a high moral price.

Ravikovitch's identification with the suffering of the refugees enables her to see and to express directly the guilt that Zach can only hint at. She describes the refugee's conditions as miserable and hopeless and also as a mortal threat, which "our own [Israeli] troops" are responsible for:

Benighted children,
at their age
they don't even have a real worldview.
And their future is shrouded too:
refugee shacks, unwashed faces,
sewage flowing in the streets,

infected eyes,
a negative outlook on life.

And thus began the flight from city to village,
from village to burrows in the hills.
As when a man did flee from a lion,
as when he did flee from a bear,
as when he did flee from a cannon,
from an airplane, from our own troops.

("On the Attitude toward Children in Times of War"
[Al hayakhas liyladim beitot milchamah], CP, 208; BK, 197–98)

The refugees' escape and their wanderings are described as attempts to escape an enormous force, just like man's attempt to escape God on Judgment Day: "And men shall go into the caves of the rocks, and into the holes of the earth, from before the terror of the Lord, and from the glory of His majesty, when He arises to shake mightily the earth" (Isaiah 2: 19). Despite the intensity of these efforts to run away, however, the refugees are forlorn; like the man who cannot escape God's power on Judgment Day, the refugee will not be able to escape his conquerors: "It will be as though a man fled from a lion, only to meet a bear, as though he entered his house and rested his hand on the wall, only to have a snake bite him" (Amos 5: 19). The uneven power relation between the refugees and "our troops" denies the refugees any chance of survival, an immoral pursuit that should prevent the victimizer from returning to his everyday life following the conflict; the moral failure of these actions, the poem says, forestalls the possibility of returning to any kind of ordinary, peaceful existence:

He who destroys thirty babies,
it is as if he'd destroyed one thousand and thirty,
or one thousand and seventy,
thousand upon thousand.
And for that alone shall he find
no peace.

(CP, 208; BK, 197–98.)

It doesn't matter how "precise" the language or the counting is; in fact, the wider and more organized the language becomes in the poem "On the Attitude toward Children in Times of War," the more specific and intense the sense of guilt in the reader.[36] Ravikovitch thus joins Zach's position of testimony, though she adds to it the dimension of responsibility and guilt.

The poem "You Can't Kill a Baby Twice" (Tinok lo horgim paamayim, in CP, 202–3; BK, 193–94) addresses the Sabra and Shatila Massacre of 1982. It blames the Israeli soldiers for not preventing the massacre that was carried out by Lebanese Maronite Christian militias, and also—as in the "On the Attitude toward Children in Times of War" poem—argues that the event will have serious implications not just for the victims but also for "those sweet soldiers of ours":

> Terror-struck women scrambled up, frantic,
> on a mound of earth:
> "They're butchering us down there,
> in Shatila."
> .   .   .   .
>
> Our own soldiers lit up the place with searchlights
> till it was bright as day.
> "Back to the camp, *marsch!*" the soldier commanded
> the shrieking women of Sabra and Shatila.
> After all, he had his orders.
>
> (CP, 202–3; BK, 193–94)

In contrast to the denial of responsibility by some Israeli leaders, Ravikovitch lays blame clearly and firmly: the Israeli soldiers knew what was happening and allowed the massacre to occur by not interfering. Even without direct contact between the Israeli soldiers and the victims, the fact that the soldiers lit up the camp illustrates their cooperation. That they were only following orders chillingly recalls the evasive moral reasoning by which others sought to extenuate collective German guilt for the Holocaust.

The main purpose of the poem, however, is not the placing of blame, the expression of bitter irony toward what happened ("And the kids were already laid out in the fetid waters,/their mouths gaping,/at peace./No one will harm them now./You can't kill a baby twice."), or even the defiance of some cosmic indifference ("A thin trail of newborn moon was hanging/over the camps.")[37] The poem's main claim comes in the last stanza:

> Those sweet soldiers of ours,
> There was nothing in it for them.

Their one and only desire
was to come home in peace.

(CP, 202–3; BK, 193–94)

Are we supposed to take this stanza as irony? An interpretation supporting an ironic reading could find evidence in the apparent gap between the
horrors described in the poem and the naïveté of its ending: the soldiers, despite what they have done, remain "sweet" and ask nothing more than to return home safely. According to Oppenheimer, the irony lies in the connection between this stanza and "Ammunition Hill" by Yoram Taharlev and Yair
Rosenblum, one of the best known songs of the Six-Day War (1967) whose
modest and naïve soldier protagonist wants only "to get home safely."[38] Other
parts of the poem can certainly be read ironically also: the number of people
who are moved from the world of the living to the world of the dead is "im-
pressive"; no one will harm the children now because "you can't kill a baby
twice."

On the other hand, a non-ironic reading of this stanza would emphasize a
central message in Ravikovitch's writing about the profound influence of any
exposure to an immoral act. The soldiers, like the people on the home front,
will carry the blame all their lives; the acts they perpetrated, witnessed, and
did not prevent have grave consequences. Unable to ignore *any* victimhood,
Ravikovitch blurs the very distinction between victim and victimizer. She
does so not by making the two equal or by reducing the victimizer's responsibility. On the contrary, by emphasizing the responsibility and guilt of the
victimizer, it comes to seem as though he too is a victim—although of a very
different kind—of the same event. The soldiers who think they can return
home safely are radically mistaken: they are returning home with a heavy burden, and they shall "find/no peace"(CP, 208; BK, 197–98). Ravikovitch stressed
a similar idea a few years after the First Intifada and the 1990 Gulf War:

> It influences the soldiers of the Givati and the Golani brigades, who
> find themselves in inhuman situations and have to react in an inhuman
> way. In this sense, I think we should feel pity not just for the battered but
> also for the ones who beat, not just for the victims but also for the victim-
> izers. What kind of men are coming out from these acts? A man is some-
> one who respects himself, but anyone who was in Hawara village or in
> Baytha, and broke legs and hands because of an order he got, is a person
> that will never be a man again. It is true that the immediate and obvious
> victim is the one whose body is hurt, but these soldiers know they are shit.

You can live a good life afterwards, and become rich and successful, but this is just self-deceit.[39]

Ravikovitch's protest poetry seeks to dispel the kind of self-deceit that lies in wait not just for the people who are directly responsible for iniquities but also for those who witness them. To ignore the responsibility and power inherent in testimony, her work contends, is to risk complicity and guilt.

chapter Nine

"Guilt-Ridden Poems"

The Contamination of Language
and the Departure from Innocence

*The poems that were written during the Lebanon War were
guilt-ridden poems. This is the uniqueness of the current political
poetry: the poets' collective recognition of guilt*
    Ravikovitch[1]

*When I hear that a child was killed, or even two students,
not exactly kids, I feel that I share the blame*
    Ravikovitch[2]

Presenting suffering from the position of the witness enables
Ravikovitch to understand, interpret, and depict the existence of evil in its
political and social contexts. This perspective exposes the social mechanisms
and arrangements that cause avoidable misery and challenges the witness to
depart from his or her imaginary innocence.

In his book *Speaking Evil: Towards an Ontology of Morals* and in the earlier
article "Beyond Good: Evil—An Outline for a Political Theory of Evils," Adi
Ophir examines the term "evil" in a social and political context. According to
Ophir, evil is not a demonic essence that transcends reality, nor is it an enig-
matic absence of good; rather, it is a product of society.[3] Defined thus, it can
be altered, or at least reduced. This theory intentionally ignores evil that is
not produced by human beings, as well as evil that is the result of abnormal
behavior. Instead, Ophir regards evil as possessing a social normalcy. The
process by which violence is normalized is the result of widespread social
indoctrination. It is a regularity that can be connected to social practices and
structural patterns of political acts.

Shoshana Felman, in her book *Testimony: Crises of Witnessing in Literature*, claims that no person can retain innocence in a world that has experienced the trauma of the Holocaust. From this standpoint, she then deconstructs our commonly held notion of history in general, and the post-Holocaust period specifically, as well as the classical meaning of testimony. "The extent of the massacre is such," she claims, "that the *witness* cannot not be in his turn *tainted*, implicated in the guilt of its occurrence by his very witnessing of it, by his very *knowledge* of the massacre—and of his own survival."[4] According to Felman, anyone who lives in an iniquitous historical age is implicated in its crimes, and she goes further by arguing that this foregone implication constitutes an existential state in which innocence means a mere lack of awareness of one's own participation in the crime. Since innocence is an illusion, innocence and guilt no longer stand in contradiction to one another, but rather represent different levels of awareness. From this perspective, "one can only be, thus, paradoxically enough, *guilty* of one's very *innocence*" (*Testimony*, 196, emphasis in the original). What Felman actually suggests is a process of dawning awareness, of awakening and relinquishing one's innocence.

Ravikovitch's protest poetry likewise unveils the political mechanism that creates iniquity. By spreading blame among varied centers of power and by applying the idea of permanent guilt, Ravikovitch's political writing does not allow anyone in Israeli society to evade responsibility or guilt.

Political regimes often seek to conceal or distort the reality of their own power and violence because without this obfuscation, their violence would require punishment. The regime uses power and violence and yet presents them in such a way as to make them appear legitimate and necessary means of punishment or self-defense. What's more, as Foucault points out, it is necessary that such violence have an invisible mechanism to facilitate its fulfillment and "normal" management, since "power is tolerable only on condition that it mask a substantial part of itself. Its success is proportional to its ability to hide its own mechanism."[5] To do so and to reinforce its standard conduct, hegemonic law uses several central ploys: euphemism, a strict binary way of thinking (us vs. them; Jewish vs. Arabic; right vs. wrong, etc.), a self-serving and objectifying definition of the victim, and the denial of the material body of the casualties.[6]

At the same time, while the hegemony constructs all these narratives to justify its violence, victims and those who identify with victims strive to deconstruct the narratives and to unveil the hidden interests they contain.[7] As part of this social and cultural arena, Ravikovitch's poetry exposes these hegemonic ploys in Israeli behavior by insisting upon the blurring of binary boundaries, by focusing on the unique suffering of the victims, and by positioning the body as an autonomous subject. These poetic acts rail against politics that enable the simultaneous creation and denial of violence. Ravikovitch's poetry thus shifts the focus from the consolatory political narrative to the very fact of this narrative's existence and its internal mechanisms. The poem "Blood Heifer" (Eglah arufah, in CP, 206–7; BB, 98–99; cf. BK 195–96), as well as other protest poems such as "They're Freezing Up North" (Batzafon kofim), "A Mother Walks Around" (Ima mithalekhet, in CP 234; BK 214–15), "The Story of the Arab Who Died in the Fire" (Hasipur al haaravi shemet basrefah, in CP, 239–40; BK, 217–18), and "Free Associating" (Asotziatzyot, in CP, 242–43; BK, 220–21), all demonstrate an awareness of hidden political mechanisms and oppose it by refusing to participate in the concealment of victims—particularly by focusing on the unique individual and the body, thus disrupting the consolatory political narrative.

The poem "A Jewish Portrait" (Portret yehudi, in CP, 198–99; BK, 189–90), which opens the political section of the book *True Love*, deals with a specific woman, "a Diaspora kind of Jew whose eyes dart around/in fear." The woman lacks a permanent home ("Any place she might stumble on/is a place that won't last") and is seemingly without political awareness ("she has no use for this business, Jerusalem"). Although she is "slowing down the caravan"— caravans of refugees and Ukrainian farmers—she finally gets to where she is staying and shuts herself in: "she will bolt the inner door,/pull the shutters closed around her./Only the soles of her feet will she bathe,/so boundless her weariness." The starting point of Ravikovitch's political writing is always the specific individual (in this case, a worried, transient woman), and not the abstract masculine hero fighting for his country. The speaker's morally penetrating eyes cannot ignore the victims' suffering and reflect a constant blame in regard to the iniquity. Turning her poetic spotlight from the hegemonic political narrative to the private and unique suffering of the victims enables Ravikovitch to unveil the political mechanism and by so doing contribute to the effort of reducing its effect.

By exposing the suffering of one individual, regardless of nationality, Ravikovitch draws attention to the moral dimension of political discussion:

She has no use for this matter, Jerusalem.
Day after day they wrangle over the Temple Mount,

each man smites and reviles his brother,
and the dead prophet shrieks,
Who hath required this at your hand, to trample My courts?

("A Jewish Portrait," CP, 198–99; BK, 189–90)

As the political discussion about Jerusalem and the Temple Mount (Har ha-bayit) becomes a violent quarrel, overshadowing the calls of the prophet Isaiah who emphasizes the moral over the formal duties (such as sacrifice, Isaiah 1: 10–17), Ravikovitch actually claims here that no religious or political idea can justify immoral behavior. Rather, loyalty to an idea requires moral conduct.

In the poem "Blood Heifer" (Eglah arufah), the identity of the poetic subject is deliberately blurred. The poem keeps from its readers two pieces of information that are usually crucial in political poetry: national identity and historical background. The poem refuses to provide information about the nationality of either the victim or the aggressor and no details are given as to the concrete historical situation. The moral position depicted in the poem is therefore not concerned with issues of nationality. Instead, it demands that the reader examine the situation without the normative evasion that a national context may provide. And rather than obscuring the power relationship or the iniquity that is its result, this blurring of concrete national identity exposes these things all the more forcefully.

BLOOD HEIFER

He took one step,
Then a few steps more.
His glasses fell to the ground,
His skullcap.
Managed another step,
bloody, dragging his feet.
Ten steps
and he's not a Jew anymore,
not an Arab—
in limbo.

Havoc in the marketplace; people shouting, Why
are you murdering us?
Others rushing
to take revenge.

And he lies on the ground: a death rattle,
A body torn open,
blood streaming out of the flesh,
streaming
out of the flesh.

He died here, or there—
no one knows for sure.
What do we know?
A dead body lying in the field.

Suffering cleanseth from sin, it is said,
man like dust in the wind,
but who was that man
lying there lonely in his blood?
What did he see,
what did he hear
with all that commotion around him?
If thou seest even thine enemy's ass
lying under its burden,
it is said, thou shalt surely help.

If a dead body is found lying in the field
if a body is found in the open,
let your elders go out and slaughter a heifer
and sacrifice its ashes in the river.

(CP, 206–7; BB, 98–99; cf. BK 195–96)

The stereotypically Jewish symbols of glasses and a skullcap characterize
the man in the poem as a type rather than a subject, yet from the moment of
his injury until his death, his religion and nationality are obscured: "and he's
not a Jew anymore,/not an Arab—/in limbo." In light of this ambiguity, the
manner in which the man's suffering is described is glaringly sharp. From the
moment he is injured, he who might have been characterized by his religion
or national identity becomes both "anyone," a human being, and "someone"
who deserves a name, a unique identity: "man like dust in the wind,/but who
was that man/lying there lonely in his blood?"

By focusing on the man's asphyxiation and gaping wounds, the poem insists that the tormented body not be left unseen. These details point to the
mechanism that disavows the material body of the subject and thereby en-

ables the routine of violence and evil to exist in the guise of necessary politics.[8] Such details insist that beyond every sophisticated social mechanism and political decision lies the suffering human being.

The obscurity at the beginning of the first stanza continues in the second:

Havoc in the marketplace; people shouting, Why
are you murdering us?
Others rushing
to take revenge.

It is not clear who is the killer and who the victim, who is shouting and who taking revenge. The endless cycle of violence, of murder and revenge, suggests that the murderer might also one day be murdered, that the victim may also one day become the victimizer. The blurring of nationality and the shift in focus from the national to the human demand an acknowledgement of the victims' suffering and of the necessary action, as relevant to both sides of the dispute. It is a situation of horrible suffering and violence, in which there is no way to identify the guilty party. Such a situation demands the ritualistic fulfillment of the biblical Blood Heifer Law.

Amid the hate and the violence Ravikovitch reminds the reader of two moral codes. One is from Exodus 23: 5, according to which there are situations in which people are obligated to help even their enemies: "Whenever you see that the ass of someone who hates you has collapsed under its load, do not leave it there. Be sure to help him with his animal." The second is the "Blood Heifer" law (from Deuteronomy 21: 1–9), which claims that bloodshed in and of itself is not atonement. According to this law, a ritual of absolution must be carried out (after any violent act) even if it is impossible to determine who is to blame or if the real culprit cannot be found. Indeed, Ravikovitch makes it impossible to decide who is the "good" and who the "bad"; both sides at once suffer from and create violence. The conclusion must nevertheless be not to continue the cycle of violence, with each side defensively protesting its innocence, but rather, to take heed of the biblical law and—in the spirit of Felman's insight[9]—acknowledge that no individual is entirely free from blame.

It should be noted that only two of the duties of the biblical blood heifer law are mentioned in the poem: to slaughter a heifer and to scatter its ashes in a river.[10] The main requirement of the ritual—that the leaders of the city wash their hands in the river and declare that they neither committed nor witnessed the crime—however, is missing. The omission of such a crucial detail from the poem would seem to imply the guilt of modern Israeli leaders:

in the First Lebanon War they could carry out the violent part of the ritual, but they cannot cleanse themselves of the blame—because they actually do have some part in the violence and unquestionably see it happen. The participation of the leaders in the ritual therefore constitutes a demagogic use of the innocent party's position, and not a real innocence. Similarly, to create a situation that explains war as a mere military operation or as a matter of necessity, intended only to defend citizens, is to reinforce the consolatory political narrative that presents the evil as unavoidable.[11] By creating a situation in which religious and national identities are obscured while ostensibly accepting the consolatory narrative, Ravikovitch exposes its falsifying effects and the danger buried within it. Indeed, the situation in the poem (and more so in reality) is complex, and it is impossible to define who is "the good" and who "the bad"; the two sides both inflict violence and both are victims. But the poem asserts that one cannot derive from this any kind of justification for the continuation of violence. On the contrary: the necessary conclusion is that *no one is free from guilt.*

It is possible to argue that blaming the leaders constitutes an un-blurring of national identity and an assignment of guilt to a specific side. According to this point of view, the blurring in the poem functions merely as a rhetorical element that emphasizes the guilt of the Israeli leaders. But this is mistaken. The blurring that characterizes the poem allows for the simultaneous existence of various types of guilt: the guilt of the leadership, for example, does not cancel out the guilt of the public.

It is the poem's biblical allusions that determine the presentation of the various types of guilt. The expression "disturbance" (Mehumat elohim) in the second stanza, for example, offers nationalism as one possible source of evil. This unique biblical expression appears in a violent description of Judgment Day in Zechariah 14: 13, which focuses on the establishment of a Hebrew national identity (mainly by excluding all other nations), and on the centrality of Jerusalem to this national identity. The root A.L.A (Ayin. Lamed. Ayin) in the fifth stanza ("but who was that man/lying there lonely in his blood?") implies another cause of evil. This is a unique root in the Bible, which appears in Job's answer to God (Job 39: 27–30). The allusion reminds the reader of the existence of unpreventable violence, for which only God or nature can be held responsible.

By presenting multiple sources of evil and violence, the poem blurs the question of responsibility for the crime. It is important to notice, however, that it is not a blurring that enables evasion of responsibility; rather, it embraces many types of guilt. It also forestalls the possibility of innocence. Raviko-vitch's political poetry presents the unavoidable culpability of all human beings who live in a historical period in which an atrocity is committed. As Felman asserts, "on the site of 'one of the greatest crimes in history', innocence can only mean lack of awareness of one's participation in the crime."[12]

Ravikovitch's poetry uncovers the mechanism that makes the illusion of innocence possible. The multiplicity of guilt present in "Blood Heifer" de-constructs the political mechanism that is based on the binary separation between guilt and blamelessness. Ravikovitch refuses to take part in the dom-inant political narrative, which forms the victimized Israeli and which de-fends only its own existence. Hers is a refusal to credit the Israeli claim that the Jewish state goes to war only when it has no other choice, that the First Lebanon War was not a war but rather "a military operation to protect the northern settlements," to use the language of the Israeli government, media, and population at the time of the events.[13]

Guilt in Ravikovitch's political poetry, then, is inseparable from her protest against the political mechanism that enables the existence of evil. The poem "Get out of Beirut" (Latzet mibeirut, in CP, 204–5; BK, 194–95) serves as an-other apt example of the way in which her work does not settle merely for the expression of a moral position toward what has occurred. Rather, the poem both indirectly accuses the guilty party and unveils the linguistic mechanism that enables the immoral act.

As Ofra Yeglin has shown, the role of language in obscuring brutality is a recurring issue in Ravikovitch's poetry. The linguistic mechanism that is adapted to justify evil supplies arguments of legitimization and rationaliza-tion that help to maintain situations of suffering while simultaneously deny-ing their existence.[14] Ravikovitch herself was clear about her public mission to resist such obfuscation, responding to a question from Ilan Lotenberg: "My role is to protest against the cheapening of terms . . . If someone is claim-ing that Jews do not run wild, mistreat and murder, that is an inverse anti-Semitism. It is a contamination of the thought, and one who knows some his-tory, also knows it led to very distorted acts. That is why, if I ask myself what I have been doing here—and for many years I have done several things in this country—I think that in total I was trying to contribute my part in keeping the clarity of thought and to be cautious about contaminating terms."[15]

This is exactly what the speaker in the poem "Get out of Beirut" does: she protests against the cheapening of terms and maintains clarity of thought by exposing the historical points at which language is used to create iniquities.

The poem infuses the suffering of refugees with the blame of those responsible for it. It also exposes the linguistic manipulation that justifies this suffering. By making use of a kind of free indirect discourse, in which several voices are integrated,[16] the poem enables multiple voices to be spoken by activating many speakers, positions, and attitudes. Most relevant to this discussion, however, is that this particular technique results in various kinds of blurring. The blurring in the poem—both of the victim and the victimizer's identities, and of the combined discourse—is the central poetic device that exposes suffering and injustice, and the mechanism that creates them. The description of the refugee's suffering is combined with the act of blaming; the poem presents both the misery of the individuals (babies with purulence on their eyes, the R.P.G children, and "unaccounted for people") and the political, linguistic, and logical mechanism that caused and enabled this misery.

The last stanza of the poem gives an extremely stark description of the refugees:

You will not be accepted anywhere
You are deported people.
You are unaccounted for people
You are uncalled for people.
You are a handful of louses
Stinging and itching
Maddeningly.

(CP, 204–5; BK, 194–95, my translation)

The exaggeration of this description requires a critical reading. The language of genocide penetrates the speech of the expellers, creating a dissonance that requires one to read the stanza as combined discourse, and not as evidence of the speaker's position. In fact, the combined discourse reflects attitudes that were common during the First Lebanon War and were formed with the help of conscious and subconscious linguistic mechanisms that dehumanized the enemy and created a convenient distraction from the morally problematic aspects of the war. Referring to the refugees as "a handful of louses" recalls the media's common use of the expression "purification of terrorists' nests" (a pun that is based on the Hebrew homonym of *Kinim*, which with a different spelling means both louses and nests). The metaphoric use of "nests" as a synonym for terror organizations contributes to the dehumanization of the enemy and therefore legitimizes "necessary" violence to combat them. The poem unveils the mechanism that "purifies the terrorists' nests" for the "protection of the northern settlements" by creating the illusion that Israel is not killing human beings, but rather, exterminating vermin. In this sense the refugees are no longer people who were ejected from their homes but merely a "waspish handful of louses."

The poem exposes another aspect of the sociopolitical mechanism that enables suffering: the mistaken order of cause and effect. The speaker's description of the refugees' suffering and their bitter conditions is not intended disrespectfully, but rather as a way of expressing the consequences of occupation and the experience of being a refugee. Ugliness, poverty, and helplessness are not, the poem contends, innate characteristics of the enemy but the results of military domination and the ejection of people from their homes. One does not expel the "repulsive" enemy; rather, expulsion creates another individual's repulsive situation.

By suffusing this poem—and many other political poems such as "You Can't Kill a Baby Twice" (Tinok lo horgim paamayim), "Laying Upon the Waters" (Shokhevet al hamayim), and "Mother Is Walking" (Ima mithalekhet)— with ambiguity and the combined discourse technique, Ravikovitch seemingly "quotes" the language that is used in order to obscure brutality and to maintain and justify the existing social order. By so doing, however, she actually exposes the manipulative and destructive power of language and subverts the political mechanism that is supported by this same language.

Ravikovtch's protest poetry exposes the system that creates societal evil and, in so doing, expresses her moral attitude. This poetry accepts the responsibility of the witness for establishing the historical narrative and courageously acknowledges the end of Zionist innocence, thereby facilitating the process of moral awakening.

chapter Ten

"Stinging and Itching/ Maddeningly"

The Palestinians as
the Israeli Abjection

Ravikovitch's use of ambiguity and blurring of boundaries contributes to one of the most radical statements in her protest poetry. This statement, concerning the establishment of Israeli national identity, suggests the possibility of a national identity based not on the exclusion of the Other but on a recognition of affinity with this other and its inclusion. This alternative has the potential to challenge the hegemonic discourse about crucial issues such as the Israeli self-image, national ego and super-ego, Jewish identity and morality, and the relationship between Palestinian identity and contemporary Zionism.

This claim can be best understood through the notion of "abjection," which Kristeva discusses in her book *Powers of Horror: An Essay on Abjection.*[2] The word "abject" means to expel, to cast out or away. As Anne McClintock shows, Freud—in *Totem and Taboo* and *Civilization and Its Discontents*—was the first to suggest that civilization is founded on the repudiation of certain pre-Oedipal pleasures and incestuous attachments. Following Freud (as well as Mary Douglas's work on boundary rituals), Kristeva argues that one's social being is constituted through the force of expulsion. As part of the socialization process, the self has to conceal certain bodily excretions that society deems impure, such as tears, urine, menstrual blood, semen, vomit, and so on. Because these expelled elements can never be fully eliminated, they haunt the edges of the subject's identity with the threat of disruption or even dissolution. Kristeva calls this process abjection: "The abject is everything that the subject seeks to expunge in order to become social; it is also a symptom of the failure of this ambition. As a compromise between 'condemnation and yearning,' abjection marks the borders of the self; at the same time, it threatens the self with perpetual danger. . . . the expelled abject haunts the subject as its inner constitutive boundary; that which is repudiated forms the self's internal limit. The abject is 'something rejected from which one does not part.'"[3]

The ambiguity that Ravikovitch creates in her political writing, in poems like "Blood Heifer" (Eglah arufah), "On the Attitude toward Children in Times of War" (Al hayakhas liyladim beitot milchamah), "A Poem in an Arabic Style, Maybe" (Shir besignon aravi, ulai), "Lying Upon the Waters" (Shokhevet al hamayim), "Lullaby" (Shir eres), and "Free Associating" (Asotziatzyot), subverts the normative binary classification that establishes the political mechanism and points up the ways in which the construction of Israeli identity is inextricably bound up with the construction of Palestinian identity. The Palestinian presence is the abjection of Israeli self-establishment in that the Palestinians are what Israel seeks to expunge and exclude in order to become social (not to say Western). The abjection signifies the constant tension between exclusion and inclusion, interior and exterior, and the self and other, and emphasizes the inability to exclude the other entirely, as the other is also similar and included; the other is like us, and in us. Therefore, even though the Palestinians are what Israeli society tries to exclude in order to establish a proper social existence, they are also the element that haunts the boundaries of Israeli identity, in a threatening and disruptive way.[4]

In the poem "Get out of Beirut" (Latzet mibeirut), for example, after representing the attempt to exclude the repugnant Palestinians—"we want to see you sailing away on the water" (CP, 204–5; BK 194–95, my translation)—there is a recognition of the presence of what cannot be expelled: "You are a handful of louses/Stinging and itching/Maddeningly" (my translation). Note that it is the person with lice who loses his mind. The Palestinian refugees, and the effort to exclude them, will not sail away on the water. Rather, they will remain, a troubling and subversive element in the establishment of Israeli identity. Ravikovitch's political writing suggests that the Israelis should replace the ongoing effort to exclude the Palestinians with a recognition of their similarity and mutual dependence.

Ravikovitch also intertwines her Jewish Israeli feminine voice with Palestinian voices (or, considering the fact that Ravikovitch was not familiar with Arabic, with what she imagined as Palestinian voices). The poem "Hamlet, Supreme Commander" (Hamlet, matzbi elyon) opens with first-person singular, "My protest is not in bitterness," and ends with third-person singular: "For who would bear the whips and scorns of time,/. . ./without growing—

sedulous, in secret—/a nail sharp-whetted as a cat's paw/to wipe out with one swift swipe of the hand/that affront."

This transition from first to third person is subtly handled and blends the speaker's protest with the Palestinian uprising. The insult to the one who witnesses the atrocities merges with the affront to the oppressed victims; the poet's protest and the Palestinian campaign become one. This it not to say that Ravikovitch does not distinguish between her position as an Israeli and the Palestinian position, but rather that the motivation for their protests is similar. The need to protest stems from a similar sensitivity to transgression and from a common refusal to accept injustice.

Ravikovitch articulates the driving force behind protest by quoting *Hamlet*: "For who would bear the whips and scorns of time,/The oppressor's wrong, the proud man's contumely,/The insolence of office, and the spurns/ That patient merit of th'unworthy takes." Ravikovitch thereby locates her own protest and that of the Palestinians in an immortal time, in the universal history of humanity, and by so doing distances the analysis of those protests from the familiar discourse of the Israeli-Palestinian conflict. This poetic move not only enables her readers to rethink the occupation in human terms rather than in those of nationalist Zionism, but also makes possible a process of identification with the victims. The Israeli reader starts his or her journey at the realm of protest by identifying with the speaker and then with the universal truths articulated by Hamlet. Only at the end of the poem is the reader brought to recognize her identification with the Palestinians.

We go through a similar process in the poem "On the Attitude toward Children in Times of War" (Al hayakhas liyladim beitot milchamah). Its first stanza reads:

He who destroys thirty babies
It is as if he'd destroyed three hundred babies,
and toddlers too,
or even eight-and-a-half year-olds;
in a year, God willing, they'd be soldiers
in the Palestine Liberation Army.

The opening line "He who destroys thirty children" recurs in the final stanzas of the poem. The allusion to *Sanhedrin* 4: 5—"whoever destroys a single life in Israel, it is as though he has destroyed an entire universe, and whoever saves a single life in Israel, it is as if he has saved an entire universe"— reminds the reader of the enormous importance of human life in Jewish culture and hints at the Israeli double standard in regard to the Palestinian people. Even more significantly, however, Ravikovitch's use of this well-known Talmudic reference activates in the reader a sophisticated emotional mechanism: the Hebrew reader who is familiar with the phrase "whoever saves a single life *in Israel,* it is as if he has saved an entire universe" is likely to assume that the hurt babies in the poem are Jewish victims (from "Israel"), and therefore to feel sympathy and sorrow for them. Only at the end of the first stanza is the actual nationality of these victims exposed: "in a year, God willing, they'd be soldiers/in the Palestine Liberation Army," at which point the reader must redirect her mercy toward victims of a different nationality.

A similar literary device is used in the poem "Hovering at a Low Altitude" (Rechifah begovah namuch). According to Chana Kronfeld, Ravikovitch constitutes the girl in the poem as Arab and as Other "only after the reader has found it difficult to ignore her humanity—in other words, can no longer emotionally accept her as other."[5] This device, characteristic of Ravikovitch's writing, is not just a rhetorical tool but an expression of her approach to the Israeli-Palestinian relationship more broadly, an approach that holds that national, moral, and political identity cannot be separated from the relationship with the Palestinian people. Even the aggressive aspects of Israeli behavior, including its complicity in violating human rights, is part of its identity. To use Ravikovitch's sarcastic language: "No point hiding it any longer:/We're an experiment that went awry,/a plan that misfired,/tied up with too much murderousness" ("Two Isles Hath New Zealand" [Shnei iyim lenew ziland], CP, 209–10; BK, 198–99).

This blurring of the separation between Israeli and Palestinian identities and the creation of a hybrid realm between the two reaches its apex in the poem "Lying Upon the Waters" (Shokhevet al hamayim), which describes a 'Stinking Mediterranean city/stretched out over the waters/head between her knees,/her body befouled with smoke and dunghills." But which city is it? Even though the immediate reaction (especially among Hebrew readers) would be to relate the poem to Tel Aviv, it is also possible that the poem actually refers to Beirut. Each of the possibilities gives a slightly different meaning to the last stanza:

Filthy Mediterranean city,
how my soul is bound up with her soul.
Because of a lifetime,
an entire lifetime.

If we take these lines to be about Tel Aviv, "Lying Upon the Waters" becomes a love poem to the supposedly secular Hebrew city, a modern monument to Israeli urbanism. Unlike the common depiction of Tel Aviv as the place where Israel meets the modern world (usually vis-à-vis Jerusalem), however, Ravikovitch locates Tel Aviv in the Middle East and does not allow her Israeli readers to distinguish themselves from that reality by identifying themselves as Westerns Europeans.

The lines could also be seen as referring to Beirut. The 1980s were an especially bleak time for the Lebanese capital: much of the city lay in ruins as a result of the 1976 Karantina Massacre carried out by the Lebanese Front, the Syrian army shelling of Christian neighborhoods in 1978 and 1981, and the Israeli invasion in 1982. It could be, then, that the dire condition of Beirut has caused the speaker's soul to be "bound up with her [Beirut's] soul." As in all of Ravikovitch's oeuvre, the speaker identifies with suffering, regardless of nationality or political discourse.

Even though Tel Aviv and Beirut could each be taken as the subject of the poem, I believe that the real subject is both of them together; in fact, at the center of the poem stands a recognition of the inability to distinguish between the two cities. The poem arouses in the reader various historical, social, emotional, and cultural associations, associations that are both related to the fact that the cities are widely perceived as enemies and that sometimes contradict each other. Nevertheless, the poetic setting prevents one association from canceling out the other entirely. The reader is compelled to face the emotional and political complexity and ambivalence that the poem provokes in her. This mechanism prevents the reader from retreating to her comforting and reassuring national boundaries. The Hebrew reader, who vacillates between various contradictory emotions, is made to experience the process of abjection in its fullness. As she tries, and fails, to expunge her relation to the enemies' "filthy Mediterranean city," her identity is modified, the boundaries of her subjectivity blurred and extended. No longer can the reader exclude the Mediterranean-Palestinian dimension from her Jewish-Israeli identity.

"The Transparent Skin That Unites Us"[1]

Photo: Dina Guna

"This Torment"[2] The Politics of Trauma

Ravikovitch's work creates a space for otherness, estrangement, and inferiority, and enables silenced voices to express their particular viewpoints and be heard. Characters that have often been marginalized in the Israeli literary and cultural milieu stand at the center of Ravikovitch's writing. The room she makes for victimhood, as well as the way her characters and speakers fail to conform or accommodate themselves to the symbolic order, creates poetic and cultural possibilities different from those established in the works of her contemporaries, like Amos Oz (b. 1939), A. B. Yehoshua (b. 1936), and David Shahar (1926–1997).

Furthermore, Ravikovitch's movement between the symbolic order and the deviant—the way in which she confronts the issues of womanhood, manic depression, madness, victimhood, and national identity from within and from outside, while revealing the inside-out and outside-in perspectives and their points of collision—is one of her most influential accomplishments in terms of the construction of deviant feminine subjectivity in Israeli culture beginning in the 1960s.

In her poem "We Had an Understanding" (Hayta beyneynu havanah), Ravikovitch describes her experience of subjectivity as having a "transparent skin": "skin that doesn't protect the flesh/not in the least." This subject experiences herself as a permanent victim (who at times has the capacity also to reveal the victimhood of others), haunted by trauma and longing but proud of her own estrangement and individualism. A kind of modern Lot's wife, perhaps. Lot's wife became a pillar of salt the moment she looked back at the burning Sodom, at the core of the catastrophe (Genesis 19, 26). Unlike Lot, the representative of the symbolic order, who could turn his gaze away from destruction, his wife was unable to ignore the catastrophe and leave her traumatic past behind. The history of Lot's wife—a narrative of petrifaction, weakness, and fragility—is comparable to Ravikovitch's poetic "historiography." It is, to use Walter Benjamin's words, a "secular explanation of history as the Passion of the world,"[3] as though the whole world were a bleeding wound and its whole existence a traumatized self: "this torment/will turn into summer and winter and spring/in a perfect circle—/will become one memory, delicate, scorching" ("Birdy," CP, 176; BK, 172).

"This torment," the focus of my book, lies at the center of Ravikovitch's unique approach to deviation. Her emotional, cultural, and ideological portrayal of a deviant subjectivity raises questions about the politics of trauma.

In various ways, this book has asked the following: What are the critical and creative challenges facing a subversive alternative to the symbolic order? What are the implications of inscribing trauma in culture? How might a traumatic event, or the speech of a victimized personality, affect the social order and bring about cultural and ethical transformation?

These questions become even more problematic when one considers involuntary subversion. According to Julia Kristeva, the semiotic—the pre-Oedipal emotional sphere tied to nonverbal impulses and instincts, the indeterminate and anarchic drive—has the potential to challenge and destabilize the symbolic order. Although signification requires both the semiotic and the symbolic, some nonverbal signifiers are constructed exclusively on the basis of the semiotic. In this sense, the semiotic is the "raw material" of signification: the corporeal, libidinal matter that must be harnessed and channeled appropriately to facilitate social cohesion and regulation. By nature, then, the semiotic is seen by Kristeva to contain subversive forces able to overflow or break down the boundaries of the symbolic order.[4] Judith Butler, however, takes issue with the notion that the subversive effects of the semiotic might be "anything more than a temporary and futile disruption of the hegemony of the paternal law." Thus, according to Butler, "Kristeva offers us a strategy of subversion that can never become a sustained political practice."[5]

I believe that questions of subversion and political practice cannot remain within the limits of common power relations (strong/weak, hegemonic/marginal, oppressor/victim); rather, they should be extended to the larger question of the politics of inferior and suppressed subjectivity. Ravikovitch's work offers us this political practice in poetic language.[6] The deviation is inherent to subjectivity, and for Ravikovitch's speakers and characters, aberrant eruptions are a crucial (if largely unconscious) part of their self-construction. They have no choice but to dispute the symbolic order. Unlike Western thought, which since the Enlightenment has advocated reason, logic, and rationality, and therefore has fostered a belief in the human capacity to choose and in our ability to influence and control our destiny, Ravikovitch's poetic and political practice is based on the assumption that personal choice is an illusion. Since the speakers and the characters have no option but to experience the world through their deviant sensibilities, their behavior is not the result of any real decision-making process. In this sense, it is possible to argue that they do gain a form of power—not the power to change the dominant order or to prevent their own repression, but the power to survive in such reality without being erased. With that in mind, one might begin to understand Ravikovitch's political practice, which focuses on and gives voice to the powerless position of those who are excluded.

The innovation of this mode becomes clear when one considers common theoretical and psychoanalytic approaches to victimhood and trauma. At the center of these stands the connection between the traumatic event and its aftermath. Some major theoretical perspectives share a commitment to assuming a linear connection between trauma, healing, and recovery, and approach trauma as something requiring rehabilitation and cure. Trauma, it is assumed, is a state the victim should seek to overcome or somehow incorporate into his or her life in a safe and even productive way. Implicitly, these approaches also share the belief that a post-traumatic personality who preserves the trauma and the victimized mentality (being unable or unwilling to incorporate the trauma into everyday life and to carry on) is thought to be in a position of weakness. Conversely, one can also find approaches to trauma that not only deny the possibility of escaping the traumatic state but actually celebrate it. All of these theories that "preserve the truth of the trauma as the failure of representation,"[7] share the idea of an endless and uncured trauma, which establishes a wounded and victimized subjectivity engaged in the ongoing process of self-construction.

This binary mapping represents the "tendency in certain contemporary approaches to eliminate or obscure the role of problematic intermediary or transitional processes."[8] This all-or-nothing tendency, the enormous yet limited range between the notion of trauma and recovery,[9] and the idea of an endless wound, between acting out and working through, raises the question of whether there might be another option, one that transcends these binaries.

Ravikovitch's work proposes a way to think about trauma without equating victimhood and weakness and, at the same time, without idealizing or romanticizing it. Her work poetically conceptualizes the traumatized personality without trapping it in binary terms. Her work presents traumatized subjectivity as an emotional mechanism that does not comply with the binary disposition of powerlessness/strength, passivity/activity, desirability/worthlessness. On the one hand, Ravikovitch's character suffers from her vulnerability and often pays a very high price for it (social exclusion, loss of custody of her daughter, hospitalization in a psychiatric ward). On the other, the character stubbornly preserves her alienation, and in fact transforms it into a sign of distinction. Furthermore, the poems and the stories express an intense desire for social engagement, and a sincere wish to be included in normative communal situations while simultaneously communicating a sense of extreme estrangement and individuality.

The protagonist of the story "The Lights of Spring" (Orot haaviv) claims that "anything I didn't know I was forced to invent from imagination." In the spirit of this endeavor, Ravikovitch invents a poetics and a unique approach that challenges and extends the conceptual norms of her time. Her work gives voice to a deviant subjectivity, creates a poetic space for estrangement, and blurs the binary differentiation between inside-out and outside-in, mania and depression, speech about madness and mad speech, and private and national identity. By doing all this, Ravikovitch reclaims the subjectivity that was taken from her speakers and characters. Moreover, she creates a cultural space that allows for the representation of deviant situations, conditions, and cases, or that at least enables the expression of the discrepancy between this deviance and the symbolic order, and the struggle for a self-definition based on the subject's own idiosyncratic criteria.

"Turn Me into Myself from Someone Else"[10]

In *True Love* Ravikovitch dedicates two poems to the poet Yona Wallach, who died in 1985: "Finally I'm Talking" (Sof sof ani medaberet, in CP, 177–78; BK, 173–74) and "True Love Isn't What It Seems" (Haahavah haamitit einah kefi shehi niret). Using Harold Bloom's theory, Michael Gluzman reads these poems as reflecting a reverse anxiety of influence, that is, as an expression of Ravikovitch's fear of Wallach's intensity.[11] The title of "Finally I'm Talking," and specifically the line "this time I'm the one who's talking/and you won't interrupt anymore," certainly express a sense of relief. When Ravikovitch describes Wallach, however, she refers not to her emasculating authority, but rather to Wallach's odd manners, "peculiar disposition," and lack of inhibition: "All of a sudden you've got manners,/you've got inhibitions." Ravikovitch thus identifies that which simultaneously binds and separates the two writers: Ravikovitch, the poet of reticence, who embraces the rigid language of the symbolic order and uses it to express her deviance, speaks to the poet who muddles and tangles the symbolic order, and articulates her aberration in a scraggly and tumultuous language. In this way, in the guise of a poet who can finally speak, Ravikovitch suggests the way in which she herself has influenced Wallach. While making clear the distance between the dead poet and the living one, she also gives a poetic map with coordinates at which the two poets meet. On this map other poets, too, are placed, at different locations that relate in various ways to the poetic alternative suggested by Ravikovitch's oeuvre.

The deep structure of victimhood in Ravikovitch's work—a structure that merges trauma, estrangement, madness, and politics—creates a mental and poetic alternative that deviates from both social and psychological norms, and that undermines the foundations of the symbolic order. This conceptual framework for thinking about disruption to the hegemony and its implications for the individual psychoanalytic process, creativity, social thought and action, and the establishment of national identity has had a lasting influence on Hebrew literature, especially on writers such as Yona Wallach (1944–1985), Raquel Chalfi (b. 1939), Agi Mishol (b. 1946), and Maya Bejerano (b. 1949).

To put it another way, Ravikovitch's innovation, the unique voice she establishes in regard to the process of constructing (a feminine, traumatized, mad, or national) subjectivity serves as a poetical-cultural platform for her contemporaries. The complex connections Ravikovitch makes between accommodating the symbolic order and manifesting aberrant, psychotic breaches create a model of poetic and intellectual engagement through which we might understand and map the voices of the foremost poets from the 1960s on. To be clear, I am not suggesting a one-way relationship between Ravikovitch and her literary milieu. Indeed, Ravikovitch was inspired by both her predecessors and her contemporaries, and her work is deeply marked by these poetic influences.[12] Nevertheless, despite the dialogic nature of Israeli literature (especially, one might argue, among the Generation of the State) it is important to note the cultural example her work established, as well as the importance of her work as a major poetic model, which writers—for better and for worse, consciously and unconsciously, intentionally or instinctively—continue to respond to.

Once again, as I hinted earlier, Ravikovitch's influence is evident in Yona Wallach's fascination with madness and peculiarity. Wallach's work is an ongoing exploration of eccentricity. Moreover, her disturbance of normative gender, sexual, and identity stances, the way she allows herself to break from conventional language and syntax, and the idea of personal identity being a constant performative act ("turn me into myself from someone else," to use Wallach's language) are all viable to some extent because of the way Ravikovitch blurs binary oppositions and challenges the reader's protected position. Ravikovitch's depictions of the entrance into and departure from insanity, as well as her various perspectives that work simultaneously, "taught" Wallach and her readers how to conduct themselves in a poetic space in which, as Wallach writes, "everything stays remains is over/my condition my nerves everything is broken bound spoken" (Wallach, 220).

Maya Bejerano emerged as a new voice in Israeli poetry in the 1970s, with her surreal, intense, and innovative sequence "Data Processing" (Ibud netunim).[13] She has published nine books of poetry and has been awarded the Prime Minister's Prize twice (in 1986 and 1996), the Bernstein Prize (in 1988), and the Bialik Prize (in 2002). Her rhythmic sequence in "Data Processing" contributes to the project of extending the plane of deviation suggested by Ravikovitch. More generally, the mechanical and routine nature associated with data processing enables the speaker in Bejerano's poems to move between prosaic and monumental situations, accepting and challenging them at the same time:

I am not defined because I am not a machine;
I am not an act's impetus

("Data Processing 54" [Ibud netunim 54])[14]

Or:

In what gentleness I tear conventions
me and my weird occupations. Void and no form

("Data Processing 8" [Ibud netunim 8])[15]

Ravikovitch influenced Agi Mishol, one of Israel's most popular living poets, in a different way. Mishol's first two books, *Nanny and Both of Us* (1972, *Nani ushneinu*) and *A Cat's Scratch* (1978, *Sritah shel chatul*), reflect a divided emotional reality, which the speaker tries to stitch together over and over again.[16] In her representation of the frustrating gap between the ideal and reality, and in instances of the split perspective (inside-out and outside-in, alternately), Mishol adopts Ravikovitch's conceptual apparatus, and in particular her ongoing sense of existential discrepancy. Even though this influence is most evident in Mishol's earlier books, an indirect dialogue with Ravikovitch's work continues in her later work, where the speaker's sense of reality is more grounded. The gap that was central to Mishol's writings in the seventies becomes a dual existence, which contains both concrete elements of everyday life and meditative aspects. The speaker walks within reality safely, while aspiring to nothingness and emptiness (see, for example, the poems

"One Hand" [Yad achat], "Brightening" [Hitbaharut], and "Meditation" [Meditatzya][17]. What manifested in Ravikovitch's writing as a gap between disappointing quotidian life (reality, "here") and utopia ("over there," reachable only in the imagination) is unified in Mishol's writing, thus becoming a different experience of existence, one that desires a Zen-like emptiness.

Ravikovitch's influence is perhaps most interesting and least discernible in the work of Raquel Chalfi. Chalfi rose to prominence in 1975, with the publication of her first book, *Shirim tat yamiyim* (Underwater and Other Poems).[18] Since then, she has published eleven more collections of poetry and won several literary awards, among them the Ashman Prize (1999) and the Bialik Prize (2006). Probably more than any other poet, Chalfi adopts Ravikovitch's ambiguity, in a way that does not duplicate the psychotic whirl of the manic episode, but rather offers a kind of rational chaos:

I tried to join water with water
but the waters were stronger than me
and I joined myself to them
and descended within them
to find there
their edges.

("Join Water with Water" [Lechaber lamayim])[19]

Chalfi's poetry creates an ongoing paradox: it tries to cross the threshold of the conflicted reality and grasp some of its essence, and at the same time, it doubts that language can adequately address the chaos of existence. To deal with this essential paradox, Chalfi challenges the cornerstones of language itself and performs exercises in logic to deconstruct and reconstruct language. In this way she gives up any control over reality, acknowledges its chaotic nature, and accepts the limitations of language and poetry. Unlike Ravikovitch's and Wallach's estrangement, which has aspects of the neurotic and the sexual, or Bejerano's repetition, Chalfi's deviation presents a lucid and logical struggle. She is "a scientist of her own dreams," to use her own words ("Knitted in the Lattice of Light" [Srugah besoragei haor]).[20]

Ravikovitch's Möbius strip of symbolic order and deviation, of underwhelming reality and utopia, of outside-in and inside-out, opens up possibilities for dissidence and deviation. The poets mentioned above respond to this challenge, each one within the confines of her own voice and poetics. Together they create a cultural plane of poetic subjectivity that maintains complex relations of both tolerance and denial of the current social-moral

order. Reading their poetry through the prism of Ravikovitch's constant movement between the symbolic order and the subversion of the symbolic order
enables an excavation of cultural interrelations, not just among these specific
poets, but also among poetry, gender, victimhood, nationalism, and literary
genealogy within the larger context of Israeli society.

Notes

Introduction

1. Michael Gluzman, "'To Endow Suffering with Elegance': Dahlia Ravikovitch and the Poetry of the Statehood Generation," *Prooftexts* 28 (2008): 282–309. Gluzman explores Ravikovitch's poetics against the background of the stylistic and ideological dynamics of the Generation of the State.

2. Miri Baruch, *Iyunim beshirat dahlia ravikovitch* [Studies in Dahlia Ravikovitch's poetry] (Tel Aviv: Eked, 1974); and Juliette Hassin, *Shirah vemitos beyetzirata shel dahlia ravikovitch* [Poetry and myth in Ravikovitch's work] (Tel Aviv: Eked, 1989).

3. Ayelet Negev, "Dahlia Ravikovitch Speaks. About It All," *Yediot aharonot*, February 23, 1996, 22, 26–28. Translated in Chana Bloch and Chana Kronfeld, trans. *Hovering At A Low Altitude: The Collected Poetry of Dahlia Ravikovitch* (New York: W. W. Norton, 2009) (subsequently BK), 19, and quoted also in Hamutal Tsamir and Tamar Hess, eds., *Khitmei or* [Sparks of light: Essays about Dahlia Ravikovitch's ouevre] (Tel Aviv: Hakibbutz Hameuchad, 2010), 14.

4. Cathy Caruth, *Trauma: Exploration in Memory* (Baltimore, MD: Johns Hopkins University Press, 1995), 4.

5. Hélène Cixous describes the *écriture féminine* as having the power to challenge logocentric and phallogocentric thought, and to create a language that will differ from the patriarchal binary hierarchy. See "The Laugh of the Medusa," trans. Keith Cohen and Paula Cohen, *Signs* 1, no. 4 (1976): 875–93. In her complex approach to the polarities of passivity and activity, Ravikovitch takes on this role, deconstructs binary structures, and establishes a different way of thinking. About the blurring of this separation, while criticizing aspects of Zionism in the poem "The Messiah's Arrival" (Biat hamashiach), see Hamutal Tsamir, "The Dead and the Living, the Believers and the Uprooted: Dahlia Ravikovitch, Mourner and Prophet" [in Hebrew], in *Mikhan* 1 (2000): 44–63; and *Beshem hanof* [In the name of the land: nationalism, subjectivity and gender in the Israeli poetry of the statehood generation] (Jerusalem: Keter Books, Beer-Sheva: Heksherim Center, 2006). About the deconstruction of binary oppositions in the poem "Even a Thousand Years" (Afilu elef shanim), see Tamar Hess, "The Poetica of the Fig Tree: Feminist Aspects in the Early Poetry of Dahlia Ravikovitch" [in Hebrew], *Mikhan* 1 (2000): 27–43.

6. Jacques Derrida, *Margins of Philosophy*, trans. Alan Bass (Chicago: University of Chicago Press, 1982).

7. Shoshana Felman, *Writing and Madness (Literature/Philosophy/Psychoanalysis)*, trans. Martha Noel Evans and the author, with the assistance of Brian Massumi (Ithaca, NY: Cornell University Press, 1994).

Part 1: Forever Beholden

1. Translated from the Hebrew by Tova Rosen, *Unveiling Eve: Reading Gender in Medieval Hebrew Literature* (Philadelphia: University of Pennsylvania Press, 2003), 67. As Rosen observes, a bilingual homonym is exploited in the name of the poem, *Shirah yetomah* (A female orphan poem), "referring also to *yatima* in the Arabic sense, namely, outstanding, one of a kind" (214).

1. Poetics of Orphanhood

1. Baruch Kurzweil, "Dahlia Ravikovitch's Poems" [in Hebrew], *Haaretz*, December 25, 1959; Yair Mazor, "A Portrait of Shame as a City of Refuge: About Dahlia Ravikovitch's Poetry" [in Hebrew], *Iton 77* 206 (1997): 19.

2. Hannah Naveh, *Bishvi haevel* [Captives of mourning: Representation of bereavement in Hebrew literature] (Tel Aviv: Hakibbutz Hameuchad, 1993), 31–36.

3. Dahlia Ravikovitch, *Kol hashirim* [The Complete Poems], eds. Giddon Ticotsky and Uzi Shavit (Tel Aviv: Hakibbutz Hameuchad, 2010) (subsequently CP) 19; Chana Bloch and Ariel Bloch, trans., *The Window: Poems by Dahlia Ravikovitch* (New York: Sheep Meadow Press, 1989) (subsequently BB) 3.

4. Caruth, *Trauma: Exploration in Memory*, 10.

5. Baruch, *Studies in Dahlia Ravikovitch's poetry*, 14.

6. Jacques Lacan, *Écrits: A Selection*, trans. Alan Sheridan (London: Tavistock, 1977).

7. For further discussion of the sonnet form in this poem and its relation to the symbolic order and the semiotic, see Ilana Szobel, "'She Tried to Escape and Lost Her Senses': Alienation and Madness in the Stories of Dahlia Ravikovitch" [in Hebrew], *Teoryah uvikoret* 28 (2006): 127–55. For a different interpretation of Ravikovitch's use of the sonnet in this poem, see Shira Stav, "The Father, the Daughter, and the Gaze" [in Hebrew], in *Khitmei or* [Sparks of light: Essays about Dahlia Ravikovitch's oeuvre], eds. Hamutal Tsamir and Tamar S. Hess (Tel Aviv: Hakibbutz Hameuchad, 2010), 284–322.

8. Chana Bloch and Chana Kronfeld translate this line as follows: "But I became damaged goods that night" (BK, 63).

9. *Baba kama* 79a; *Shulhan arukh, Hoshen mishpat* 409c.

10. Kurzweil, "Dahlia Ravikovitch's Poems."

11. See Allison Schachter, "A Lily among the Bullfrogs: Dahlia Ravikovitch and the Field of Hebrew Poetry," *Prooftexts* 28 (2008): 310–34; Zafrira Lidovsky-Cohen, "Teresa versus Shunra: The Image of the Woman in the Poems of Dahlia Ravikovitch and Yona Wallach" [in Hebrew], *Iton 77* 315 (2006): 22–26; and *"Loosen the Fetters of Thy Tongue Woman": The Poetry and Poetics of Yona Wallach* (Cincinnati: Hebrew Union College Press, 2003); Michael Gluzman, "The Joyful Elegy: Two Poems by Dahlia Ravikovitch about Yona Wallach" [in Hebrew], *Helikon* 26 (1998): 19–26; Yair Mazor, "The Poetry of Dahlia Hertz and Yona Wallach in the Comparative Context of Dahlia Ravikovitch's Poetry" [in Hebrew], *Iton 77* 220 (1998): 11–15; Lily Rattok, *Malakh haesh* [Angel of fire: The poetry of Yona Wallach] (Tel Aviv: Hakibbutz Hameuchad, 1997).

12. Ravikovitch, "Six Hundred Thirteen Commandments Plus One" (Taryag mitzvot veahat), CP, 16.

13. Dahlia Ravikovitch, *Kvutzat hakhaduregel shel wini mandelah* [Winnie Mandela's football team] (Tel Aviv: Hakibbutz Hameuchad, 1997) (subsequently *Winnie Mandela's*), 48–59.

14. Nathan Alterman, *Shirim shemikvar* [Collected works] (Tel Aviv: Hakkibutz Hameuchad, 1994), 121.

15. Ravikovitch's engagement with biblical language and themes is a fundamental characteristic of her writing. See Tamar Hess, "The Poetica"; Tsamir, "The Dead and the Living"; Juliette Hassin, *Shirah vemitos beyetzirata shel dahlia ravikovitch* [Poetry and myth in Ravikovitch's work] (Tel Aviv: Eked, 1989); Mazor, "Portrait of Shame"; and Mordechai Shalev, "Dahlia Ravikovitch: Poetess of Lamenting" [in Hebrew], *Haaretz*, April 2 and June 13, 1969.

16. Yael Feldman, "Back to Genesis: Toward the Repressed and Beyond in Israeli Identity" [in Hebrew], in *Bakhivun hanegdi* [In the counter direction: Critical essays on Mr. Mani], ed. Nitza Ben-Dov (Tel Aviv: Hakibbutz Hameuchad, 1995): 218–19; and "'And Rebecca Loved Jacob,' But Freud Did Not," in *Freud and Forbidden Knowledge*, eds. Peter L. Rudnytsky and Ellen Handler Spitz (New York: New York University Press, 1994), 14.

17. Feldman, "And Rebecca," 13–14.

18. Michel Foucault, "Of Other Spaces," *Diacritics* 16 (1986): 25.

19. Very rarely does Ravikovitch's work also present a mother's death, as in the stories "Clouds" (Ananim) and "The Lights of Spring" (Orot haaviv) in *Winnie Mandela's*.

20. Slavoj Zizek, *For They Know What They Do: Enjoyment as a Political Factor* (London: Verso, 1994), 222.

21. Ibid., 203.

22. For a different interpretation of Ravikovitch's disobedience, see Nili R. Gold Scharf, "Staying in the Place of Danger: The Disobedient, Poetic 'I' of Dahlia Ravikovitch," in *To Speak or To Be Silent: The Paradox of Disobedience in the Lives of Women*, ed. Lena B. Ross (Wilmette, IL: Chiron Publications, 1993), 97–108.

23. In this context, it is important to mention Ravikovitch's monumental poem "Hovering at a Low Altitude" (Rechifah begovah namuch) (CP, 179–81; BK, 174–78), which I will discuss in part 4. Nili R. Gold Scharf reads this poem as a response to a psychological trauma and analyzes it as "a text that touches hidden corners of the soul, a struggle to confront a memory, this time without being consumed or destroyed by it and not by escaping or repressing it." Nili R. Gold Scharf, "Hovering at a Low Altitude," *Reading Hebrew Literature: Critical Discussions of Six Modern Texts*, ed. Alan Mintz (Waltham, MA: Brandeis University Press, 2003), 228. As such, "Hovering at a Low Altitude" is another fascinating example of Ravikovitch's unique psycho-poetic voice.

24. Ravikovitch, "Three or Four Cyclamens" (Shalosh arba rakafot), CP, 272; BK, 242.

25. Dahlia Ravikovitch, *Baah vehalchah* [Come and gone] (N.p.: Modan, 2005) (subsequently *Come and Gone*), 19.

26. Nicolas Abraham and Maria Torok, *The Shell and the Kernel: Renewals of Psychoanalysis*, ed. and trans. Nicholas T. Rand (Chicago: University of Chicago Press, 1994).

27. Abraham and Torok, *The Shell*, 159.

28. Nitza Ben-Dov suggests that age six, the age at which Ravikovitch lost her father, was the real inspiration for the admiration Ravikovitch felt toward the American author Mary McCarthy, who lost both of her parents at the same age ("Father Died: An Existential Experience Pierced in Time" [in Hebrew], in *Sparks of light* 207–8).

29. Ibid., 130.

2. Orphanhood and Motherhood

1. *Winnie Mandela's*, 180.

2. For the role of irony in Ravikovitch's poetic concept of parenthood, see Tal Frankel Alroei, "Come-Gone" [in Hebrew], *Mitaam* 6 (2006): 16–29.

3. Shmuel Yosef Agnon, *8 Great Hebrew Short Novels*, trans. Gabriel Levin and eds. Alan Lelchuk and Gershon Shaked (New Milford: Toby Press, 2005), 187–245.

4. Ibid., 189.

5. Luce Irigaray, "And the One Doesn't Stir without the Other," trans. Helene Vivienne Wenzel, *Signs* 7, no. 1 (1981): 66–67.

6. Although the mother has become increasingly important in developmental psychoanalytic theory and in understanding object relations, the mother's own subjective existence was ignored in the work of major psychoanalytic thinkers such as Sigmund Freud, Sandor Ferenczi, Helena Deutsch, Melanie Klein, and Luce Irigaray. Furthermore, most of the feminist theory and the feminist psychoanalytic discourse on motherhood focus on the mother-daughter relationship. See Anat Palgi-Hecker, *Mei-mahut leimahut* [The mother in psychoanalysis: A feminist view] (Tel Aviv: Am Oved , 2005), 274. For a similar argument regarding Kristeva's representation of the mother as other, see Domna Stanton, "Difference on Trial: A Critique of the Maternal Metaphor in Cixous, Irigaray and Kristeva," *The Poetics of Gender*, ed. Nancy K. Miller (New York: Columbia University Press, 1986), 157–82; and Marianne Hirsch, *The Mother/Daughter Plot: Narrative, Psychoanalysis, Feminism* (Bloomington: Indiana University Press, 1989). For discussions of maternal subjectivity in literature, see Yael Feldman, *No Room of Their Own: Gender and Nation in Israeli Women's Fiction* (New York: Columbia University Press, 1999), 223; Janice Doane and Devon Hodges, *From Klein to Kristeva: Psychoanalytic Feminism and the Search for the "Good Enough" Mother* (Ann Arbor: University of Michigan Press, 1992); Jo Malin, *The Voice of the Mother: Embedded Maternal Narratives in Twentieth-Century Women's Autobiographies* (Carbondale: Southern Illinois University Press, 2000); Hirsch, *Mother/Daughter Plot*; Suleiman, "Writing and Motherhood," in *The (M)other Tongue: Essays in Feminist Psychoanalytic Interpretation*, eds. Shirley Nelson Garner, Claire Kahane, and Madelon Sprengnether (Ithaca, NY: Cornell University Press, 1985), 352–77.

7. Cixous, "The Laugh," 891.

8. Simone De Beauvoir, *The Second Sex*, 1949, trans. H. M. Parshley (New York: Vintage Books, 1989).

9. Shva Salhov, "The Monster of Love: Sigal Avni's Exhibition" [in Hebrew], *Studio* 108 (1999): 46.

10. Adrienne Rich, *Of Woman Born: Motherhood as Experience and Institution* (New York: W. W. Norton, 1986), 13.

11. For more about motherhood as a cultural construction, see Nancy Chodorow, *The Reproduction of Mothering* (Berkeley: University of California Press, 1978); Nancy Chodorow and Susan Contratto, "The Fantasy of the Perfect Mother," *Rethinking the Family*, eds. Barrie Thorne and Marilyn Yalom (Boston: Northeastern University Press, 1992), 191–214; Sylvia Ann Hewlett, *A Lesser Life: The Myth of Women's Liberation in America* (New York: William Morrow, 1986), especially chapter 11, "The Rise of a Cult of Motherhood," 253–86. In the years since the publication of Adrienne Rich's groundbreaking book, the topic of motherhood has emerged as a central issue in feminist scholarship. This broad academic and non-academic body of work confronts the effects of globalization and HIV/Aids, as well as the challenges and influences of third-wave feminism and low-income, queer, transgender, and lesbian perspectives. Even though the basic tension between motherhood and mothering still stands at the center of these discussions, there is an attempt in current feminist scholarship to blur the clear-cut separation that Rich draws, and to see how the two objectives might interconnect. See Andrea O'Reilly, ed., *From Motherhood to Mothering: The Legacy of Adrienne Rich's Of Woman Born* (Albany: State University of New York Press, 2004); and Andrea O'Reilly, ed. *Twenty-First Century Motherhood* (New York: Columbia University Press, 2010).

12. Needless to say, many women (and mothers) internalize these images. See Chodorow and Contratto, *Fantasy*, 192; and Donna Bassin, Margaret Honey, and Meryle Mahrer Mahrer, *Representations of Motherhood* (New Haven, CT: Yale University Press, 1994), 2–5.

13. Rich, *Of Woman Born*, 13.

14. Sandra M. Gilbert and Susan Gubar, *The Madwoman in the Attic: The Woman Writer and The Nineteenth-Century Literary Imagination* (New Haven, CT: Yale University Press, 1984), 53–59.

15. The complex connection between patriarchal dictates and "female diseases" stands at the center of the work of various feminist scholars since the 1970s. Phyllis Chesler depicts "female diseases" as establishing a worship of women's roles. See *Women and Madness* (San Diego: Harcourt Brace Jovanovich, 1989). Irigaray explores the relation between melancholy and femininity in Freud's work. See *Speculum of the Other Woman*, trans. Gillian C. Gill (Ithaca, NY: Cornell University Press, 1985), 66–73. Susan R. Bordo discusses the political meaning of "female diseases" within the construction of gender. See "The Body and the Reproduction of Femininity: A Feminist Appropriation of Foucault," in *Gender/ Body/ Knowledge*, ed. Alison M. Jaggar and Susan R. Bordo (New Brunswick, NJ: Rutgers University Press, 1990), 16. The notion of the body as non-objective entity, which cannot be understood as separated from subjectivity, gender, sexuality, ethnicity, class, age, and any other socio-historical contexts is of great significance to feminist thought. See Roland Littlewood and Maurice Lipsedge, *Aliens and Alienists: Ethnic Minorities and Psychiatry* (Harmondsworth, UK: Penguin, 1982); Peter Sedgwick, *Psycho Politics: Laing, Foucault, Goffman, Szasz, and the Future of Mass Psychiatry* (New York: Harper and Row, 1982); Lynn Payer, *Medicine and Culture: Varieties of Treatment in the United States, England, West Germany, and France* (New York: Henry Holt and Company, 1988); Jane Ussher, "A Material-Discursive," *The Psychology of the Female Body* (London: Routledge,

1989); and Elizabeth Grosz, *Volatile Bodies: Toward A Corporeal Feminism* (Bloomington: Indiana University Press, 1994).

16. Rich, *Of Woman Born*, 225.

3. Women's Symbolic Orphanhood

1. Ravikovitch, "On the road at night" (Omed al hakhevish), CP, 19; BB, 3.

2. Meir Wieseltier, "True Love Isn't What It Seems" [in Hebrew], *Haaretz*, September 6, 1995, 132.

3. Alterman, *Collected Works*, 49–50, my translation.

4. Hess, "Poetica," 39.

5. Lynda E. Boose, "The Father's House and the Daughter in It: The Structures of Western Culture's Daughter-Father Relationship," in *Daughters and Fathers*, eds. Lynda E. Boose and Betty S. Flowers (Baltimore, MD: Johns Hopkins University Press, 1989), 20.

6. Hess, "Poetica," 40–41.

7. Leah Goldberg, *Shirim* [Poems], ed. Tuvia Rivner (Tel Aviv: Sifriat Poalim, 1973), 174–83.

4. Estrangement and the Collision of Perspectives

1. Saar Dayan, "Needs a Child's Protection" [in Hebrew], *Maariv*, January 22, 1993, 6–8.

2. Jacob Agmon, "A Departure from Poetry: Jacob Agmon Asks Ravikovitch Personal Questions" [in Hebrew], *Haaretz*, January 30, 1970, 15, emphasis added.

3. Elizabeth Grosz, *Volatile Bodies: Toward A Corporeal Feminism* (Bloomington: Indiana University Press, 1994).

4. Ibid., vii. For a history of the binary distinction between body and mind in Western culture, see Nancy Jay, "Gender and Dichotomy," *Feminist Studies* 1 (1981): 36–56; Genevieve Lloyd, *The Man of Reason: "Male" and "Female" in Western Philosophy* (London: Methuen, 1984); and Grosz, *Volatile Bodies*.

5. Michel Foucault, *The History of Sexuality*, trans. Robert Hurley (New York: Pantheon Books, 1978), 85. With all of its enormous importance, Foucault's influential analysis of power, society, and subjectivity does not refer to gender, which is crucial to my interpretation of the court scenes. On law and gender, and on the masculinity of the law, see Susan Moller Okin, *Women in Western Political Thought* (Princeton, NJ: Princeton University Press, 1979), particularly the chapter "Persons, Woman, and the Law" (247–73); Catharine A. MacKinnon, *Only Words* (Cambridge, MA: Harvard University Press, 1993), "Feminism, Marxism, Method, and the State: Toward Feminist Jurisprudence," *Contemporary Critical Theory*, ed. Dan Latimer (Orlando, FL: Harcourt College Publishers., 1989), 605–63, *Toward a Feminist Theory of the State* (Cambridge, MA: Harvard University Press, 1989), and *Feminism Unmodified: Discourses on Life and Law* (Cambridge, MA: Harvard University Press, 1987); Penina Lahav, "'When the Palliative Simply Impairs': The Debate in the Knesset on the Law for Women's Rights" [in Hebrew], *Zmanin* 46–47 (1993): 149–59; Ayelet Shahar, "The Sex of the Law: Rape's Legal Discourse" [in Hebrew], *Iyunei Mishpat* 18, no. 1 (1993): 159–99; Orit Kamir, *Feminizm, zekhuyot umishpat* [Feminism, rights and law in Israel] (Tel Aviv: Broadcast University, 2002) and "What's in a

Woman's Name" [in Hebrew], *Mishpatim* 27, no. 2 (1996): 327–82; and Liora Bilsky, "Violent Silence" [in Hebrew], *Iyunei Mishpat* 23, no. 2 (2000): 427–72.

6. Hannah Naveh, "Life Outside the Canon" [in Hebrew], in *Min, migdar, politikah* [Sex, gender, politics: Women in Israel], eds. Dafnah Izraeli, et al. (Tel Aviv: Hakibbutz Hameuchad, 1999): 105.

7. Irigaray, *Speculum*.

8. Lacan, *Écrits* and *The Four Fundamental Concepts of Psychoanalysis*, trans. Alan Sheridan (London: Vintage, 1998).

9. Irigaray, *Speculum* 48, emphasis in the original.

10. Luce Irigaray, *This Sex Which Is Not One*, trans. Catherine Porter and Carolyn Burke (Ithaca, NY: Cornell University Press, 1985).

11. Dan Rabinowitz, "The Twisting Journey for the Rescue of Brown Women" [in Hebrew], *Teoryah uvikoret* 7 (1995): 6.

12. Mary Louise Pratt, *Imperial Eyes: Travel Writing and Transculturation* (London: Routledge, 1992), 4.

13. Felman, *Madness*, 20, emphasis in the original.

5. "Imaginary Geography"

1. Quoted in Agmon, "A Departure."

2. Ravikovitch, "Delight" (Chemdah), CP, 35; BK, 69.

3. Dahlia Karpel, "Another Book, True Love" [in Hebrew], *Hair*, November 28, 1986.

4. For Ravikovitch's use of eloquent language ("high language") as a filter to deal with the concrete, harmful world, see Shimon Sandbank, "A World of Disappearance: On the Poems of Dahlia Ravikovitch" [in Hebrew], *Hameorer* 4 (1998): 130.

5. Agmon, "A Departure," 14.

6. "Seats for Trial" (Khisot lemishpat), CP, 26.

7. Onno Van der Hart and Rutger Horst, "The Dissociation Theory of Pierre Janet," *Journal of Traumatic Stress* 2, no. 4 (1989): 397–412.

8. Carlo Strenger, *Individuality, the Impossible Project: Psychoanalysis and Self-Creation* (Madison, CT: International Universities Press, 1998), 124.

9. Shulamit Levo-Vardinon, "A Fall Before the Lift-off: Horrible Life in 'Death in the Family'" [in Hebrew], *Davar*, March 16, 1979, 20.

Part 3: Mania, Depression, and Madness

1. Ravikovitch, "The Lights of Spring" (Orot haaviv), *Winnie Mandela's*, 141.

2. Theodore Roethke, *The Collected Poems of Theodore Roethke* (Seattle: University of Washington Press, 1982), 239.

6. Poetics of *Mobilité*

1. Kay R. Jamison, *Touched with Fire: Manic-Depressive Illness and the Artistic Temperament* (New York: The Free Press, 1993), 13.

2. Jamison, *Touched with Fire*, 125.

3. Marina Van Zuylen, *Monomania: The Flight from Everyday Life in Literature and Art* (Ithaca, NY: Cornell University Press, 2005), 14.

4. Edgar Allan Poe, *The Poems of Edgar Allan Poe*, ed. Killis Campbell (Boston: Ginn and Company, 1917), 49.

5. Both quotes are translated by Marina Van Zuylen in *Monomania* (35, 30). The first is a quotation of Pierre Janet, and the second a quotation of Simone, a patient of his.

6. Rachel Bluwstein Sela, *Flowers of Perhaps: Selected Poems of Ra'hel*, trans. Robert Friend and Shimon Sandbank (London: Menard Press, 1994), 46.

7. Dan Miron, *Imahot meyasdot, achayot chorgot* [Founding mothers, stepsisters: The emergence of the first Hebrew poetesses] (Tel Aviv: Hakibbutz Hameuchad, 1991), 17.

8. Bluwstein, *Flowers of Perhaps*, 46.

9. Van Zuylen, *Monomania*, 2.

10. Ibid., 29, emphasis in the original.

11. Ibid., 6. This fear of the unexpected, and the sense that that which is out of our control is menacing, is a major characteristic of people suffering from obsessive behavior. Karl Abraham refers to it as a phobic fear of asymmetry (see also Van Zuylen, *Monomania*, 6). Ravikovitch's style of expressing the deviant and the dissident by using an organized and strict language (a topic I explore at length in chapters 1 and 2) can be understood also as an expression of this phobic fear of asymmetry. Accordingly, the rigid and logical structure, syntax, and argumentation of Ravikovitch's poetry can be seen as the speaker's poetic and mental way of controlling or covering up her obsessive, impulsive, and anxious personality.

12. Ibid., 39.

13. Sigmund Freud, "Beyond the Pleasure Principle" in *The Standard Edition of the Complete Psychological Works of Sigmund Freud*, ed. James Strachey, in collaboration with Anna Freud, assisted by Alix Strachey and Alan Tyson, vol. 18 (London : Hogarth Press, 1953), 38.

14. Baruch, *Studies in Dahlia Ravikovitch's poetry*, 39.

15. Hassin, *Poetry and myth*, 59, 61.

16. A few scholars in various contexts have referred to the poem "The Love of an Orange" (*Ahavat tapuah hazahav*) as a fundamental poem in Ravikovitch's work. Mordechai Shalev, for instance, reads it as the ultimate expression of the oral dimension of love characteristic of Ravikovitch's writings, and sees in it the "hymn of her entire poetry" (Shalev, "Poetess of Lamenting"). Tamar Hess agrees that the poem represents a basic approach in Ravikovitch's poetry, but defines this approach as an adaptation of patriarchal norms and values, which by the very act of writing from a woman's perspective, subverts this same patriarchy ("The Poetica," 35).

17. "If his master gives him [the slave] a wife and she bears him sons or daughters, the woman and her children shall belong to her master, and the man shall go away alone. But if the slave should say, 'I love my master, my wife, and my children; I will not go free,' then his master shall bring him to God, he shall bring him to the door or the door-post, and his master shall pierce his ear with an awl, and the man shall be his slave for life" (Exodus 21: 4–6).

18. Baruch Kurtzweil, "Dahlia Ravikovitch's Poems" [in Hebrew], *Haaretz*, December 25, 1959.

19. The psychiatrist Pierre Janet, in his book of 1903, *Les Obsessions et la Psychasthénie* (which has not been translated into English), was the first to establish a cogent connec-

tion between the desperate quest for harmony (by turning the world into a compact personal obsession) and obsessive behavior (Van Zuylen, *Monomania*, 8).

20. CP, 46; BK, 76–77.

21. Poe, *Poems*, 49.

22. The poem actually contains a third voice as well: the manic voice itself. It thus combines speech about mania and manic speech.

23. Jamison, *Touched with Fire*, 34.

24. *The Encyclopedia Mythica*, s.v. "Tammuz," by Micha F. Lindemans, last modified February 8, 1999, www.pantheon.org/articles/t/tammuz.html; *Encyclopaedia Judaica*, vol. 15., s.v. "Tammuz," by Raphael Kutscher (Jerusalem: Keter, n.d.), 787–88.

25. Quoted in Foucault, *History of Madness*, trans. Jonathan Murphy and Jean Khalfa (London: Routledge, 2006), 200.

7. Speech about Madness, and Mad Speech

1. *Winnie Mandela's*, 141.

2. René Girard points out that every individual has a tendency to think of himself as different from others, and that every culture entertains this feeling of difference among its individuals. It is not this difference within the system that culture cannot tolerate, but rather a difference outside the system. This external difference is "the potential for the system to differ from its own difference, in other words not to be different at all, to cease to exist as a system." *The Scapegoat*, trans. Yvonne Freccero (Baltimore, MD: The Johns Hopkins University Press, 1986), 21. This external difference frightens the system "because it reveals the truth of the system, its relativity, its fragility, and its morality" (ibid.). Thus, paradoxically, "persecutors are never obsessed by difference but rather by its unutterable contrary, the lack of difference" (ibid., 22).

3. Foucault, *Sexuality*, 5; Ophir, "About Michel Foucault, and His Book *History of Madness*" [in Hebrew], in *History of Madness*, trans. Aaron Amir (Jerusalem: Keter, 1986), 219.

4. Joan Busfield, *Men, Women, and Madness: Understanding Gender and Mental Disorder* (New York: New York University Press, 1996), 52.

5. Quoted in Sander L. Gilman, *Difference and Pathology: Stereotypes of Sexuality, Race, and Madness* (Ithaca, NY: Cornell University Press, 1985), 225.

6. Felman, *Madness*, 14.

7. Dwight Fee, "The Project of Pathology: Reflexivity and Depression in Elizabeth Wurtzel's 'Prozac Nation,'" in *Pathology and the Postmodern: Mental Illness as Discourse and Experience*, ed. Dwight Fee (London: Sage Publications, 2000), 87.

8. Felman, *Madness*, 14.

9. Foucault, *Madness*.

10. Thomas J. Scheff, ed. *Labeling Madness* (New Jersey: Prentice-Hall, 1975), 7.

11. Foucault, *Madness*, 233.

12. *Winnie Mandela's*, 57. The occupation of the friend defining, characterizing, and judging the disease (and Ehud's behavior) is not surprising at all in the context of Ravikovitch's work: he is a lawyer. In this manner, as a symbolic representation, Ehud's relationship with his friend duplicates the power relationships in the trials of Nurit ("The Summer

Vacation Tribunal" [Hatribunal shel hachofesh hagadol]), Rama ("Winnie Mandela's Football Team" [Kvutzat hakhaduregel shel wini mandelah]), and the prisoner in the story "The Lights of Spring"[Orot haaviv]. Again, even by using an almost trivial nugget of information, Ravikovitch reveals the unbreakable connection between the individual's construction and the social order within which she exists, between "personal" experience and various organizing mechanisms: "Thus, what may be described as a problem of will with respect to the individual becomes, in an institutional context, primarily a problem in social organization." Robert M. Cover, "Violence and the Word," *Yale Law Journal* 95, no. 8 (1986): 1601.

13. James M. Glass, *Shattered Selves: Multiple Personality in a Postmodern World* (Ithaca, NY: Cornell University Press, 1993), xix.

14. Rivka Feldhay, "A Feminine Midrash" [in Hebrew], *Teoryah uvikoret* 2 (1992): 77.

15. Foucault, *Madness*, 227.

16. Felman, *Madness*, 14.

17. Ravikovitch, "Prepare for the Messiah's Arrival" (Hikhonu lebiat hamashiach), *Winnie Mandela's*, 38.

18. Gabriel Moked, "About Two New Books By Dahlia Ravikovitch—in Poetry and Prose" [in Hebrew], *Yediot Aharonot*, July 30, 1976, 3.

19. Foucault, *Madness*, 232.

20. Felman, *Madness*, 67.

21. Chesler, *Women and Madness*, 56.

22. See Barbara Ehrenreich and Deirdre English, *Witches, Midwives, and Nurses: A History of Women Healers* (Old Westbury, NY: Feminist Press, 1973); Julia Kristeva, *Revolution in Poetic Language*, trans. Margaret Waller (New York: Columbia University Press, 1984); Carol Gilligan, *In a Different Voice: Psychological Theory and Women's Development* (Cambridge, MA: Harvard University Press, 1982); Elaine Showalter, *The Female Malady: Women, Madness, and English Culture, 1830–1980* (New York: Pantheon Books, 1985); Felman, *Madness*; Jane Ussher, *Women's Madness: Misogyny or Mental Illness?* (Amherst: The University of Massachusetts Press, 1992).

23. Fee, *The Postmodern*, 14.

24. Claims about the liaison between gender and the professional aspect of the mental health system were also emphasized by Barbara Ehrenerich and Deirdre English in *Complaints and Disorders: The Sexual Politics of Sickness* (Old Westbury, NY: Feminist Press, 1973).

25. Chesler, *Women and Madness*, 69.

26. By showing how Ravikovitch's writing subverts the hegemonic system, I do not intend to glorify the state of mind of actual or fictional madness. James M. Glass's critique about the idealization of schizophrenia proposed by Deleuze and Guattari, brings to mind the danger of glorifying and idolizing the anguished subject, a danger that lies within any attempt to analyze madness (and any other kind of human suffering) in an ideological sense. I believe that my reading of Ravikovitch's representations of madness does not fall into this category. See Glass, *Shattered Selves*, especially the chapter "Placelessness and Asylum."

27. Felman, *Madness*, particularly 14.

28. Ravikovitch, "The Seasons of the Year" (Tkufot hashanah), CP, 43; BK, 73.

29. Foucault, *Sexuality*, 5.

30. Chesler, *Women and Madness*, 60.

31. For interpretations of madness, see Gilbert and Gubar, *Madwoman in the Attic*; Foucault, *Madness*; Kristeva, "Women's Time," trans. Alice Jardine and Harry Blake, *Signs* 7, no. 1 (1981): 13–35; Felman, *Madness*.

Part 4: Unveiling Injustice

1. Quoted in Idith Zertal, "Poetry—A Soul without a Body" [in Hebrew], *Davar*, July 8, 1966.

8. Witnessing and Complicity

1. "Hovering at a Low Altitude" (Rechifah begovah namuch), CP, 179–81; BK, 174–76.

2. The exact number of the Sabra and Shatila victims is not clear. The Kahan Commission, established by the Israeli government in September 1982 to investigate the events of the massacre, talks about hundreds of victims. Bayan Nuwayhed al-Hout, however, in her book *Sabra and Shatila: September 1982* (London: Pluto Press, 2004), claims that at least 3,500 people were killed (289).

3. Alterman, *Collected works*, 189–91.

4. Quoted in Bat-Ami Bar On. "Meditations on National Identity," *Hypatia* 9, no. 2 (1994): 43.

5. David Hoffman, "Israeli Society Falls under MTV's Spell," *Washington Post Foreign Service,* July 17, 1993, A10.

6. I capitalize the word "wrong" here and throughout the chapter because I am using it as a concept, to connote the Hebrew word *Avel*, which encapsulates evil, wrongdoing, and injustice.

7. Shapiro, quoted in Jose Brunner, "Comments on Political Evil" [in Hebrew], *Teoryah uvikoret* 1 (1991): 88.

8. Levo-Vardinon, "A Fall," 20.

9. Tsamir, "The Dead" and *In the name.*

10. "Hovering at a Low Altitude" (Rechifah begovah namuch) is usually considered a political poem. For a reading of it as a personal, lyrical poem, see Gold Scharf, "Hovering." For the juxtaposition of nationalism, ars-poetica, and gender in the poem, see Dana Olmert, "'I Am Not Here': The Political Position and the Threat over Subjectivity in the Poetry of Dahlia Ravikovitch" [in Hebrew], in *Sparks of light.*

11. Ravikovitch, "They're Freezing Up North" (Batzafon kofim), CP, 200–201; BK, 191–92, my translation.

12. Ravikovitch quoted in Ilana Zukerman, ed. "True Love: Printed Excerpts from a Radio Broadcast" [in Hebrew], *Proza* 100 (1988): 108–11.

13. For a discussion of her earlier political writing, especially in regard to the poem "What's Happening" ([Ma koreh], CP, 125–26; BK, 136–37), see Yochai Oppenheimer, *Hazchut hagdola lomar lo: shira politit beisrael* [Political poetry in Israel] (Jerusalem: The HU Magnes Press, 2003), 334–40.

14. Ravikovitch quoted in Zukerman, "True Love," 109.

15. Israel Eldad, "An Interpellation to Dahlia Ravikovitch" [in Hebrew], *Haaretz*, February 5, 1987, 9.

16. Karpel, "Another Book."

17. Naomi Gotkind, "Poems like 'a Sharpened Claw'" [in Hebrew], *Hatzofe*, February 6, 1987, 6.

18. "Behold, this was the iniquity of thy sister Sodom: pride, fullness of bread, and quiet ease was in her and in her daughters; neither did she strengthen the hand of the poor and needy" (Ezekiel 16: 49).

19. Sima Kadmon, "I Am Always the Defeated Side" [in Hebrew], *Maariv*, February 8, 1991, 22.

20. Nissim Calderon describes the different stages in the publication of "Hovering at a Low Altitude." Ravikovitch first submitted it to the periodical *Hadarim* before the First Lebanon War. After the war she gave her permission to include it in the collection *There's No End to the Battles and Slaughter: Political Poetry of the Lebanon War*, but in her book *True Love* she chose to locate it in the section "The Window," and not in the section dedicated to her political writing, "Issues in Contemporary Judaism." Calderon, *Hargasha shel makom* [A sense of place] (Tel Aviv: Hakibbutz Hameuchad, 1988), 12.

21. Ariel Hirschfeld, "Ravikovitch After a Decade" [in Hebrew], *Yediot Aharonot*, January 9, 1987, 21, emphasis added.

22. Jean-Paul Sartre, "The Search for the Absolute," in *Giacometti: A Catalogue* [in Hebrew] (Tel Aviv: Tel Aviv University Art Gallery, 1984), 8.

23. Barbara Mann, "Hovering at a Low Altitude," *Reading Hebrew Literature: Critical Discussions of Six Modern Texts*, ed. Alan Mintz (Waltham, MA: Brandeis University Press, 2003), 218, 220.

24. Ana Douglass and Thomas A. Vogler, eds. *Witness and Memory: The Discourse of Trauma* (New York: Routledge, 2003), 36.

25. For the difference between women's low gaze and men's high gaze, and especially for the feminist-political potential within this low gaze, see Orly Lubin, "Low Gaze, Freed Gaze," in *Igael Shemtov: Low Landscape Low Reality* (Tel Aviv: Loushy Art and Editions, 2004).

26. Adi Ophir, "Beyond Good: Evil—An Outline for a Political Theory of Evils" [in Hebrew], *Teoryah uvikoret* 1 (1991): 63.

27. See Derrida's discussion of Herman Melville's story "Bartleby the Scrivener," mainly about Bartleby's "I would prefer not to" in *The Gift of Death*, trans. David Wills (Chicago: University of Chicago Press, 1995), 74–77.

28. Oppenheimer, *Political Poetry in Israel*, 340.

29. The lines from Auden's "September 1, 1939" come to mind here: "Waves of anger and fear/Circulate over the bright/And darkened lands of the earth,/Obsessing our private lives." I thank Giles Harvey for this reference.

30. Quoted in Negev, "Dahlia Ravikovitch Speaks."

31. Emmanuel Levinas, *Otherwise Than Being: Or Beyond Essence*, trans. Alphonso Lingis (New York: Springer, 1981).

32. Quoted in Dahlia Karpel, "After the Silence" [in Hebrew], *Haaretz*, October 24, 1986.

33. Mann, "Hovering," 220.

34. Nathan Zach, *Anti-mechikon* [Hard to remember] (Tel Aviv: Hakibbutz Hameuchad, 1984). Translated in Esther Raizen, ed. and trans., *No Rattling of Sabers: An Anthology of Israeli War Poetry* (Austin: Center for Middle Eastern Studies at the University of Texas, 1995), 138.

35. Yochai Oppenheimer, "The Right to Say No: Auden, Zach, and Laor in a Political Context" [in Hebrew], *Alpayim* 10 (1994): 241.

36. The linguistic organization in the poem "On the Attitude toward Children in Times of War" (Al hayakhas liyladim beitot milchamah) is noticeable in the escalating numbers, and in the use of typological numbers: three, seven, and ten. The ever-increasing guilt, on the other hand, is manifested by the format of the last stanza, in which the lines become shorter and shorter.

37. See also Olmert, "'I Am Not Here,'" 426–27.

38. Yochai Oppenheimer, "Political Competence: On the Lyrical and the Political in the Poetry of Dahlia Ravikovitch" [in Hebrew], *Siman kriah* 22 (1991): 427.

39. Quoted in Ilan Lotenberg, "Half a Poet" [in Hebrew], *Hadashot*, June 4, 1993, 61.

9. Contamination of Language, Departure from Innocence

1. Quoted in Karpel, "Another Book."

2. Quoted in Zukerman, "True Love."

3. See also Michael Walzer, *Spheres of Justice: A Defense of Pluralism and Equality* (New York: Basic Books, 1983); Pierre Bourdieu, *Distinction: A Social Critique of the Judgment of Taste*, trans. Richard Nice (Cambridge, MA: Harvard University Press, 1984); Pierre Bordieau et al, *The Weight of the World: Social Suffering in Contemporary Society*, trans. Priscilla Parkhurst Ferguson et al (Stanford: Stanford University Press, 1999).

4. Felman, *Madness*, 185, emphasis in the original.

5. Foucault, *Sexuality*, 86.

6. Many scholars address this effort to unveil the mechanisms that enable the existence of evil and violence. For works that focus on questions of social and political ethics, see Hannah Arendt, *Eichmann in Jerusalem: A Report on the Banality of Evil* (New York: Penguin Books, 1977); Foucault, *Discipline & Punish: The Birth of the Prison*, trans. Alan Sheridan (New York: Vintage Books, 1995), *The History of Sexuality*, trans. Robert Hurley (New York: Pantheon Books, 1978), and *Madness*; Cover, "Violence and the Word"; Brunner, "Political Evil," 79–90; and Idith Zertal, "Hannah Arendt Versus the State of Israel" [in Hebrew], *Teoryah uvikoret* 12–13 (1999): 159–67.

7. Ophir, "Beyond Good," 67.

8. When addressing questions of physicality and violence, especially in the writing of a female poet, it is hard to avoid issues of gender. By referring to the connection between Ravikovitch's political writing, gender, and grammar, Kronfeld shows how the poem "Hovering at a Low Altitude" "rejects the view of the national subject (as Jew and male) on the metaphorical model of female sexuality, and suggests instead the flesh-and-blood girl (as Arab and female) as a (literal) national subject, a subject who can no longer be dehumanized by an ethics and aesthetics of 'hovering.'" "A Lebanon War Poem?" in *Reading Hebrew Literature: Critical Discussions of Six Modern Texts*, ed. Alan Mintz (Waltham, MA: Brandeis University Press, 2003), 244.

9. Shoshana Felman and Dori Laub, *Testimony: Crises of Witnessing in Literature, Psychoanalysis, and History* (New York: Routledge, 1992).

10. The scattering of the heifer's ashes to the river is Ravikovitch's addition to the original biblical ritual. Hassin claims that this addition refers to the scattering of the ash in II Kings 23: 4-6 during the burning of Asherah by Hilkiah the Cohen as part of his purification of the Temple. Hassin understands this biblical reference as part of Ravikovitch's general interest in questions of bloodshed and redemption (*Poetry and Myth*, 166).

11. See Ophir, "Beyond Good," 67, 72.

12. Felman, *Testimony*, 196.

13. "Operation Peace for Galilee" [Mivtza shlom hagalil] was the official Israeli name for the Israel Defense Force's invasion of Lebanon on June 6, 1982.

14. Ofra Yeglin, "Did I Forget? Well, Who Cares? On Three Poems by Dahlia Ravikovitch" [in Hebrew], *Rehov* 2 (1995): 71-81.

15. Quoted in Lotenberg, "Half a Poet," 58.

16. Even though the poem is a testimony of concrete events, Ravikovitch is not a direct witness to those events; rather, she listens to them. According to Adam Smith, this position of indirect witnessing demands the listener imaginatively fill in the gaps; sympathy can thus be seen as dependent on a kind of imaginative playfulness (in Douglass, *Witness and Memory*, 39). In view of this, we might understand Ravikovitch's choice of free indirect speech as form of imaginative playfulness necessary to comprehend and internalize the trauma she witnesses.

10. Palestinians as the Israeli Abjection

1. "Get out of Beirut" (Latzet mibeirut) (CP, 204–5; BK, 194–95; my translation).

2. This argument is inspired by McClintock's suggestion that we view modern industrial imperialism through the term "Abjection." According to McClintock, the Abject people, "whom industrial imperialism rejects but cannot do without," return to haunt modernity as its inner repudiation. Anne McClintock, *Imperial Leather: Race, Gender and Sexuality in the Colonial Contest* (New York: Routledge, 1995), 72.

3. McClintock, *Imperial Leather*, 71. See also Julia Kristeva, *Powers of Horror: An Essay on Abjection*, trans. Leon S. Roudiez (New York: Columbia University Press, 1982).

4. In his 1993 article "About Uncles and Arabs," the writer S. Yizhar presents a similar argument, focusing on the moral aspect of the Israeli conquest, rather than on the psychological one: "The Palestinian Question is nothing but the Jewish Question ... And instead of continuing to run away from it, one must stop and turn to face it, turn and look at it closely. Since to resolve the Palestinian Question incorrectly means not to resolve the Question of the Jews and the Question for Judaism, and this really means to forfeit the future of the Jews and the future of Judaism." "About Uncles and Arabs," *Hebrew Studies* 47 (2006): 326.

5. Kronfeld, "A Lebanon War Poem?" 241.

Conclusion

1. Ravikovitch, "We Had an Understanding" (Hayta beyneynu havanah), CP, 189–90; BK, 181–82.

2. Ravikovitch, "Birdy," CP, 176; BK, 172.

3. Walter Benjamin, *The Origin of German Tragic Drama*, trans. John Osborne (London: NLB, 1977), 166.

4. Julia Kristeva, *Revolution*.

5. Judith Butler, *Gender Trouble: Feminism and the Subversion of Identity* (New York: Routledge, 1990), 81.

6. See Chana Bloch and Chana Kronfeld, "Dahlia Ravikovitch: An Introduction," *Prooftexts* 28 (2008): 249–81; Hamutal Tsamir, "Jewish-Israeli Poetry, Dahlia Ravikovitch, and the Gender of Representation," *Jewish Social Studies* 14, no. 3 (2008): 85–125; and "The Dead and the Living, the Believers and the Uprooted: Dahlia Ravikovitch, Mourner and Prophet" [in Hebrew], *Mikhan*, 1 (2000): 44–63; Hess, "The Poetica"; Szobel, "Alienation and Madness."

7. Leys, *Trauma*, 253.

8. Dominick LaCapra, "Trauma, Absence, Loss," *Critical Inquiry* 25, no. 4: 717.

9. Judith Lewis Herman, *Trauma and Recovery: The Aftermath of Violence—From Domestic Abuse to Political Terror* (New York: Basic Books, 1992).

10. Yona Wallach, "Matzavim transformatoriyim" [Transformative conditions] in *Tat hakharah niftachat khmo menifa* [Selected poems 1963–1985] (Tel Aviv: Hakibbutz Hameuchad, 1992), 220.

11. Michael Gluzman, "The Joyful Elegy: Two Poems by Dahlia Ravikovitch about Yona Wallach" [in Hebrew], *Helikon* 26 (1998): 19–26.

12. To Hayyim Nachman Bialik's influences on Ravikovitch's poetics, see Schachter, "Lily Among Bullfrogs" and Yaara Shehori, "*A Sixty-Meter Dash from Bialik's Tomb*": *Dahlia Ravikovitch Refers to H.N. Bialik's Poetry* [in Hebrew], in Sparks of light, 354–90.

13. Maya Bejerano, *Tedarim* [Frequencies] (Tel Aviv: Hakibbutz Hameuchad, 2005), 11–92.

14. Ibid., 81.

15. Ibid., 17.

16. Dan Miron, "A Comic Sibyl," *Agi Mishol: Mivchar vechadashim* [Agi Mishol: New and selected Poems] (Tel Aviv: Hakibbutz Hameuchad, 2003), 294.

17. All poems in Agi Mishol, *Mivchar vechadashim* [Agi Mishol: New and selected Poems] (Tel Aviv: Hakibbutz Hameuchad, 2003), 144, 151, 152.

18. Raquel Chalfi, *Shirim tat yamiyim* [Underwater and other poems] (Tel Aviv: Hakibbutz Hameuchad, 1975).

19. Raquel Chalfi, *Miklaat hashemesh: mivchar 1975–1999* [Solar plexus: Poems 1975–1999] (Tel Aviv: Hakibbutz Hameuchad, 2002), 37.

20. Ibid., p. 159.

Bibliography

The titles of Dahlia Ravikovitch's poems and short stories are given both in translation and in transliteration, for those who wish to consult them in the original. The page numbers of the poems in Hebrew are from Dahlia Ravikovitch, *Kol hashirim* [The complete poems], eds. Giddon Ticotsky and Uzi Shavit (Tel Aviv: Hakibbutz Hameuchad, 2010). The page numbers of the stories from Dahlia Ravikovitch, *Mavet bamishpahah* [Death in the family] (Tel Aviv: Am Oved, 1976) refer to Dahlia Ravikovitch, *Kvutzat hakhaduregel shel wini mandelah* [Winnie Mandela's football team] (Tel Aviv: Hakibbutz Hameuchad, 1997). Most of the translations of the poems are taken either from *The Window: Poems by Dahlia Ravikovitch*, trans. Chana Bloch and Ariel Bloch (New York: Sheep Meadow Press, 1989), or from *Hovering At A Low Altitude: The Collected Poetry of Dahlia Ravikovitch*, trans. Chana Bloch and Chana Kronfeld (New York: W. W. Norton, 2009) (the latter volume annotates and extensively revises the poems in the former). Unless otherwise stated, other translations throughout the book are mine, kindly reviewed by Taly Ravid and Daniel Banai.

Quotations from Ravikovitch's work are cited in the text with the abbreviations listed below.

BB   Chana Bloch and Ariel Bloch, trans. *The Window: Poems by Dahlia Ravikovitch*. New York: Sheep Meadow Press, 1989.

BK   Chana Bloch and Chana Kronfeld, trans. *Hovering At A Low Altitude: The Collected Poetry of Dahlia Ravikovitch*. New York: W. W. Norton, 2009.

CP   *Kol hashirim* [The complete poems]. Eds. Giddon Ticotsky and Uzi Shavit. Tel Aviv: Hakibbutz Hameuchad, 2010.

Winnie Mandela's   *Kvutzat hakhaduregel shel wini mandelah* [Winnie Mandela's football team]. Tel Aviv: Hakibbutz Hameuchad, 1997.

Abraham, Karl. "Contribution to the Theory of the Anal Character." In *Selected Papers on Psychoanalysis*, 370–92. Vol. 1 of *Selected Papers of Karl Abraham*. Trans. Douglas Bryan and Alix Strachey. New York: Basic Books, 1953.

Abraham, Nicolas, and Maria Torok. *The Shell and the Kernel: Renewals of Psychoanalysis*. Ed. and Trans. Nicholas T. Rand. Chicago: University of Chicago Press, 1994.

Agmon, Jacob. "A Departure from Poetry: Jacob Agmon Asks Ravikovitch Personal Questions" [in Hebrew]. *Haaretz* January 30, 1970: 14–15.

Agnon, Shmuel Yosef. "In the Prime of Her Life," trans. Gabriel Levin. In *8 Great Hebrew Short Novels*, ed. Alan Lelchuk and Gershon Shaked, 187–245. New Milford: Toby Press, 2005.

Alterman, Nathan. *Shirim shemikvar* [Collected works]. Tel Aviv: Hakibbutz Hameuchad, 1994.

Arendt, Hannah. *Eichmann in Jerusalem: A Report on the Banality of Evil.* 1963. New York: Penguin Books, 1977.

Arnon, Lina. "Myths and Archetypes in the Poetry of Dahlia Ravikovitch." Master's thesis, Tel Aviv University, 1987.

Bar On, Bat-Ami. "Meditations on National Identity." *Hypatia* 9, no. 2 (1994): 40–62.

Baruch, Miri. *Iyunim beshirat dahlia ravikovitch* [Studies in Dahlia Ravikovitch's poetry]. Tel Aviv: Eked, 1974.

Bassin, Donna, Margaret Honey, and Meryle Mahrer Kaplan, eds. *Representations of Motherhood.* New Haven, CT: Yale University Press, 1994.

Baudelaire, Charles. *Paris Spleen.* 1869. Trans. Louise Varese. New York: New Directions Publishing Corporation, 1970.

Bean, Jennifer M. Rev. of *Trauma: A Genealogy,* by Ruth Leys. *Modernism/Modernity* 8.3 (2001): 525–27.

Bejerano, Maya. *Tedarim* [Frequencies]. Tel Aviv: Hakibbutz Hameuchad, 2005.

Ben-Dov, Nitza. "Father Died: An Existential Experience Pierced in Time" [in Hebrew]. In *Khitmei or* [Sparks of light: Essays about Dahlia Ravikovitch's oeuvre], eds. Hamutal Tsamir and Tamar S. Hess, 203–215. Tel Aviv: Hakibbutz Hameuchad, 2010.

Benjamin, Walter. *The Origin of German Tragic Drama.* Trans. John Osborne. London: NLB, 1977.

Ben-Naftali, Michal. *Khronikah shel preda* [A chronicle of separation: On deconstruction's disillusioned love]. Tel Aviv: Resling, 2000.

Bilsky, Liora. "Violent Silence" [in Hebrew]. *Iyunei mishpat* 23, no. 2 (2000): 427–72.

Bloch, Chana, and Ariel Bloch, trans. *The Window: Poems by Dahlia Ravikovitch.* New York: Sheep Meadow Press, 1989.

Bloch, Chana, and Chana Kronfeld, trans. *Hovering At A Low Altitude: The Collected Poetry of Dahlia Ravikovitch.* New York: W. W. Norton, 2009.

———. "Dahlia Ravikovitch: An Introduction." *Prooftexts* 28 (2008): 249–81.

Bluwstein Sela, Rachel. *Flowers of Perhaps: Selected Poems of Ra'hel.* Trans. Robert Friend and Shimon Sandbank. London: Menard Press, 1994.

Boose, Lynda E. "The Father's House and the Daughter in It: The Structures of Western Culture's Daughter-Father Relationship." In *Daughters and Fathers,* eds. Lynda E. Boose and Betty S. Flowers, 19–74. Baltimore, MD: Johns Hopkins University Press, 1989.

Bordo, Susan R. "The Body and the Reproduction of Femininity: A Feminist Appropriation of Foucault." In *Gender/Body/Knowledge,* eds. Alison M. Jaggar and Susan R. Bordo, 13–33. Piscataway, NJ: Rutgers, 1990.

Bourdieu, Pierre. *Distinction: A Social Critique of the Judgment of Taste.* Trans. Richard Nice. Cambridge, MA: Harvard University Press, 1984.

Bourdieu, Pierre, Alain Accardo et al. *The Weight of the World: Social Suffering in Contemporary Society.* Trans. Priscilla Parkhurst Ferguson et al. Palo Alto, CA: Stanford University Press, 1999.

Brison, Susan J. "The Aftermath of Violence." *Polylog: Forum for Intercultural Philosophy* 5 (2004), http://them.polylog.org/5/cbs-en.htm.

———. *Aftermath: Violence and the Remaking of a Self.* Princeton, NJ: Princeton University Press, 2002.

Brunner, Jose. "Comments on Political Evil" [in Hebrew]. *Teoryah uvikoret* 1 (1991): 79–90.

Busfield, Joan. *Men, Women, and Madness: Understanding Gender and Mental Disorder.* New York: New York University Press, 1996.

Butler, Judith. *Gender Trouble: Feminism and the Subversion of Identity.* New York: Routledge, 1990.

Calderon, Nissim. *Hargashah shel makom* [A sense of place]. Tel Aviv: Hakibbutz Hameuchad, 1988.

Caruth, Cathy. *Unclaimed Experience: Trauma, Narrative, and History.* Baltimore, MD: Johns Hopkins University Press, 1996.

———. *Trauma: Exploration in Memory.* Baltimore, MD: Johns Hopkins University Press, 1995.

Chalfi, Raquel. *Miklaat hashemesh: Mivchar 1975–1999* [Solar plexus: Poems 1975–1999]. Tel Aviv: Hakibbutz Hameuchad, 2002.

———. *Shirim tat yamiyim* [Underwater and other poems]. Tel Aviv: Hakibbutz Hameuchad, 1975.

Chesler, Phyllis. *Women and Madness.* 1972. San Diego: Harcourt Brace Jovanovich, 1989.

Chodorow, Nancy. *The Reproduction of Mothering.* Berkeley: University of California Press, 1978.

Chodorow, Nancy, and Susan Contratto. "The Fantasy of the Perfect Mother." 1980. In *Rethinking the Family,* eds. Barrie Thorne and Marilyn Yalom, 191–214. Boston: Northeastern University Press, 1992.

Cixous, Hélène. *"Coming To Writing" And Other Essays.* Cambridge, MA: Harvard University Press, 1991.

———. "The Laugh of the Medusa." Trans. Keith Cohen and Paula Cohen. *Signs* 1, no. 4 (1976): 875–93.

Cover, Robert M. "Violence and the Word." *Yale Law Journal* 95, no. 8 (1986): 1601–29.

Dayan, Saar. "Needs a Child's Protection" [in Hebrew]. *Maariv,* January 22, 1993: 6–8.

De Beauvoir, Simone. *The Second Sex.* 1949. Trans. H. M. Parshley. New York: Vintage Books, 1989.

Deleuze, Gilles. *Difference and Repetition.* Trans. Paul Patton. New York: Columbia University Press, 1994.

Deleuze, Gilles, and Félix Guattari. *Anti-Oedipus: Capitalism and Schizophrenia.* Trans. Robert Hurley, Mark Seem, and Helen R. Lane. New York: Viking Press, 1977.

Derrida, Jacques. *The Gift of Death.* Trans. David Wills. Chicago: The University of Chicago Press, 1995.

———. *Margins of Philosophy.* Trans. Alan Bass. Chicago: University of Chicago Press, 1982.

Doane, Janice, and Devon Hodges. *From Klein to Kristeva: Psychoanalytic Feminism and the Search for the "Good Enough" Mother.* Ann Arbor: University of Michigan Press, 1992.

Douglass, Ana, and Thomas A. Vogler, eds. *Witness and Memory: The Discourse of Trauma.* New York: Routledge, 2003.

Ehrenreich, Barbara, and Deirdre English. *Complaints and Disorders: The Sexual Politics of Sickness.* Old Westbury, NY: Feminist Press, 1973.

———. *Witches, Midwives, and Nurses: A History of Women Healers.* Old Westbury, NY: Feminist Press, 1973.

Eldad, Israel. "An Interpellation to Dahlia Ravikovitch" [in Hebrew], *Haaretz*, February 5, 1987: 9.

Fee, Dwight, ed. *Pathology and the Postmodern: Mental Illness as Discourse and Experience.* London: Sage Publications, 2000.

———. "The Project of Pathology: Reflexivity and Depression in Elizabeth Wurtzel's 'Prozac Nation.'" In *Pathology and the Postmodern: Mental Illness as Discourse and Experience,* ed. Dwight Fee, 74–99. London: Sage Publications, 2000.

Feldhay, Rivka. "A Feminine Midrash" [in Hebrew]. *Teoryah uvikoret* 2 (1992): 69–88.

Feldman, Yael. *No Room of Their Own: Gender and Nation in Israeli Women's Fiction.* New York: Columbia University Press, 1999.

———. "Back to Genesis: Toward the Repressed and Beyond in Israeli Identity" [in Hebrew]. In *Bakhivun hanegdi* [In the counter direction: Critical essays on Mr. Mani], ed. Nitza Ben-Dov, 204–22. Tel Aviv: Hakibbutz Hameuchad, 1995.

———. "'And Rebecca Loved Jacob,' But Freud Did Not." In *Freud and Forbidden Knowledge,* eds. Peter L. Rudnytsky and Ellen Handler Spitz, 7–25. New York: New York University Press, 1994.

Felman, Shoshana. *Writing and Madness (Literature/Philosophy/Psychoanalysis).* 1985. Trans. Martha Noel Evans and the author, with the assistance of Brian Massumi. Ithaca, NY: Cornell University Press, 1994.

Felman, Shoshana, and Dori Laub. *Testimony: Crises of Witnessing in Literature, Psychoanalysis, and History.* New York: Routledge, 1992.

Fischer, Yona, ed. *Moshe Kupferman: Works from 1962 to 2000.* Jerusalem: Israel Museum, 2002.

Flax, Jane. *Disputed Subjects: Essays on Psychoanalysis, Politics and Philosophy,* New York: Routledge, 1993.

Foucault, Michel. *Discipline & Punish: The Birth of the Prison.* 1975. Trans. Alan Sheridan. New York: Vintage Books, 1995.

———. *The History of Sexuality.* Vol. 1: An Introduction. Trans. Robert Hurley. New York: Pantheon Books, 1978.

———. "Of Other Spaces." *Diacritics* 16 (1986): 22–27.

———. *History of Madness.* 1961. Trans. Jonathan Murphy and Jean Khalfa. London: Routledge, 2006.

Frankel Alroei, Tal. "Come-Gone" [in Hebrew]. *Mitaam* 6 (2006): 16–29.

Freud, Sigmund. *Beyond the Pleasure Principle.* 1920. Vol. 18 of *The Standard Edition of the Complete Psychological Works of Sigmund Freud.* Ed. James Strachey, in collaboration with Anna Freud, assisted by Alix Strachey and Alan Tyson. London: Hogarth Press, 1953.

———. *Case Histories.* 1893. Vol. 2 of *The Standard Edition of the Complete Psychological Works of Sigmund Freud.* Ed. James Strachey, in collaboration with Anna Freud, assisted by Alix Strachey and Alan Tyson. London: Hogarth Press, 1953.

Friedman, Ariela. *Baah meahavah* [Coming from love: Intimacy and power in female identity]. Tel Aviv: Hakibbutz Hameuchad, 1996.

Gilbert, Sandra M., and Susan Gubar. *The Madwoman in the Attic: The Woman Writer and The Nineteenth-Century Literary Imagination.* New Haven, CT: Yale University Press, 1984.

Gilligan, Carol. *In a Different Voice: Psychological Theory and Women's Development.* Cambridge, MA: Harvard University Press, 1982.

Gilman, Sander L. *Difference and Pathology: Stereotypes of Sexuality, Race, and Madness.* Ithaca, NY: Cornell University Press, 1985.

Girard, René. *The Scapegoat.* Trans. Yvonne Freccero. Baltimore, MD: The Johns Hopkins University Press, 1986.

Glass, James M. *Shattered Selves: Multiple Personality in a Postmodern World.* Ithaca, NY: Cornell University Press, 1993.

Gluzman, Michael. "'To Endow Suffering with Elegance': Dahlia Ravikovitch and the Poetry of the Statehood Generation." *Prooftexts* 28 (2008): 282–309.

———. "The Joyful Elegy: Two Poems by Dahlia Ravikovitch about Yona Wallach" [in Hebrew]. *Helikon* 26 (1998): 19–26.

Gold Scharf, Nili R. "Hovering at a Low Altitude." In *Reading Hebrew Literature: Critical Discussions of Six Modern Texts,* ed. Alan Mintz, 221–29. Waltham, MA: Brandeis University Press, 2003.

———. "Staying in the Place of Danger: The Disobedient, Poetic 'I' of Dahlia Ravikovitch." in *To Speak or to Be Silent: The Paradox of Disobedience in the Lives of Women,* ed. Lena B. Ross, 97–108. Wilmette, IL: Chiron Publications, 1993.

Goldberg, Leah. *Shirim* [Poems]. Ed. Tuvia Rivner. 3 vols. Tel Aviv: Sifriat Poalim, 1973.

Gotkind, Naomi. "Poems like 'A Sharpened Claw'" [in Hebrew], *Hatzofe,* February 6, 1987: 6.

Grosz, Elizabeth. *Volatile Bodies: Toward A Corporeal Feminism.* Bloomington: Indiana University Press, 1994.

Hassin, Juliette. *Shirah vemitos beyetzirata shel dahlia ravikovitch* [Poetry and myth in Ravikovitch's work]. Tel Aviv: Eked, 1989.

Heidegger, Martin. *Being and Time.* 1926. Trans. John Macquarrie and Edward Robinson. Oxford: Basil Blackwell, 1967.

Herman, Judith Lewis. *Trauma and Recovery: The Aftermath of Violence—From Domestic Abuse to Political Terror.* New York: Basic Books, 1992.

Hess, Tamar. "The Poetica of the Fig Tree: Feminist Aspects in the Early Poetry of Dahlia Ravikovitch" [in Hebrew]. *Mikhan* 1 (2000): 27–43.

Hever, Hannan. *Pitom mareh hamilchamah* [Suddenly, the sight of war: nationality and violence in Hebrew poetry of the 1940's]. Tel Aviv: Hakibbutz Hameuchad, 2001.

Hever, Hannan, and Moshe Ron, eds. *Veein tikhla lakravot ulahereg* [There's no end to the battles and slaughter: Political poetry of the Lebanon War]. Tel Aviv: Hakibbutz Hameuchad, 1983.

Hewlett, Sylvia Ann. *A Lesser Life: The Myth of Women's Liberation in America.* New York: William Morrow, 1986.

Hirsch, Marianne. *The Mother/Daughter Plot: Narrative, Psychoanalysis, Feminism.* Bloomington: Indiana University Press, 1989.

Hirschfeld, Ariel. "Ravikovitch After a Decade" [in Hebrew]. *Yediot acharonot,* January 9, 1987: 21.

Hoffman, David. "Israeli Society Falls under MTV's Spell." *Washington Post Foreign Service,* July 17, 1993: A10, www.washingtonpost.com/wp-srv/inatl/longterm/mia/tvo71793.htm.

Hout, Bayan Nuwayhed. *Sabra and Shatila: September 1982.* London: Pluto Press, 2004.

Irigaray, Luce. *Speculum of the Other Woman.* 1974. Trans. Gillian C. Gill. Ithaca, NY: Cornell University Press, 1985.

——. *This Sex Which Is Not One.* Trans. Catherine Porter and Carolyn Burke. Ithaca, NY: Cornell University Press, 1985.

——. "And the One Doesn't Stir without the Other." Trans. Helene Vivienne Wenzel. *Signs* 7, no. 1 (1981): 60–67.

Jamison, Kay R. *Touched with Fire: Manic-Depressive Illness and the Artistic Temperament.* New York: The Free Press, 1993.

Janet, Pierre. *The Major Symptoms of Hysteria: Fifteen Lectures Given in the Medical School of Harvard University.* New York: Macmillan, 1907.

Jay, Nancy. "Gender and Dichotomy." *Feminist Studies* 1 (1981): 36–56.

Kadmon, Sima. "I Am Always the Defeated Side" [in Hebrew]. *Maariv,* February 8, 1991: 22–23.

Kamir, Orit. *Feminizm, zekhuyot umishpat* [Feminism, rights and law in Israel]. Tel Aviv: Broadcast University, 2002.

——. "What's in a Woman's Name" [in Hebrew]. *Mishpatim* 27, no. 2 (1996): 327–82.

Karpel, Dahlia. "Another Book, True Love" [in Hebrew]. *Hair,* November 28, 1986.

——. "After the Silence" [in Hebrew]. *Haaretz,* October 24, 1986.

Kristeva, Julia. *New Maladies of the Soul.* Trans. Ross Guberman. New York: Columbia University Press, 1995.

——. *In the Beginning Was Love: Psychoanalysis and Faith.* Trans. Arthur Goldhammer. New York: Columbia University Press, 1987.

——. *About Chinese Women.* Trans. Anita Barrows. New York: Marion Boyars, 1986.

——. *Revolution in Poetic Language.* 1974. Trans. Margaret Waller. New York: Columbia University Press, 1984.

——. *Powers of Horror: An Essay on Abjection.* Trans. Leon S. Roudiez. New York: Columbia University Press, 1982.

——. "Women's Time." Trans. Alice Jardine and Harry Blake. *Signs* 7, no. 1 (1981): 13–35.

——. *Desire in Language: A Semiotic Approach to Literature and Art.* Trans. Thomas Gora, Alice Jardine, and Leon S. Roudiez. New York: Columbia University Press, 1980.

Kronfeld, Chana. "A Lebanon War Poem?" In *Reading Hebrew Literature: Critical Discussions of Six Modern Texts,* ed. Alan Mintz, 232–45. Waltham, MA: Brandeis University Press, 2003.

Kurtzweil, Baruch. "Dahlia Ravikovitch's Poems" [in Hebrew]. *Haaretz*, December 25, 1959.

Kutscher, Raphael. "Tammuz." *Encyclopaedia Judaica*. Vol. 15, 787–88. Jerusalem: Keter, n.d.

Lacan, Jacques. *The Four Fundamental Concepts of Psycho-Analysis*. Trans. Alan Sheridan. London: Vintage, 1998.

———. "Seminar on The Purloined Letter." 1966. In *The Purloined Poe: Lacan, Derrida, and Psychoanalytic Reading*, trans. J. Mehlman, eds. John P. Muller and William J. Richardson, 28–54. Baltimore, MD: Johns Hopkins University Press, 1988.

———. *Écrits: A Selection*. Trans. Alan Sheridan. London: Tavistock, 1977.

LaCapra, Dominick. "Trauma, Absence, Loss." *Critical Inquiry* 25, no. 4 (1999): 696–727.

Lahav, Penina. "'When the Palliative Simply Impairs': The Debate in the Knesset on the Law for Women's Rights" [in Hebrew]. *Zmanim* 46–47 (1993): 149–59.

Laing, Ronald David. *The Politics of Experience*. New York: Ballantine, 1970.

———. *The Politics of the Family*. New York: Vintage, 1969.

———. *The Divided Self: An Existential Study in Sanity and Madness*. New York: Penguin, 1960.

Laing, Ronald David, and Aaron Esterson. *Sanity, Madness, and the Family: Families of Schizophrenics*. London: Tavistock, 1964.

Levinas, Emmanuel. *Otherwise Than Being: Or Beyond Essence*. 1974. Trans. Alphonso Lingis. New York: Springer, 1981.

Levo-Vardinon, Shulamit. "A Fall before the Lift-off: Horrible Life in 'Death in the Family'" [in Hebrew]. *Davar*, March 16, 1979: 20.

Leys, Ruth. "Image and Trauma." *Science in Context* 19 (2006): 137–49.

———. *Trauma: A Genealogy*. Chicago: University of Chicago Press, 2000.

Lidovsky-Cohen, Zafrira. "Teresa Versus Shunra: The Image of the Woman in the Poems of Dahlia Ravikovitch and Yona Wallach" [in Hebrew]. *Iton 77* 315 (2006): 22–26.

———. *"Loosen the Fetters of Thy Tongue Woman": The Poetry and Poetics of Yona Wallach*. Cincinnati: Hebrew Union College Press, 2003.

Lieblich, Amia. *El leah* [Towards Leah]. Tel Aviv: Hakibbutz Hameuchad, 1995.

Lindemans, Micha F. "Tammuz." *The Encyclopedia Mythica*. 1997, www.pantheon.org/articles/t/tammuz.html.

Littlewood, Roland, and Maurice Lipsedge. *Aliens and Alienists: Ethnic Minorities and Psychiatry*. Harmondsworth, UK: Penguin, 1982.

Lloyd, Geneveie. *The Man of Reason: "Male" and "Female" in Western Philosophy*. London: Methuen, 1984.

Lotenberg, Ilan. "Half a Poet" [in Hebrew]. *Chadashot*, June 4, 1993: 58–61.

Lubin, Orly. "Low Gaze, Freed Gaze." In *Igael Shemtov: Low Landscape Low Reality*. Tel Aviv: Loushy Art & Editions, 2004.

Lyotard, Jean-François. *The Differend: Phrases in Dispute*. Trans. Georges Van Den Abbeele. Minneapolis: University of Minnesota Press, 1988.

MacKinnon, Catharine A. *Only Words*. Cambridge, MA: Harvard University Press, 1993.

———. "Feminism, Marxism, Method, and the State: Toward Feminist Jurisprudence."
     1983. In *Contemporary Critical Theory*, ed. Dan Latimer, 605-33. Orlando, FL:
     Harcourt College Publishers, 1989.

———. *Toward a Feminist Theory of the State*. Cambridge, MA: Harvard University Press,
     1989.

———. *Feminism Unmodified: Discourses on Life and Law*. Cambridge, MA: Harvard
     University Press, 1987.

Malin, Jo. *The Voice of the Mother: Embedded Maternal Narratives in Twentieth-Century
     Women's Autobiographies*. Carbondale: Southern Illinois University Press, 2000.

Mann, Barbara. "Hovering at a Low Altitude." In *Reading Hebrew Literature: Critical
     Discussions of Six Modern Texts*, ed. Alan Mintz, 213-20. Waltham, MA: Brandeis
     University Press, 2003.

Mazor, Yair. "The Poetry of Dahlia Hertz and Yona Wallach in the Comparative Context
     of Dahlia Ravikovitch's Poetry" [in Hebrew]. *Iton 77* 220 (1998): 11-15.

———. "A Portrait of Shame As a City of Refuge: About Dahlia Ravikovitch's Poetry"
     [in Hebrew]. *Iton 77* 206 (1997): 16-19, 42.

McClintock, Anne. *Imperial Leather: Race, Gender and Sexuality in the Colonial Contest*.
     New York: Routledge, 1995.

Miron, Dan. "A Comic Sibyl" [in Hebrew]. In *Agi Mishol: mivchar vechadashim* [Agi
     Mishol: Selection and new poems], 291-443. Tel Aviv: Hakibbutz Hameuchad, 2003.

———. *Imahot meyasdot, achayot chorgot* [Founding mothers, stepsisters: The emer-
     gence of the first Hebrew poetesses]. Tel Aviv: Hakibbutz Hameuchad, 1991.

Mishol, Agi. *Mivchar vechadashim* [Agi Mishol: New and selected poems]. Tel Aviv:
     Hakibbutz Hameuchad, 2003.

———. *Sritah shel chatul* [A cat's scratch]. Tel Aviv: Hakibbutz Hameuchad, 1978.

———. *Nani ushneinu* [Nanny and both of us]. Tel Aviv: Akad, 1972.

Mitchell, Juliet. *Psychoanalysis and Feminism*. New York: Vintage, 1974.

Moi, Toril, ed. *The Kristeva Reader*. New York: Columbia University Press, 1986.

Moked, Gabriel. "About Two New Books By Dahlia Ravikovitch—in Poetry and Prose"
     [in Hebrew]. *Yediot acharonot*, July 30, 1976: 3.

Moorjani, Angela. *Beyond Fetishism and Other Excursions in Psychopragmatics*. New York:
     St. Martin's Press, 2000.

Mujica-Jenkins, Harrison. "Schizoanalysis." *Schizo's Web*, www.latephilosophers.com/
     schizo.html.

Naveh, Hannah. *Nosim venosot* [Women and men traveling: The travel narrative in
     Hebrew literature].Tel Aviv: Ministry of Defense Publishing House, 2002.

———. "Life Outside the Canon" [in Hebrew]. In *Min, migdar, politikah* [Sex, gender,
     politics: Women in Israel], eds. Dafnah Izraeli, et al., 49-106. Tel Aviv: Hakibbutz
     Hameuchad, 1999.

———. *Bishvi haevel* [Captives of mourning: Representation of bereavement in Hebrew
     literature]. Tel Aviv: Hakibbutz Hameuchad, 1993.

Negev, Ayelet. "Dahlia Ravikovitch Speaks. About It All" [in Hebrew]. *Yediot acharonot*,
     February 23, 1996: 22, 26-28.

Okin, Susan Moller. *Women in Western Political Thought.* Princeton, NJ: Princeton
University Press, 1979.

Olmert, Dana. "'I Am Not Here': The Political Position and the Threat over Subjectivity
in the Poetry of Dahlia Ravikovitch" [in Hebrew]. In *Khitmei or* [Sparks of light:
Essays about Dahlia Ravikovitch's oeuvre], eds. Hamutal Tsamir and Tamar S. Hess,
416–43. Tel Aviv: Hakibbutz Hameuchad, 2010.

Ophir, Adi. *Lashon lara* [Speaking evil: Towards an ontology of morals]. Tel Aviv: Am
Oved, 2000.

———. "Beyond Good: Evil—An Outline for a Political Theory of Evils" [in Hebrew].
Teoryah uvikoret 1 (1991): 41–77.

———. "About Michel Foucault and His Book *History of Madness*" [in Hebrew]. In
History of Madness, trans. Aaron Amir, 215–30. Jerusalem: Keter, 1986.

Oppenheimer, Yochai. *Hazkhut hagdolah lomar lo* [Political poetry in Israel]. Jerusalem:
Hebrew University Magnes Press, 2003.

———. "The Right to Say No: Auden, Zach, and Laor in a Political Context" [in Hebrew].
Alpayim 10 (1994): 238–59.

———. "Political Competence: On the Lyrical and the Political in the Poetry of Dahlia
Ravikovitch" [in Hebrew]. *Siman kriah* 22 (1991): 415–30.

O'Reilly, Andrea, ed. *Twenty-first Century Motherhood.* New York: Columbia University
Press, 2010.

———. *From Motherhood to Mothering: The Legacy of Adrienne Rich's Of Woman Born.*
Albany: State University of New York Press, 2004.

Palgi-Hecker, Anat. *Mei-mahut leimahut* [The mother in psychoanalysis: A feminist
view]. Tel Aviv: Am Oved Press, 2005.

Payer, Lynn. *Medicine and Culture: Varieties of Treatment in the United States, England,
West Germany, and France.* New York: Henry Holt, 1988.

Poe, Edgar Allan. *The Poems of Edgar Allan Poe.* Ed. Killis Campbell. Boston: Ginn and
Company, 1917.

Pratt, Mary Louise. *Imperial Eyes: Travel Writing and Transculturation.* London:
Routledge, 1992.

Rabinowitz, Dan. "The Twisting Journey for the Rescue of Brown Women" [in Hebrew].
Teoryah uvikoret 7 (1995): 5–19.

Raizen, Esther, ed. and trans. *No Rattling of Sabers: An Anthology of Israeli War Poetry.*
Austin: Center for Middle Eastern Studies at the University of Texas, 1995.

Rattok, Lily. *Malakh haesh* [Angel of fire: The poetry of Yona Wallach]. Tel Aviv:
Hakibbutz Hameuchad, 1997.

Ravikovitch, Dahlia. *Kol hashirim* [The complete poems]. Eds. Giddon Ticotsky and Uzi
Shavit. Tel Aviv: Hakibbutz Hameuchad, 2010.

———. *Mayim rabim: shirim 1995–2005* [Many waters: Poems 1995–2005]. Eds. Dana
Olmert and Uzi Shavit. Tel Aviv: Hakibbutz Hameuchad, 2006.

———. *Baah vehalchah* [Come and gone]. N.p.: Modan, 2005.

———. *Chatzi shaah lifnei hamonsun* [Half an hour before the monsoon]. Raanana: Even
Hoshen Publishers, 1998.

———. *Kvutzat hakhaduregel shel wini mandelah* [Winnie Mandela's football team]. Tel Aviv: Hakibbutz Hameuchad, 1997.

———. *Hinneh* [Behold: Poetry collection] 1. Ed. Nathan Zach. 1995.

———. *Kol hashirim ad khoh.* [The complete poems so far]. Tel Aviv: Hakibbutz Hameuchad, 1995.

———. *Ima im yeled* [Mother with child]. Tel Aviv: Hakibbutz Hameuchad, 1992.

———. *The Window: Poems by Dahlia Ravikovitch.* Trans. Chana Bloch and Ariel Bloch. New York: Sheep Meadow Press, 1989.

———. *Ahavah amitit* [True Love]. Tel Aviv: Hakibbutz Hameuchad, 1987.

———. *Mavet bamishpahah* [Death in the family]. Tel Aviv: Am Oved, 1976.

———. *Tehom kore* [Deep calleth unto deep]. Tel Aviv: Hakibbutz Hameuchad, 1976.

———. *Hasefer hashlishi* [The third book]. N.p.: Modan, 1970.

———. *Choref kasheh* [A hard winter]. Tel Aviv: Dvir, 1964.

———. *Ahavat tapuach hazahav* [The love of an orange]. Merhavia: Sifriat Poalim Publishing Group, 1959.

Rich, Adrienne. *Of Woman Born: Motherhood as Experience and Institution.* New York: W. W. Norton, 1986.

Roethke, Theodore. *The Collected Poems of Theodore Roethke.* Seattle: University of Washington Press, 1982.

Rosen, Tova. *Unveiling Eve: Reading Gender in Medieval Hebrew Literature.* Philadelphia: University of Pennsylvania Press, 2003.

Rothblum, Esther D., and Ellen Cole, eds. *A Woman's Recovery from the Trauma of War: Twelve Responses from Feminist Therapists and Activists.* New York : Haworth Press, 1986.

Salhov, Shva. "The Monster of Love: Sigal Avni's Exhibition" [in Hebrew]. *Studio* 108 (1999): 40–46.

Sandbank, Shimon. "A World of Disappearance: On the Poems of Dahlia Ravikovitch" [in Hebrew]. *Hameorer* 4 (1998): 126–32.

———. *Megamot yesod bashirah hamodernit* [Major trends in modern poetry]. Tel Aviv: The Ministry of Defense Publishing House, 1990.

Sartre, Jean-Paul. "The Search for the Absolute." In *Giacometti: A Catalogue,* 8–12 [in Hebrew]. Tel Aviv: Tel Aviv University Art Gallery, 1984.

Schachter, Allison. "A Lily among the Bullfrogs: Dahlia Ravikovitch and the Field of Hebrew Poetry." *Prooftexts* 28 (2008): 310–34.

Scheff, Thomas J., ed. *Labeling Madness.* New Jersey: Prentice-Hall, 1975.

Schwartz, Murray M. "Locating Trauma." Rev. of *Trauma: A Genealogy,* by Ruth Leys. *American Imago* 59, no. 3 (2002): 367–84.

Sedgwick, Peter. *Psycho Politics: Laing, Foucault, Goffman, Szasz, and the Future of Mass Psychiatry.* New York: Harper and Row, 1982.

Shacham, Chaya. *Nashim vemasekhot* [Women and masks]. Tel Aviv: Hakibbutz Hameuchad, 2001.

———. "A Female Poet in the Company of Males Poets: On the Acceptance of Leah Goldberg and Dahlia Ravikovitch's Poetry by the Critics of Their Time" [in Hebrew]. *Sadan* 2 (1996): 203–40.

Shahar, Ayelet. "The Sex of the Law: Rape's Legal Discourse" [in Hebrew]. *Iyunei mishpat* 18, no.1 (1993): 159-99.

Shalev, Mordechai. "Dahlia Ravikovitch: Poetess of Lamenting" [in Hebrew]. *Haaretz*, April 2 and June 13, 1969.

Shehori, Yaara. *"A Sixty-Meter Dash from Bialik's Tomb": Dahlia Ravikovitch Refers to H. N. Bialik's Poetry* [in Hebrew]. In *Khitmei or* [Sparks of light: Essays about Dahlia Ravikovitch's oeuvre], eds. Hamutal Tsamir and Tamar S. Hess, 354-90. Tel Aviv: Hakibbutz Hameuchad, 2010.

Showalter, Elaine. *The Female Malady: Women, Madness, and English Culture, 1830-1980.* New York: Pantheon Books, 1985.

Stanton, Domna. "Difference on Trail: A Critique of the Maternal Metaphor in Cixous, Irigaray and Kristeva." *The Poetics of Gender,* ed. Nancy K. Miller, 157-82. New York: Columbia University Press, 1986.

Stav, Shira. "The Father, the Daughter, and the Gaze" [in Hebrew]. In *Khitmei or* [Sparks of light: Essays about Dahlia Ravikovitch's oeuvre], eds. Hamutal Tsamir and Tamar S. Hess, 284-322. Tel Aviv: Hakibbutz Hameuchad, 2010.

Strenger, Carlo. *Individuality, the Impossible Project: Psychoanalysis and Self-Creation.* Madison, CT: International Universities Press, 1998.

Suleiman, Rubin, S. "Writing and Motherhood." In *The (M)other Tongue: Essays in Feminist Psychoanalytic Interpretation,* eds. Shirley Nelson Garner, Claire Kahane, and Madelon Sprengnether, 352-77. Ithaca, NY: Cornell University Press, 1985.

Szobel, Ilana. "Forever Beholden: The State of Orphanhood in the Work of Dahlia Ravikovitch." *Nashim: A Journal of Jewish Women's Studies & Gender* 19 (2010): 228-47.

———. "'Hovering at a Low Altitude': Testimony and Complicity in the Political Writing of Dahlia Ravikovitch" [in Hebrew]. In *Khitmei or* [Sparks of light: Essays about Dahlia Ravikovitch's oeuvre], eds. Hamutal Tsamir and Tamar S. Hess, 444-69. Tel Aviv: Hakibbutz Hameuchad, 2010.

———. "'She Tried to Escape and Lost Her Senses': Alienation and Madness in the Stories of Dahlia Ravikovitch" [in Hebrew]. *Teoryah uvikoret* 28 (2006): 127-55.

Tsamir, Hamutal. "Jewish-Israeli Poetry, Dahlia Ravikovitch, and the Gender of Representation." *Jewish Social Studies* 14, no. 3 (2008): 85-125.

———. *Beshem hanof* [In the name of the land: Nationalism, subjectivity and gender in the Israeli poetry of the statehood generation]. Jerusalem: Keter Books, 2006.

———. "The Dead and the Living, the Believers and the Uprooted: Dahlia Ravikovitch, Mourner and Prophet" [in Hebrew]. *Mikhan* 1 (2000): 44-63.

Tsamir, Hamutal, and Tamar S. Hess, eds. *Khitmei or* [Sparks of light: Essays about Dahlia Ravikovitch's oeuvre]. Tel Aviv: Hakibbutz Hameuchad, 2010.

Ussher, Jane. "Women's Madness: A Material-Discursive-Intrapsychic Approach." *Pathology and the Postmodern: Mental Illness as Discourse and Experience,* ed. Dwight Fee, 207-30. London: Sage Publications, 2000.

———. *Women's Madness: Misogyny or Mental Illness?* Amherst: University of Massachusetts Press, 1992.

———. *The Psychology of the Female Body.* London: Routledge, 1989.

Van der Hart, Onno, and Rutger Horst. "The Dissociation Theory of Pierre Janet." *Journal of Traumatic Stress* 2, no. 4 (1989): 397–412.

Van der Kolk, Bessel A. *Psychological Trauma*. Washington, DC: American Psychiatric Press, 1987.

Van der Kolk, Bessel A., Alexander C. MacFarlane, and Lars Weisæth, eds. *Traumatic Stress: The Effects of Overwhelming Experience on Mind, Body, and Society*. New York: Guilford Press, 1996.

Van Zuylen, Marina. *Monomania: The Flight from Everyday Life in Literature and Art*. Ithaca, NY: Cornell University Press, 2005.

Wallach, Yona. *Tat hakharah niftachat khmo menifa* [Selected poems 1963–1985]. Tel Aviv: Hakibbutz Hameuchad, 1992.

Walzer, Michael. *Spheres of Justice: A Defense of Pluralism and Equality*. New York: Basic Books, 1983.

Wieseltier, Meir. "True Love Isn't What It Seems" [in Hebrew]. *Haaretz*, September 6, 1995: 132.

Yeglin, Ofra. "Did I Forget? Well, Who Cares? On Three Poems by Dahlia Ravikovitch" [in Hebrew]. *Rechov* 2 (1995): 71–81.

Yizhar, Smilansky. "About Uncles and Arabs." 1993. *Hebrew Studies* 47 (2006): 321–26.

Zach, Nathan. *Anti-mechikon* [Hard to remember]. Tel Aviv: Hakibbutz Hameuchad, 1984.

Zertal, Idith. "Hannah Arendt Versus the State of Israel" [in Hebrew]. *Teoryah uvikoret* 12–13 (1999): 159–67.

———. "Poetry—A Soul without a Body." *Davar*, July 8, 1966.

Zizek, Slavoj. *For They Know What They Do: Enjoyment as a Political Factor*. London: Verso, 1994.

Zukerman, Ilana, ed. "True Love: Printed Excerpts from a Radio Broadcast" [in Hebrew]. *Prozah* 100 (1988): 108–11.

Index

Note: All titles of works without author attribution are those of Ravikovitch.

estrangement: collision of perspectives, 39–51; imaginary geography, 52–60, 63–64; and madness, 63–64, 77–78, 87, 88, 89

evil as human responsibility, 99, 108, 116

exclusion of the insane estranged, 77–78, 91

existential anxiety, 68

external and internal experience: in "Clockwork Doll," 11; collision of in self-definition, 41–48; collision of perspectives, 50–51; estrangement and deviant subjectivity, 40–42; "here" and "over there," 52–60, 69–70, 72, 74, 148n17; interfusion of, 89–90; madness and mad speech, 79–85, 88, 89; manic-depressive cycle, 73–76; in protest poetry, 108; Ravikovitch's blurring of, 80–85

fantasy and reality, Ravikovitch's blurring of. *See* external and internal experience

"Faraway Land" (poem), 64, 67

father, loss of: missing link and symbolic rewriting, 15–17; and mother and daughters as orphans, 29; psychosis, legacy of, 5–7, 10–11; Ravikovitch's poetic expression of, 3–4; state of doom due to, 12–15, 17–20

"The Father of—" (story), 17, 20

Feldhay, Rivka, 81

Feldman, Yael, ix, 13–14

Felman, Shoshanna, xix, 50, 78, 79, 82–83, 84, 117, 123

femininity, rebellion against hegemonic definition, 34, 44–46, 86, 132–33

"Finally I'm Talking" (poem), 135

"The Firstborn Grandchild" (story), 20

First Intifada (1987), 96–98, 128

First Lebanon War (1982), 95–115, 122, 123, 124

fixation and obsession. *See* obsession and fixation

form, poetic. *See* symbolic order

Foucault, Michel, 15, 43, 77, 78, 80, 83–84, 117, 146n5

"The Four Hundred Thousand Protest," 96

"Free Associating" (poem), 118, 127

Freud, Sigmund, 78, 126

"From Day to Night" (poem), 65

Galron, Nurit, 97–98

gaze: and power relations, 44, 45–46, 47, 50; in witnessing and complicity, 99, 101–2

Gemayel, Bashir, 95

gender: female disease, 26, 145n15; femininity, rebellion against hegemonic definition, 34, 44–46, 86, 132–33; insanity discourse, 86–87, 90; loss of subjectivity in motherhood, 24–27; motherhood, 21–29, 45, 144n6, 145n11; symbolic order's perpetuation of inequality, 47–48; violence and "Hovering at a Low Altitude," 153n8. *See also* patriarchy

Generation of the State, xii

"Get out of Beirut" (poem), 123–24, 127

Giacometti, Alberto, 105

Gilbert, Sandra M., 90, 145n14

Gilman, Sander L., 78

Girard, René, 149n2

Gluzman, Michael, 135

Goldberg, Leah, 12, 34

Gorea vezoreach, 64, 67

Grosz, Elizabeth, 41–42

Gubar, Susan, 90, 145n14

guilt-ridden poems, 116–25. *See also* moral responsibility

Gvaot melach, 64

Haahavah haamitit einah kefi shehi niret, 107, 135

Hachalon, 102

Hachishuk hadimyoni, 83–84

Half an Hour before the Monsoon (1998), 74

Hamaarav hakhachol, 67, 68, 69

obsession and fixation: in manic depression cycle, 65, 68–69, 70, 148n11; and orphanhood, 5, 8, 16–17, 30; as quest for harmony, 148–49n19; self-annihilation desire as, 70, 72; as subversive of hegemonic symbolic order, 7–8

occupation, Israeli, questioning of, 96, 98, 125, 128

Omed al hakhevish, 3, 5–7, 19, 30, 33–34, 70

"On the Attitude toward Children in Times of War" (poem), 110–14, 127, 128–29, 153n36

"On the Desire to Be Precise" (Zach), 110–11

"On the road at night" (poem), 3, 5–7, 19, 30, 33–34, 70

Ophir, Adi, 106, 116

Oppenheimer, Yochai, 107, 111, 114

Orot haaviv, 23, 24–25, 80, 84–85, 135

orphanhood: doom, state of, 12–15, 27–28, 32, 34; and dysfunctional motherhood, 21–29; and obsession and fixation, 5, 8, 16–17, 30; overview, xviii–xix; women's symbolic, 30–35. *See also* mourning as endless quest

Other, inclusion of, and Israeli national identity, xiv–xv, 126–30

outside-in/inside-out, mediating, 41–42, 90–91. *See also* external and internal experience

"over there" and "here." *See* external and internal experience

Palestinian Arabs, 96–98, 127–30

patriarchy: cultural expectations of motherhood, 25, 26, 28; external-internal dichotomy and gender, 43–48; insanity definitions as instrument of repression, 86; as perpetuator of women's orphanhood, 30–35; symbolic order as hegemonic discourse, 7

peace and human rights activism, xiii

Peace Now, 96

personal, the: *Likrat* poets' embrace of, xii; and national trauma, shifting between, xiv, 99–100, 107–8; witnessing victimhood from universal and, 99

personal choice as illusion, 133

Phalangist militias, 95

phantom aspect of psychological mourning mechanism, 18, 19, 20

Pizmon hakhokhav harachok, 34

"A Poem in Arabic Style, Maybe" (poem), 127

politics: abjection and Israeli-Palestinian conflict, 126–30; human vs. national perspective, 118–21; merging with the personal, xiv, 99–100, 107–8; protest poetry, 99–115, 117–25, 127–30; Ravikovitch's contribution to meaning of trauma, 132–35. *See also* witnessing and complicity

Portret yehudi, 118–19

power relations: and gaze, 44, 45–46, 47, 50; hegemonic rationalization of violence, 117–22; and madness, 78–79, 86–87, 91; and national moral responsibility, 110; power in deviant subjectivity, 133–34; in "A Short Delay," 48–51; trial scenes in Ravikovitch's work, 43–48. *See also* patriarchy

Powers of Horror: An Essay on Abjection (Kristeva), 126

Pratt, Mary Louise, ix, 50

"Prepare for the Messiah's Arrival" (story), 77, 85, 86–89

protest poetry, 99–115, 117–25, 127–30

psychiatric hospitals in Ravikovitch's work, 63

psychic dissociation caused by trauma, 55–56

psychoanalytic perspective: on abjection, 126–27; being-with vs. being-against society, 56–57; bereavement and orphanhood, 5-7; and compulsion of repetition, 14; mother's lack of subjectivity, 144n6; obsessive behavior, 148n11; psychosis as originating in loss of father, 13; secret, crypt, and phantom, 18-20; self-annihilation, desire for, 70, 72; and subversion of symbolic order, 133; visibility vs. invisibility, 46

psychosis. *See* madness

"Pure Memory" (poem), 19

Ramat Gan, xii, 19

Rashi (Shlomo Yitzhaqi), 75

Ravikovitch, Dahlia: and Alterman, 13, 30-34, 96; and Bejerano, 137; biographical sketch, xii-xiii; canonization of, xii; and Chalfi, 138; and Goldberg, 12, 34; on her poetic legacy, xiii; on Israeli moral responsibility, 100-101; legacy of, xii, 131-39; lifetime production, xi-xii; and Mishol, 137-38; overview of oeuvre, xiv-xvii; peace and human rights activism, xiii; political activism, 96; prizes awarded, xii; on protest poetry, 102, 109, 123; and Wallach, 135, 136-37. *See also* estrangement; madness; orphanhood; politics

Ravikovitch, Levi (father), xii-xiii, 3-4

reality and fantasy, Ravikovitch's blurring of. *See* external and internal experience

Rechifah begovah namuch, 101, 102-5, 109-10, 129, 143n23, 153n8

refusal vs. rebellion, protest poetry, 106

reorganization of past in mourning, lack of access to, 15-17

repetition, 7-12, 16, 17-18

repetition-in-variation in biblical narrative, 14

repression, 77-79, 85-86, 89-90, 91, 133-34

Rich, Adrienne, 25, 27, 145n11

"The Roar of the Waters" (poem), 70

Rosenblum, Yair, 114

"Royal Gifts" (poem), 70

Sabra and Shatila Massacre (1982), 95, 113, 151n2

Sartre, Jean-Paul, 105

Saviv liyrushalaim, 65

"Seats for Trial" (poem), 56, 59-60

secret aspect of psychological mourning mechanism, 18-20

self-annihilation, desire for, 69-72

self-production: abjection and borders of self, 126-27; collision of in external and internal experience, 41-48; estrangement as act of, 39-40; madness as site of, 65, 79-81; and social order, 80-81, 149-50n12; and subversion of symbolic order, 10, 11, 133; wounded subjectivity's role in, 134. *See also* external and internal experience; subjectivity

self-world dynamic, creation of, 46

semiotic, the, and subversion of symbolic order, 133

Shalosh arba rakafot, 18

Sharon, Ariel, 95

Sheon hamayim, 70

Shir besignon aravi, ulai, 127

Shir eres, 127

Shirim tat yamiyim (Chalfi), 138

Shlonsky, Avraham, 30, 31

Shnei iyim lenew ziland, 98, 129

Shnei shirei ginah, 66-67, 69

Shokhevet al hamayim, 125, 127, 129-30

"Shooting and Crying" (Himan), 96-97

"A Short Delay" (story), 48-51, 57-58, 87

signification and symbolic vs. semiotic, 133

silencing of eccentric voices, 77-79

"Six Hundred Thirteen Commandments Plus One" (poem), 17

"A Small House at the 'Ganim' Neighborhood" (story), 63-64

"Two Isles Hath New Zealand" (poem),
98, 129
Tzaar halaylah, 56

unmothered, feeling of being, 27–28

Van Zuylen, Marina, 65, 68
victimhood: blurring of binary boundaries,
xvi–xvii, 134; and deconstruction of
state-sanctioned violence, 118–21;
overview, xv–xvii; in protest poetry,
98–100, 108, 109, 111–12, 114–15,
124–25; Ravikovitch's structure of,
136. *See also* orphanhood; witnessing
and complicity
violence, normalizing of, 116

Wallach, Yona, 12, 135, 136–37
"Waning and Waxing" (poem), 64, 67
"We Had an Understanding" (poem), 108,
132
"Where Will We Carry the Shame?"
(Alterman), 96
Wieseltier, Meir, 30, 31
"The Wild Geese" (story), 58
Willis, Thomas, 76
"The Window" (poem), 102

"Winnie Mandela's Football Team"
(story), 26, 28, 43–46, 47, 49, 77,
87, 88
witnessing and complicity: as critique of
social order, 98–99, 100–101, 105–6,
118–21; distance and engagement,
99, 102–9, 111; identification with
suffering, 111–13; imaginary
innocence, 114–15, 116; indirect
nature of Ravikovitch's, 154n16;
moral responsibility of witness,
102–7, 108–10, 111–15, 117, 128
women. *See* gender
Writing and Madness (Felman), 78
writing madness, 80–84

Yeglin, Ofra, 123
Yitzhaqi, Rabbi Shlomo (Rashi), 75
Yizhar, S., 154n4
Yom leyom yabia omer, 65
"You Can't Kill a Baby Twice" (poem),
113–14, 125

Zach, Nathan, xii, 4, 110
Zikaron tamim, 19
Zionist ideology of trauma, xv–xvi
Žižek, Slavoj, 15

Library of Congress Cataloging-in-Publication Data
Szobel, Ilana.
A poetics of trauma: the work of Dahlia Ravikovitch / Ilana Szobel.
    p. cm. — (HBI series on Jewish women & Schusterman series in
Israel studies)
Includes bibliographical references and index.
ISBN 978-1-61168-354-7 (cloth: alk. paper)—
ISBN 978-1-61168-355-4 (pbk.: alk. paper)—
ISBN 978-1-61168-356-1 (ebook)
    1. Ravikovitch, Dahlia, 1936–2005—Criticism and interpretation.
2. Psychic trauma in literature. 3. Alienation (Social psychology)
in literature. 4. Identity (Psychology) in literature. 5. Nationalism
in literature. I. Title. II. Title: Work of Dahlia Ravikovitch.
PJ5054.R265Z87   2013
892.4'16—dc23   2012025573

5 4 3 2 1